Is Inequality the Problem?

Is Inequality the Problem?

LANE KENWORTHY

OXFORD
UNIVERSITY PRESS

Oxford University Press is a department of the University of Oxford.
It furthers the University's objective of excellence in research, scholarship,
and education by publishing worldwide. Oxford is a registered trade mark of
Oxford University Press in the UK and in certain other countries.

Published in the United States of America by Oxford University Press
198 Madison Avenue, New York, NY 10016, United States of America.

© Lane Kenworthy 2025

All rights reserved. No part of this publication may be reproduced, stored in a retrieval system, transmitted, used for text and data mining, or used for training artificial intelligence, in any form or by any means, without the prior permission in writing of Oxford University Press, or as expressly permitted by law, by license or under terms agreed with the appropriate reprographics rights organization. Inquiries concerning reproduction outside the scope of the above should be sent to the Rights Department, Oxford University Press, at the address above.

You must not circulate this work in any other form
and you must impose this same condition on any acquirer.

CIP data is on file at the Library of Congress

ISBN 9780197817100

ISBN 9780197817094 (hbk.)

DOI: 10.1093/oso/9780197817094.001.0001

Paperback printed by Marquis Book Printing, Canada

Hardback printed by Lightning Source, Inc., United States of America

The manufacturer's authorized representative in the EU for product safety is
Oxford University Press España S.A., Parque Empresarial San Fernando de Henares,
Avenida de Castilla, 2 – 28830 Madrid (www.oup.es/en).

Contents

1. Inequality Isn't the Problem — 1
2. Is Income Inequality Bad for Living Standards? — 15
3. Does Income Inequality Degrade Democracy? — 28
4. Does Income Inequality Obstruct Opportunity? — 37
5. Does Income Inequality Lessen Longevity? — 49
6. Does Income Inequality Hinder Happiness? — 62
7. Is Income Inequality Harmful? — 71
8. People Want Less Inequality, But It's Not a Priority for Them — 79
9. Inequality Reduction in Rich Nations May Impede Reduction of Worldwide Inequality — 84
10. What About Wealth? — 89
11. Inequality Reduction Should Be a Secondary Goal — 93
12. How to Reduce Inequality — 109

Acknowledgments — 129
Appendix — 130
Notes — 136
References — 147

1
Inequality Isn't the Problem

To a host of thoughtful observers, economic inequality is one of our most important problems and needs to be fixed.

> The problems in rich countries are not caused by the society not being rich enough (or even by being too rich) but by the scale of material differences between people within each society being too big. . . . Attempts to deal with health and social problems through the provision of specialized services have proved expensive and, at best, only partially effective. . . . Greater equality can address a wide range of problems across whole societies.
> —Richard Wilkinson and Kate Pickett, 2009[1]

> Extreme concentration of income is incompatible with real democracy. Can anyone seriously deny that our political system is being warped by the influence of big money, and that the warping is getting worse as the wealth of a few grows ever larger?
> —Paul Krugman, 2011[2]

> Inequality is the ill that underlies all the others. Like an odorless gas, it pervades every corner of the United States. . . . Inequality creates a lopsided economy, which leaves the rich with so much money that they can binge on speculation, and leaves the middle class without enough money to buy the things they think they deserve, which leads them to borrow and go into debt. These were among the long-term causes of the financial crisis and the Great Recession. Inequality hardens society into a class system, imprisoning people in the circumstances of their birth—a rebuke to the very idea of the American dream. Inequality divides us from one another in schools, in neighborhoods, at work, on airplanes, in hospitals, in what we eat, in the condition of our bodies, in what we think, in our children's futures, in how we die. Inequality makes it harder to imagine the lives of others. . . . Inequality corrodes trust among

fellow citizens, making it seem as if the game is rigged. Inequality provokes a generalized anger that finds targets where it can—immigrants, foreign countries, American elites, government in all forms—and it rewards demagogues while discrediting reformers. Inequality saps the will to conceive of ambitious solutions to large collective problems, because those problems no longer seem very collective. Inequality undermines democracy.

—George Packer, 2011[3]

We are paying a high price for the inequality that is increasingly scarring our economy—lower productivity, lower efficiency, lower growth.

—Joseph Stiglitz, 2012[4]

Three decades of accelerating inequality have produced a deformed social order and a set of elites who cannot help but be dysfunctional and corrupt.

—Christopher Hayes, 2012[5]

As the economic gap between the plutocrats and everyone else becomes a chasm, they are coming to inhabit their own global gated community. . . . This increases the political myopia of the plutocrats. Add to that ordinary greed and a society that has turned its capitalists into popular heroes and you have an economic elite primed to repeat the mistake of the Venetian merchants . . . to conflate its own self-interest with the interests of society as a whole. Low taxes, light-touch regulation, weak unions, and unlimited campaign donations are certainly in the best interests of the plutocrats, but that doesn't mean they are the right way to maintain the economic system.

—Chrystia Freeland, 2012[6]

Inequality of this extent—of the sort we are now experiencing—is very dangerous for our economy and it's very dangerous for our society and our democracy.

—Robert Reich, 2013[7]

Inequality is the root of social evil.

—Pope Francis, 2014[8]

A lot of money can buy you a lot of political speech, particularly now that the Supreme Court is systematically dismantling the limits on buying political speech. This is a doom loop of oligarchy: wealth buys power, power buys more wealth, more wealth means more power, more power means more wealth, and on and on and on we go until a very small fraction of the population has a whole lot of the power and a whole lot of the money.

–Ezra Klein and Joe Posner, 2014[9]

A way out of the decades of inequality . . . is the most urgent of projects.

–Jefferson Cowie, 2016[10]

Traditionally, policy experts have focused on finding specific solutions to one issue at a time. Medical experts seek to improve health. Criminologists formulate policies to reduce crime. Education experts design ways to improve schools, and so on. There are surely unique aspects to each of the societal troubles we face. But so many of them have extreme economic inequality as a common denominator that it would be foolish not to try to confront it directly.

–Keith Payne, 2017[11]

The consequences of large income differences for income anxiety, health, life satisfaction, and social mobility are clearly and strongly negative.

–Carsten Jensen and Kees van Kersbergen, 2017[12]

We've been taught . . . that the bulwark against barbarism is human rights. But that may be mistaken. It provides a bulwark against some barbarism. But unlike socialism or other potentially egalitarian languages, it doesn't lead to a movement that talks about, let alone obstructs, another barbarity of our time, which is the victory of the rich.

–Samuel Moyn, 2018[13]

There should be no billionaires.

—Bernie Sanders, 2019[14]

Runaway inequality has remade American politics, reorienting power and policy toward corporations and the superrich. . . . The rise of plutocracy is the story of post-1980 American politics.

–Jacob Hacker and Paul Pierson, 2020[15]

Income and earnings disparities have risen considerably. . . . And most people in most countries are strenuously calling for greater equality of economic outcome and opportunity.

–Organization for Economic Cooperation and Development (OECD), 2021[16]

Inequality is widening, posing major moral, social, and political challenges to which policymakers must react. . . . Reacting to this evidence, we organized a major conference on inequality at the Peterson Institute for International Economics in October 2019. . . . There was widespread (if often implicit) agreement on many aspects of inequality that would have been more contentious some years earlier. For one thing, nobody at the conference challenged the view that inequality is a first-order problem requiring significant policy attention. . . . We sensed a much stronger belief than in the past that inequality is an urgent issue and should be at the top of policymakers' agendas.

–Olivier Blanchard and Dani Rodrik, 2021[17]

Inequality denial is as dangerous as climate denial.

—Thomas Piketty, 2023[18]

Today's extreme inequality is hampering Americans' freedom in ways large and small. Most children who grow up in poverty are not free to escape it. . . . Many children are not free to achieve their potential because they attend inadequate schools. Workers are not free to earn wages that reflect their economic contributions. Consumers are not free to avoid surprise medical bills and sneaky mobile phone fees. Americans are not free to travel around the country as rapidly or easily as the citizens of other affluent countries move around theirs. Nor do we live as long as they do. In each of these cases, the main culprit is our highly unequal economy.

–David Leonhardt, 2023[19]

Given that extreme wealth often translates into political power, the concentration of wealth in few hands is anathema to democracy. This is particularly evident in the age of Big Tech, when billionaires can gain an outsize influence on public discourse by taking over critical media platforms or manipulating search results.

–Kaushik Basu, 2023[20]

Economic inequality inevitably leads to political inequality, albeit to varying degrees across countries. In a country like the United States, which has virtually no constraints on campaign contributions, "one person, one vote" has morphed into "one dollar, one vote."

–Joseph Stiglitz, 2023[21]

The superrich stride the world like giants, and the rest of us quiver in their wake. . . . The superrich are pirates, pillaging the common wealth. We can and should abolish them. . . . The highest income one can earn should be limited to, say, 10 or 20 times the minimum wage (implying a maximum wage of $200,000 or $400,000 per year) and the maximum wealth that anyone is ever allowed to accumulate should be limited to roughly 200 or perhaps 400 times the median wealth (i.e., $20 million or $40 million).

–Tom Malleson, 2023[22]

Every billionaire is a policy failure.

—Oxfam, 2023[23]

Time is running out for the world to implement policies that work for the majority of us, not a handful of rich people. . . . Inequality should be at the top of the agenda. Governments, the IMF, the World Bank, and the UN must find practical solutions to address the inequality crisis. This will solve most of the challenges the world is facing. . . . All countries should aim for an income Gini index of 0.3 or less.

–Anthony Kamande, 2024[24]

Rising inequality has become a major cause for concern, even in affluent postindustrial societies. Rising inequality contributes to rising poverty; at any level of affluence in a society, the more unequal the distribution of resources, the higher the levels of poverty. Poverty has lasting effects on children's chances to develop to their full capacity, and thus on the human capital in their generation and ultimately on the productive capacity of the society. Where in the income distribution someone is born profoundly shapes their options in life. If the benefits from economic growth are captured by a small share of the population at the top of the income distribution, even those in the middle may be held back. A case in point is the United States, where real median household incomes remained stagnant for some three decades while the top 1 percent greatly increased their share of national income. Rising inequality generates higher levels of relative deprivation, which is associated with feelings of social exclusion and susceptibility to populist appeals. High levels of income inequality are accompanied by high levels of political inequality—e.g., in campaign financing and paying lobbyists—which violates democratic principles.

–Evelyne Huber and John Stephens, 2024[25]

Inequality is bad because it has bad consequences. It produces differences in social status and thereby creates stigma and undermines social cohesion. It leads to the abuse of power and domination of the political process by the elite, which then results in unfair policies that help the rich more than the poor. It undermines equality of opportunity. It generates stress and has negative effects on people's health. . . . I am advocating a political limit of, roughly, ten million per person. . . . Via policies and institutional design, governments should try to make sure that no one accumulates more money than this.

–Ingrid Robeyns, 2024[26]

The inequality at issue here isn't inequality between groups such as women and men, young and old, native-born and immigrant, Black and white. It's the overall amount of inequality of income or wealth in a society—the distance between the top and the bottom. I'll refer to this as "income inequality" or "wealth inequality," though I'll also frequently use the more generic terms "economic inequality" or just "inequality."

Is there a compelling case for reducing inequality in the world's affluent longstanding-democratic countries? If so, how high should this be on policymakers' priority list?

Inequality Is Unfair

Much of what determines a person's income and wealth—intelligence, creativity, physical and social skills, motivation, persistence, confidence, connections, inherited assets, discrimination—is a product of genetics, parents' assets and traits, and the quality of one's childhood neighborhood and schools. These aren't chosen; they are a matter of luck. A nontrivial portion of economic inequality is therefore, arguably, undeserved.[27]

Is Inequality Harmful?

Historically, the belief that inequality is unfair was the main reason for objection to it. In recent decades the source of opposition has shifted. A prominent concern now, perhaps the dominant one, is that inequality may have harmful effects on a range of outcomes we value, from democracy to opportunity to health and more.

The case for inequality reduction surely is much stronger if this is true. Is it true?

There are plausible reasons to suspect that economic inequality will have damaging consequences. One outcome of concern is living standards. Income inequality might reduce economic growth, the key driver of living standards over the long term. This could be because the rich tend to save a larger share of their income than do others, so more income inequality may yield inadequate consumption. Or the perceived unfairness of high income inequality may cause people to work less diligently or share less information with their managers. Whether economic growth is fast or slow, inequality may reduce income growth for households in the middle and at the bottom. When more of the income growth goes to those at the top, there is less available to go to those below the top. Another important component of living standards is household balance sheets. Income inequality might cause middle- and low-income households to take on more debt in an attempt to emulate spending by the affluent or simply because their own incomes aren't growing very rapidly.

Income inequality may interfere with a core element of democracy: equality of opportunity to influence government policy. Those with more income can use their money to buy political influence by lobbying, donating to campaigns, shaping opinion through the media and think tanks, getting themselves elected to policymaking positions, and in other ways.

A third key outcome is economic opportunity. Income can influence a variety of things that determine children's chances in life, including family structure, school quality, parents' spending, health, and neighborhoods. Greater inequality of income may therefore result in greater inequality of economic opportunity.

One of the most common concerns about income inequality's consequences has to do with health and longevity. More income inequality may cause us to stress more about our status position. Stress can harm health directly, and it may lead people to engage in behaviors that are bad for health, such as smoking, overeating, drug and alcohol abuse, and violence to oneself or to others.

Economic inequality may also hinder happiness. We tend to compare ourselves to others, so rising income inequality might cause us to perceive that we're no better off than before even when living standards and well-being are increasing.

A Focus on Countries

In assessing inequality's effects, I'll focus on countries. I examine developments within the rich democratic nations and compare across them. There are many ways we can go about assessing inequality's consequences, but if our interest is in the implications for government policy, we ought to privilege country-level evidence. Most of the relevant levers for influencing economic inequality are at the level of the national government. That's why when someone hypothesizes that less income inequality would improve living standards or democracy or health or some other outcome, they typically mean less inequality in their country, rather than in their school or workplace or neighborhood or city or region.

Some analyses of inequality's effects look at individuals. This can be relevant and helpful. A lab experiment that finds people are more likely to cheat or to become stressed when they're in a context of high inequality tells us something. So too can analyses of survey data from individuals. However, relying on individual-level evidence comes with a critical limitation: we don't know whether effects we observe will scale up. If our aim is to guide policy, this is very important.

Consider this example. A prominent hypothesis holds that lower tax rates will increase economic growth. Many studies of individuals find that people respond to financial incentives in a way that is consistent with this hypothesis. Yet when we look at the world's rich democratic countries, the patterns across countries and the patterns over time within countries aren't consistent with the lower-taxes-are-good-for-economic-growth hypothesis.[28] The incentive effect for individuals evidently is relatively small, or it may be offset by other effects of taxes that are conducive to growth. Either way, this information—the impact of taxes on aggregate outcomes for the country—is what citizens and policymakers need to know.

The same is true for inequality. If analyses of individuals find evidence consistent with the inequality-is-harmful hypothesis, that lends support to the hypothesis. But if the country-level evidence tells a different story, we should be very cautious before recommending to policymakers that reducing income inequality is a good strategy for improving living standards or opportunity or health or some other outcome.

The Era of Rising Inequality

Figure 1.1 shows the share of income that goes to the top 1 percent of households in each of the world's affluent longstanding-democratic nations. This tells us about income inequality between those at the top and everyone else. It's one of the two main ways social scientists typically measure income inequality. If income were distributed equally across all households, the top 1 percent of households would get 1 percent of the income. Instead, in most of these nations this group gets around 10 percent of the income.

These data come mainly from income tax records, and for some countries they're available all the way back to the 1800s.[29] As we can see in figure 1.1, the trend in top-end income inequality has shifted over time. Between the late 1800s and the early 1900s it was increasing in most of the countries for which we have data. Then it decreased nearly everywhere for about seventy years, from 1910 until around 1979. Since the late 1970s, inequality has risen in most countries.[30]

The post-1979 rise in inequality hasn't been the same everywhere.[31] The top 1 percent's income share has increased quite rapidly in Australia, Canada, Denmark, Finland, Italy, New Zealand, the United Kingdom, and the United States. It has risen less rapidly in France, Germany, Ireland, Japan, Korea, Norway, Portugal, and Sweden. It's increased only minimally or not at all in Austria, Belgium, the Netherlands, Spain, and Switzerland. The book's appendix has a separate graph for each country that makes it easier to see these differing trends.

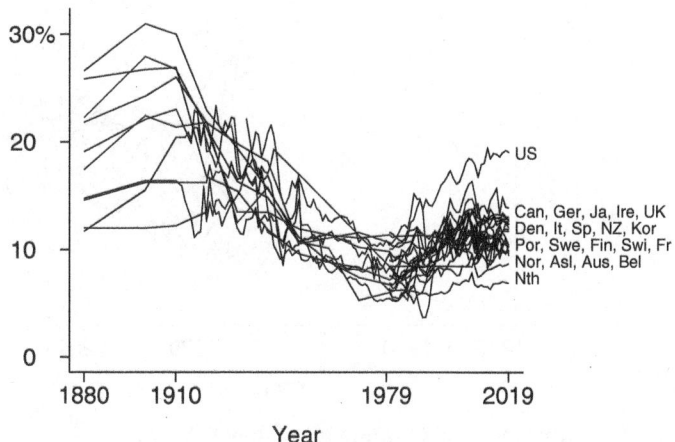

Figure 1.1 Income inequality between the top 1 percent and the bottom 99 percent
Top 1 percent's share of income. Pretax income. Excludes capital gains. Data source: World Inequality Database. "Asl" is Australia; "Aus" is Austria.

10 IS INEQUALITY THE PROBLEM?

The second way social scientists measure income inequality is within the bottom 99 percent. The standard measure here is the Gini coefficient, which is equal to zero if everyone's income is the same and 100 if a single household gets all of the income. These data come mainly from household surveys in which people are asked what their income was in the previous year.

Figure 1.2 shows the data for bottom-99-percent income inequality. Because many countries didn't begin conducting regular income surveys until the 1960s or 1970s, these data don't go nearly as far back in time as the top-1-percent-income-share data. Even so, we can see the same pattern of falling inequality in the period prior to the late 1970s and rising inequality since then.

And here too we observe a good bit of variation across the countries in the degree to which income inequality has increased since 1979 (again the appendix has a chart for each nation). Inequality rose sharply in Australia, Finland, Germany, Japan, New Zealand, Sweden, and the United States. It rose less rapidly in Austria, Belgium, Canada, Denmark, Italy, the Netherlands, Norway, Spain, and the United Kingdom. It remained flat or declined slightly in France, Ireland, Korea, Portugal, and Switzerland.

It would be nice to have a single, unified measure of income inequality. However, the data for these two measures come from different sources—one from income tax records, the other from surveys. In recent years some analysts have made efforts to merge them.[32] But these efforts rely on a number of assumptions

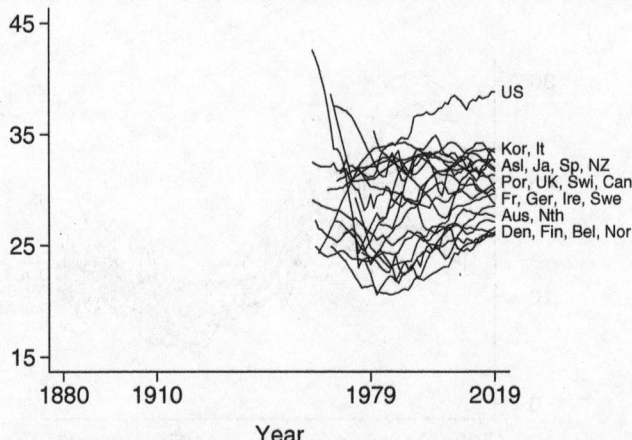

Figure 1.2 Income inequality within the bottom 99 percent

Gini coefficient. Posttransfer-posttax income, adjusted for household size. The vertical axis doesn't begin at zero. Data source: Frederick Solt, Standardized World Income Inequality Database, version 9.5, using data from the Luxembourg Income Study, the OECD, and other sources. "Asl" is Australia; "Aus" is Austria.

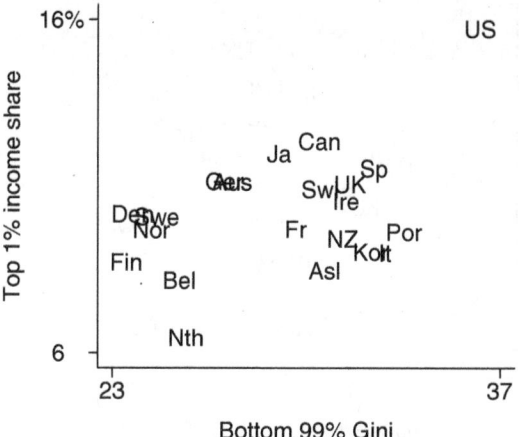

Figure 1.3 Level of income inequality within the bottom 99 percent and level of income inequality between the top 1 percent and the bottom 99 percent

Average for the years 1979 to 2019. For data description and sources, see figures 1.1 and 1.2. "Asl" is Australia; "Aus" is Austria. The correlation is +.46.

and imputations. We don't yet know how valid and reliable these combined measures are.

More important, perhaps, there are a number of countries for which these two measures of inequality, which focus on different points in the income distribution, tell differing stories. Figure 1.3 shows the average top 1 percent income share by the average bottom-99-percent Gini across the countries over the period from 1979 to 2019. These two measures are positively correlated—nations that are higher on one of the measures tend to be higher on the other. But the correlation isn't especially strong. The same is true when we look at change over this period, shown in figure 1.4. Indeed, here the correlation is even weaker. Quite a few countries that had relatively little rise on one measure of income inequality saw much greater increase on the other measure.

Given these considerations, it makes more sense to examine income inequality's effects using these two separate measures rather than a single combined measure. That's what I'll do throughout the book.

Reducing Inequality Probably Won't Do Much to Solve Other Problems

I examine the country evidence on the effect of income inequality on living standards, democracy, equality of opportunity, longevity, and happiness (chapters 2

12 IS INEQUALITY THE PROBLEM?

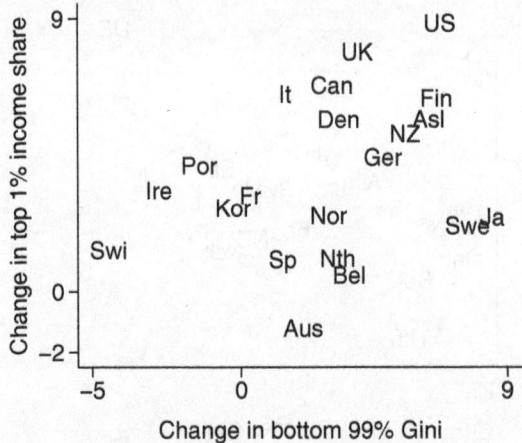

Figure 1.4 Change in income inequality within the bottom 99 percent and change in income inequality between the top 1 percent and the bottom 99 percent

Change from 1979 to 2019. Rather than calculate pure change scores (ending-year value minus beginning-year value), I regress each variable on year to calculate average yearly change and then multiply by 40 (the number of years). This avoids potential problems due to quirks in beginning or ending values. For data description and sources, see figures 1.1 and 1.2. "Asl" is Australia; "Aus" is Austria. The correlation is +.31.

through 7). As it turns out, support for the notion that reducing inequality will improve other outcomes is underwhelming.

Rich democratic nations with higher levels of income inequality or larger increases in income inequality haven't tended to have slower economic growth, lower or slower-growing household income, or worse household balance sheets.

Government policy decisions tend to reflect the preferences of people with high incomes more than those of people with middle or low incomes. That's inconsistent with what we'd like in a democracy—equal opportunity for political influence. However, in the United States, which has experienced a large rise in income inequality since the late 1970s, the amount of inequality in political influence hasn't increased. Nor does it appear to differ notably from other nations that have far lower levels of income inequality. So even if the United States was able to reduce income inequality back to the level of the late 1970s, its lowest level ever, there is little reason to expect that would reduce inequality of political influence.

There are a number of pathways through which income inequality might increase inequality of opportunity, from family structure to family expenditures to schools and neighborhoods. Yet evidence that reducing income inequality will significantly reduce inequality of opportunity is quite thin.

The notion that income inequality is harmful for health has received substantial attention from researchers, and some now take it for granted that inequality reduces longevity. But the country evidence offers very little support for this conclusion.

Does income inequality and its rise account for why the rich democratic nations have had so little improvement in life satisfaction since the 1970s despite rising incomes and living standards? Inequality might be a contributor, but if so it appears to be a minor one.

None of this tells us that inequality isn't a problem. But it does strongly suggest that inequality isn't *the* problem. Reducing income inequality isn't likely to significantly boost living standards for the poor or the middle class. It probably won't do much to equalize political influence. It's unlikely to help much with equalization of economic opportunity. It probably won't make much difference for our health. And it's doubtful that it will facilitate a rise in happiness.

We have less data with which to assess the consequences of wealth inequality (chapter 10). But two key facts from the country experience recommend skepticism about the wealth-inequality-is-harmful hypothesis. One is the success of the Nordic countries in creating good outcomes despite comparatively high wealth inequality. The other is the massive advance in well-being in France over the past two centuries despite the small and stagnant wealth share held by the bottom half of the French population.

We're likely to make more progress in living standards, democracy, opportunity, health, and happiness by pursuing these outcomes directly, rather than by hoping to achieve them indirectly via a reduction in income inequality or wealth inequality.

Within-Country Inequality and Global Inequality

Egalitarians have tended to focus on economic inequality within countries.[33] That's understandable. Most of the available inequality data are for countries, and inequality-shaping policy is made mostly by national governments. However, new data suggest that in recent decades global income inequality has been decreasing even as inequality within most of the rich democratic nations has been rising (chapter 9).

A key contributor to the decline in worldwide inequality is globalization—in particular, trade between poor countries and rich ones and migration from poor countries to rich ones. But trade and migration tend to boost income inequality within rich nations. Egalitarian policymakers in the rich democracies therefore must, at least to some extent, prioritize one type of inequality reduction over the other. Fairness considerations lean strongly in favor of prioritizing worldwide equality rather than equality within the affluent nations.

Inequality Reduction Should Be a Secondary Goal

Much of the gap in income and wealth between people is undeserved, because most of what determines where each of us ends up on the socioeconomic ladder is beyond our control. Less economic inequality would be fairer. Moreover, lots of people would like there to be less inequality (chapter 8). Reducing inequality of income and wealth is therefore a sensible goal. I'll offer suggestions for how to do this (chapter 12).

At the same time, inequality reduction shouldn't be a top-level priority (chapter 11). We don't need the Gini coefficient or the top 1 percent's income share to be among our headline economic and social indicators. We don't need to enact a policy whereby tax rates shift automatically in order to hold income inequality at a constant level. I don't think we should impose a cap on the amount of income or wealth a person can have. It wouldn't be wise to decrease spending on government services in order to fund a universal basic income, even though doing so would sharply reduce income inequality. And while widespread homeownership is an effective way to reduce wealth inequality, we should hesitate to encourage that.

Our principal aim should be to make people's lives better, especially by bringing up the floor of living standards and well-being. A key element of this is public goods and services. These don't show up in measures of income or wealth, so they don't contribute to reduction of income inequality or wealth inequality. But they matter greatly for our capabilities and quality of life.

2
Is Income Inequality Bad for Living Standards?

For a growing number of observers, the chief concern about income inequality is that it may have harmful effects on a range of outcomes we value. Does it?

Chapters 2 through 7 examine the evidence. In this chapter I look at the effect of income inequality on living standards. Chapter 3 explores democracy. Chapter 4 examines opportunity. Chapter 5 turns to health. In chapter 6 I look at happiness. Chapter 7 draws conclusions and considers some potential objections.

How Should We Assess Income Inequality's Effects?

I examine twenty-one affluent longstanding-democratic nations for which we have data on income inequality and on many of the outcomes of interest: Australia, Austria, Belgium, Canada, Denmark, Finland, France, Germany, Ireland, Italy, Japan, Korea (South), the Netherlands, New Zealand, Norway, Portugal, Spain, Sweden, Switzerland, the United Kingdom, and the United States.

Data are available for some middle-income and poor countries as well. But it doesn't make sense to include them because inequality's effects are likely to be very different in rich countries than in poor and middle-income ones. For instance, in less-affluent countries, income inequality tends to reduce economic growth,[1] but the ways in which it does so are specific to those countries. It hampers educational attainment, as parents force their children to work instead of going to school, and it fosters political instability. Neither of these causal paths applies in rich democracies. Few families keep their children out of elementary or secondary school due to financial need, and governments aren't threatened or toppled by groups demanding less inequality. If we want to understand the impact of income inequality in affluent democratic nations, we need to confine the analysis to such nations.[2]

Much existing country-level study of the effects of income inequality is comparative but static; it is based on patterns across countries at a single point in time. These "cross-sectional" correlations can be informative, but they also can be misleading, because nations differ culturally and in other ways that we can't measure very well and that might be the true cause of differences in outcomes such as economic growth, opportunity, or happiness.

Imagine we want to know the effect of a vitamin supplement on people's health. One approach would be to collect information from a large number of people about whether they take the vitamin supplement and about their health. Suppose we do this and we find that people who take the supplement tend to have better health. It could be a mistake to conclude that the supplement caused the better health, because those who take the supplement may differ from those who don't in ways that contribute to good health. Similarly, countries with lower income inequality may differ from countries with higher inequality in a variety of ways that affect economic, social, and political outcomes.

A better design for testing the impact of the vitamin supplement is to measure the health of a set of people, then have a randomly selected subset of them take the supplement, and then measure everyone's health again at a later point in time. If those who began taking the vitamin supplement see their health improve more than those who didn't take the supplement, we can have greater confidence that the vitamin has a genuine causal effect on health.

We can't do this kind of experiment with countries, but we can approximate it. As we saw in chapter 1, the degree to which income inequality changed between 1979 and 2019 varies markedly across the rich democratic countries. This variation in changes—this "difference in differences," as statisticians call it—is useful for analytical purposes. If nations with larger increases in inequality experienced greater worsening of an outcome than countries with smaller increases in inequality, we can be more confident that inequality has a causal effect. A correlation between changes in the hypothesized cause and changes in the outcome is less likely to be caused by culture or other constant, potentially influential, difficult-to-measure differences between countries.[3]

A difference-in-differences approach is appropriate when we have significant over-time change in the hypothesized cause, when there is variation across nations in that change, and when the change is mainly unidirectional rather than up and down. For income inequality in the world's rich countries during the period from 1979 to 2019, all three of these conditions apply (see figures 1.1 through 1.4 in chapter 1).

Effects of income inequality are likely to take a while to play out, so I focus on change over the full period of rising inequality, from 1979 to 2019, rather than change over a single year or a few years. Four decades should be a sufficiently lengthy time period for an impact of income inequality to show up if one exists. Both 1979 and 2019 were business-cycle peak years, so they are useful starting and ending points.

For each of the outcomes, I try controlling for some other potential influences: change in gross domestic product (GDP) per capita, change in educational attainment, change in the elderly population share, and change in the immigrant population share.[4] To keep the presentation simple, I mention this only when adding such controls alters a finding.

Does Income Inequality Reduce Economic Growth?

Let's begin with economic growth, the most important determinant of living standards over the long run.[5] It has become increasingly common to conclude or assert that income inequality reduces economic growth.[6]

There are several hypotheses about why inequality might be bad for growth in affluent democratic nations.[7] One points to the fact that consumer demand is important for growth. The rich spend a smaller fraction of their income than the middle class and the poor, so if a larger share of income goes to those at the top, consumer demand may weaken. On the other hand, investment also is important for growth, and those with high incomes tend to save and invest more than the middle class and the poor. We don't know what mix of consumption and investment is best for economic growth, so while it's perfectly reasonable to suspect that a rise in income inequality will move us away from the optimal point, this suspicion has to take a back seat to the data.

A second way in which income inequality might reduce economic growth is that if people perceive the distribution of pay and income to be unfair, their resentment may spur productivity-decreasing behavior. They may not work as hard. They may be less likely to share valuable information with management. They may be more likely to steal from their employer. However, while there are supportive experiments and anecdotes,[8] we don't have economy-wide evidence that more inequality tends to result in less productive workers.

Third, income inequality may increase the likelihood of financial crises that reduce economic growth in the short or long run. Households with stagnant incomes might increase borrowing in order to sustain consumption growth, eventually leading to unsustainable debt levels. Or as the rich get a larger and larger portion of the income, they may end up with excess savings, fueling speculative investment and financial bubbles. Or the rich might use their money and consequent political influence to press policymakers to loosen regulations on finance. This too could lead to bubbles.

Then again, the most comprehensive study of financial crises across countries and over time concludes that "the history of systemic banking crises in different countries around the world does not suggest that either rising or high inequality is a significant causal factor."[9] What about the 2008 financial crisis in particular? While analysts continue to debate its causes, there are grounds for skepticism about income inequality's contribution.[10] In the United States, the epicenter of the crisis, there was growing demand for loans by middle- and low-income households, but that may have been driven more by the rising cost of homes and college, along with relaxed lending standards and the availability of home equity loans, than by slow household income growth. (We'll look more closely at this later in the chapter.) There was risky lending by financial institutions, but this may have been spurred by the creation of new financial instruments that appeared to spread risk and by rising pressure for profits in publicly owned investment firms. Finally, the Federal Reserve could have quashed the housing bubble, the proximate precipitant of the crisis, had it wanted to. That it chose not to do so arguably owed more to Fed chair Alan Greenspan's ideological predilections than to the political influence of America's rich.

So we have some plausible hypotheses predicting a negative impact of income inequality on economic growth but also grounds for skepticism. What does the country-level evidence say? Prior studies have reached varying conclusions, but few have concluded that inequality is bad for growth.[11]

Figure 2.1 shows countries' average rate of economic growth over 1979 to 2019 (vertical axes) by their average level of income inequality over that period (horizontal axes). Economic growth is adjusted for countries' starting level of GDP per capita, because nations that begin less affluent have been able to grow more rapidly—to "catch up"—by borrowing technology from the leading nations.[12]

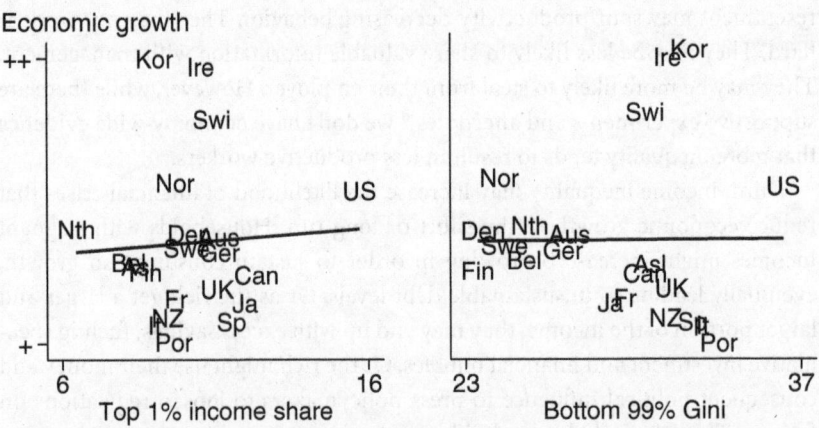

Figure 2.1 Income inequality and economic growth

Average for 1979–2019. Horizontal axes: income inequality. For data description and sources, see figures 1.1–1.4. Vertical axes: average rate of growth of inflation-adjusted and purchasing-power-parity-adjusted gross domestic product (GDP) per capita, 1979 to 2019. Economic growth is adjusted for starting level of GDP per capita; the vertical-axis measure is the residuals from a regression of average economic growth on 1979 level of GDP per capita. + = growth; ++ = faster growth. Data source: OECD, "Growth in GDP per Capita, Productivity, and ULC," stats.oecd.org. "Asl" is Australia; "Aus" is Austria. The lines are linear regression lines.

IS INCOME INEQUALITY BAD FOR LIVING STANDARDS?

The vertical axis is the same in both charts. The horizontal axis in the chart on the left uses income inequality between the top 1 percent and everyone else, while in the chart on the right it uses income inequality within the bottom 99 percent.

If the inequality-is-harmful hypothesis is correct, the pattern of countries should slope down to the right—countries with greater income inequality should have lower (catch-up adjusted) economic growth. However, that's not what we observe. Neither chart suggests that economic growth has been any slower in high-inequality countries than in low-inequality ones. Each chart includes a regression line that summarizes the association between income inequality and economic growth. The fact that these lines are flat tells us the two things aren't correlated with one another.

Figure 2.2 switches from levels to changes. It shows the association between changes in income inequality and changes in economic growth between 1979 and 2019. Most of these countries experienced a decline in economic growth during this period. The inequality-is-harmful hypothesis predicts that economic growth will have decreased more in countries with larger increases in income inequality. But that didn't happen. There was a similar decrease in economic growth in countries with little or no change in income inequality, in those with small or moderate increases in inequality, and in those with large increases in inequality.

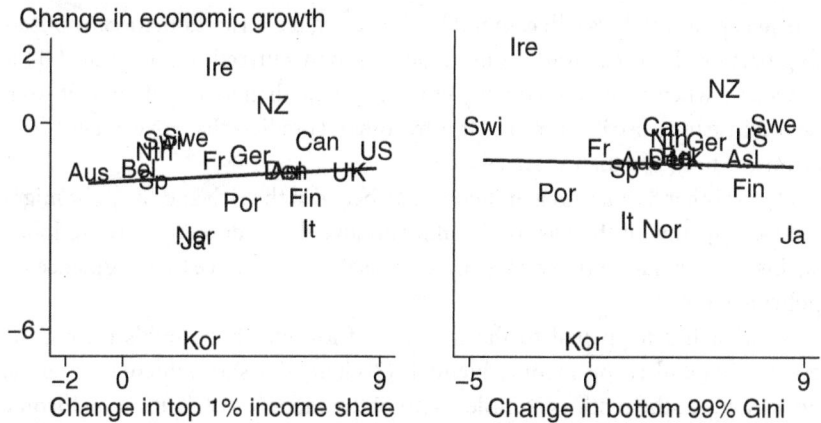

Figure 2.2 Change in income inequality and change in economic growth

Change from 1979 to 2019. Horizontal axes: change in income inequality. For data description and sources, see figures 1.1–1.4. Vertical axes: change in the rate of growth of inflation-adjusted and purchasing-power-parity-adjusted gross domestic product (GDP) per capita. The values on both axes are for average change per year multiplied by 40. Data source: OECD, "Growth in GDP per Capita, Productivity, and ULC," stats.oecd.org. "Asl" is Australia; "Aus" is Austria. The lines are linear regression lines.

Overall, the experience of the rich democracies suggests that income inequality hasn't tended to be bad for economic growth.

It's also worth emphasizing that, contrary to much theorizing from a generation ago,[13] there is no indication in the data that inequality is good for growth.

Does Income Inequality Reduce Low-End Household Income Growth?

If the rich or the upper middle class capture a large share of a country's economic growth, the incomes of low-end households are likely to increase more slowly than economic growth allows. This is a matter of simple arithmetic. As the pie grows, the poor's slice may increase in absolute size, but not as much as it would if the pie were divided more equally.

Now, this could be offset if rising income inequality causes economic growth to increase. If that were to happen, the faster increase in the size of the pie might compensate for the shrinking share of the pie going to those at the bottom. But as we saw in the previous section, there is no indication that income inequality has, in fact, produced faster economic growth in the world's affluent democratic countries.

Another potential counteracting force is government redistribution. An influential hypothesis holds that if the market distribution of income becomes more unequal, policymakers will respond by increasing redistribution, thereby offsetting part or all of the shortage of income growth suffered by the poor.[14] This is because when income inequality goes up, the median voter will benefit from an increase in redistribution, and this hypothesis predicts that governments will acquiesce to the median voter's wishes.

On the other hand, a greater income gap between the rich and the poor might reduce empathy on the part of the affluent, give them more incentive to lobby against redistribution (they have more to lose), and enhance their influence on policymaking.[15]

So what has happened to the incomes of low-end households during the era of high and rising income inequality? Figure 2.3 shows income levels of households at the tenth percentile (p10) of the income distribution by income inequality levels. In the chart on the left, we see little if any association with inequality measured as the share going to the top 1 percent. In the chart on the right, with inequality measured within the bottom 99 percent, there is a fairly strong negative correlation. In nations with greater bottom-99-percent income inequality, the incomes of poor households tend to be lower, which is what the inequality-is-harmful hypothesis predicts.

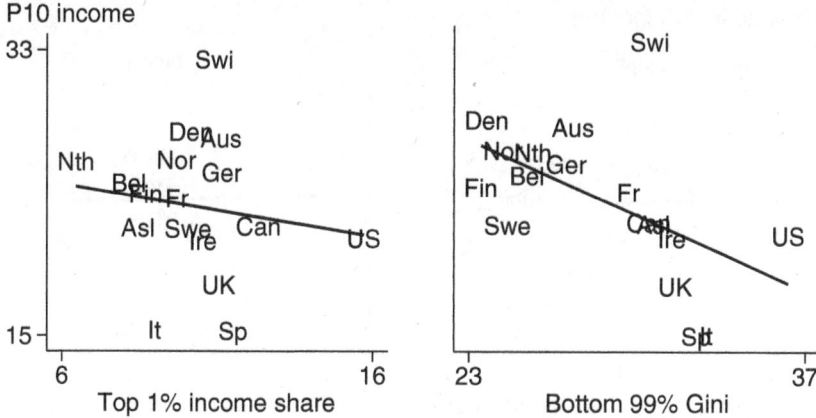

Figure 2.3 Income inequality and low-end household incomes

Average for 1979–2019. Horizontal axes: income inequality. For data description and sources, see figures 1.1–1.4. Vertical axes: posttransfer-posttax income at the tenth percentile of the income distribution. The incomes are adjusted for household size and then rescaled to reflect a three-person household, adjusted for inflation, and converted to US dollars using purchasing power parities. The numbers on the vertical axis are thousands of US dollars; "33" = $33,000. Data source: Luxembourg Income Study, "LIS Key Figures." "Asl" is Australia; "Aus" is Austria. Japan, Korea, New Zealand, and Portugal are missing due to limited data. The lines are linear regression lines.

This could, however, owe to characteristics of particular countries—especially those that have higher inequality and lower p10 incomes, such as the United States, the United Kingdom, Italy, and Spain. So it will help to examine changes over time. The charts in figure 2.4 show changes in low-end household incomes by changes in income inequality. Here we see no association at all. Countries with larger increases in income inequality haven't tended to experience slower growth of low-end household incomes.[16]

Why is that? Although we often think of economic growth trickling down to low-end households via rising employment and rising wages, since the late 1970s government transfers have played a more prominent role. This shouldn't surprise us. In most rich countries 20 to 35 percent of all households have no earnings, and this includes quite a few people on the low rungs of the income ladder. They are disabled, sick, caring for children or other family members, temporarily unemployed, or elderly. They rely heavily on government transfers, and so their incomes rise to the extent that those transfers rise.[17]

Policy choices about whether to increase government transfers to low-income households have been largely independent of income inequality. The contrast between the United States and the United Kingdom is illustrative. Both countries have had comparatively high and rising income inequality in the period since the late 1970s. But whereas government transfers to the poor increased only a little

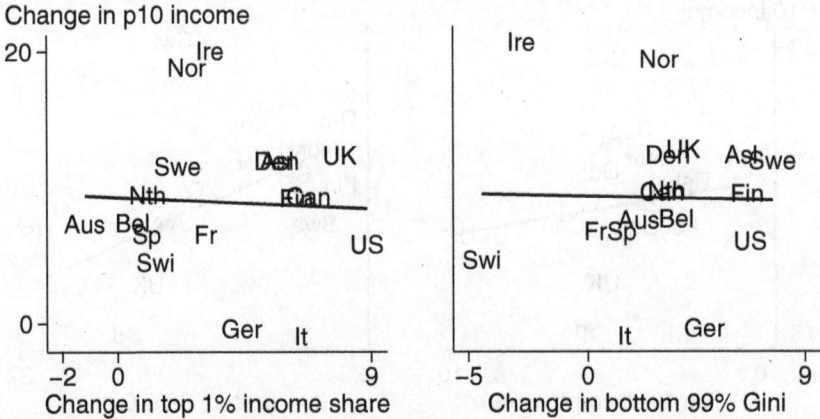

Figure 2.4 Change in income inequality and change in low-end household incomes

Change from 1979 to 2019. Horizontal axes: change in income inequality. For data description and sources, see figures 1.1–1.4. Change in posttransfer-posttax income at the tenth percentile of the income distribution. The incomes are adjusted for household size and then rescaled to reflect a three-person household, adjusted for inflation, and converted to US dollars using purchasing power parities. The numbers on the vertical axis are thousands of US dollars; "20" = $20,000. Data source: Luxembourg Income Study, "LIS Key Figures." "Asl" is Australia; "Aus" is Austria. Japan, Korea, New Zealand, and Portugal are missing due to limited data. The lines are linear regression lines

in the United States, in the United Kingdom they rose sharply, at least during the New Labour governments between 1997 and 2010. Those governments, headed by Tony Blair and Gordon Brown, focused much of their rhetoric on employment and economic opportunity, but they also increased benefits and reduced taxes for low earners, single parents, and pensioners.[18]

In short, changes in government transfers have been the chief determinant of changes in low-end household incomes in the rich democratic nations over the past several decades, and political decisions, rather than income inequality, have determined the degree to which those transfers increased. As a result, income inequality has had no systematic impact on the incomes of low-end households.

Does Income Inequality Reduce Middle-Class Household Income Growth?

Disproportionately large income gains at the top may come at least partly at the expense of those in the middle, resulting in slower middle-class income growth than would have been the case in the absence of high inequality.[19]

Figure 2.5 shows middle-class income levels by income inequality levels. On the vertical axis of each chart is posttransfer-posttax income for the median (p50)

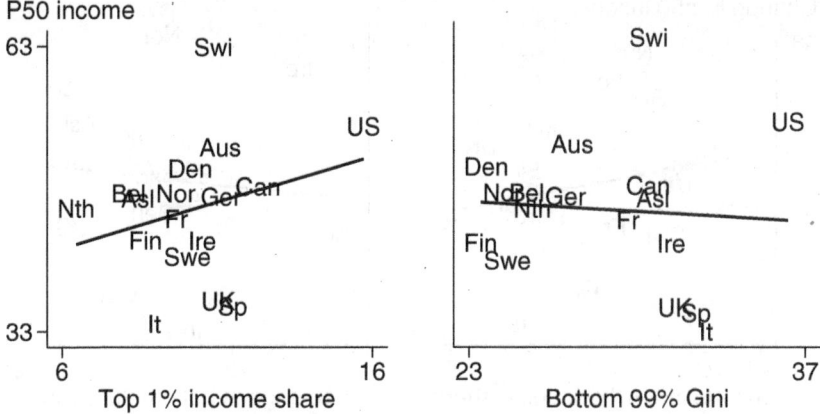

Figure 2.5 Income inequality and middle-class household incomes

Average for 1979–2019. Horizontal axes: Income inequality. For data description and sources, see figures 1.1–1.4. Vertical axes: Posttransfer-posttax income at the fiftieth percentile (median) of the income distribution. The incomes are adjusted for household size and then rescaled to reflect a three-person household, adjusted for inflation, and converted to US dollars using purchasing power parities. The numbers on the vertical axis are in thousands of US dollars; "63" = $63,000. Data source: Luxembourg Income Study, "LIS Key Figures." "Asl" is Australia; "Aus" is Austria. Japan, Korea, New Zealand, and Portugal are missing due to limited data. The lines are linear regression lines

household. On the horizontal axis is the average level of income inequality. Neither chart shows the predicted negative association. Nations with greater income inequality don't tend to have lower middle-class incomes. (In the first chart the line slopes slightly upward, but that's due entirely to a single country, the United States, and so isn't representative of the broader pattern across the countries.)

The same is true when we turn to changes, in figure 2.6. Countries with larger increases in income inequality haven't tended to experience smaller increases in middle-class incomes. Studies examining shorter time periods have reached a similar conclusion.[20]

Does Income Inequality Worsen Household Balance Sheets?

Rising income inequality may cause households to reduce their saving, increase their borrowing, and thereby run up debt. There are two ways this can happen.

One is that low- and middle-income households borrow more in order to keep their absolute consumption increasing in the face of slow income growth.[21] People come to expect a certain rate of increase in their spending over time, and when this expectation is frustrated due to stagnant or slowly rising earnings, they

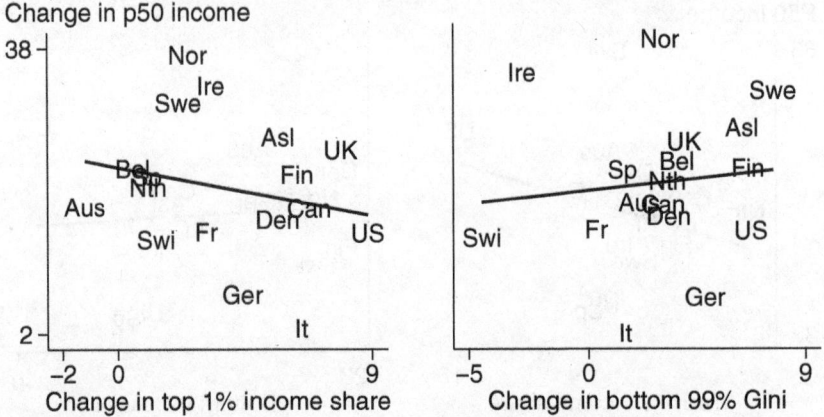

Figure 2.6 Change in income inequality and change in middle-class household incomes

Change from 1979 to 2019. Horizontal axes: Change in income inequality. For data description and sources, see figures 1.1–1.4. Change in posttransfer-posttax income at the fiftieth percentile (median) of the income distribution. The incomes are adjusted for household size and then rescaled to reflect a three-person household, adjusted for inflation, and converted to US dollars using purchasing power parities. The numbers on the vertical axis are in thousands of US dollars; "38" = $38,000. Data source: Luxembourg Income Study, "LIS Key Figures." "Asl" is Australia; "Aus" is Austria. Japan, Korea, New Zealand, and Portugal are missing due to limited data. The lines are linear regression lines.

turn to borrowing as a substitute. We've just seen, however, that the country evidence suggests no systematic tendency for income inequality to reduce economic growth or low-end or middle-class household income growth, so this hypothesis seems unlikely to play out.

The second is that middle-class households borrow more in order to maintain or improve their relative position in the status hierarchy, especially in housing.[22] Housing is a "positional" good. To a greater degree than for goods such as toothpaste and cereal, people's happiness with their home depends on how it compares to other homes. Rapidly rising income inequality allows the well-to-do to purchase increasingly large and elaborately equipped homes. Because housing satisfaction depends on relative comparison, middle-class homebuyers and homeowners may feel compelled to follow suit, leading to dramatic increases in home prices and housing expenditures. To afford these expensive homes and home renovations, middle-class buyers might have no choice but to take on higher and higher levels of debt.[23]

For comparing across countries, the best measure of household borrowing is savings as a share of household disposable income. Increased borrowing will show up as reduced saving. Figure 2.7 plots average levels of household saving by levels of income inequality. There is no noteworthy correlation. Figure 2.8 shows changes in household saving by changes in income inequality. (Change here is measured over 1995 to 2019, because household savings data for several countries begin in 1995.) Once again there is no association. So the cross-country and over-time experience of the rich democratic nations doesn't suggest that income inequality is bad for household balance sheets.

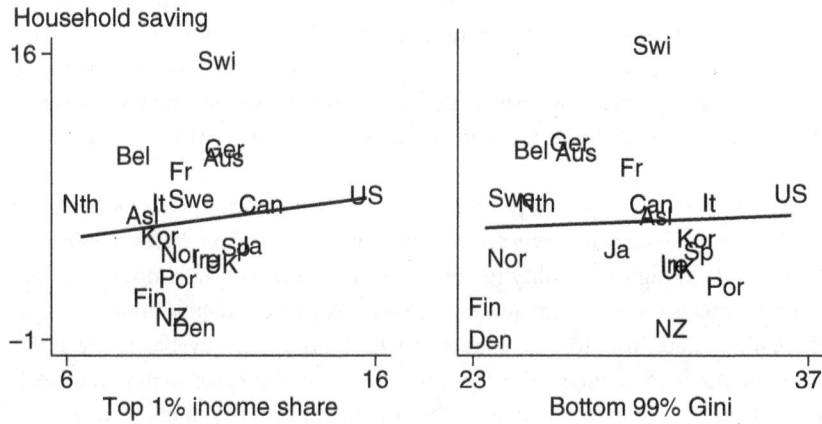

Figure 2.7 Income inequality and household saving

Average for 1979–2019. Horizontal axes: income inequality. For data description and sources, see figures 1.1–1.4. Vertical axes: net household saving as a share of disposable household income. Data source: OECD, "Household Savings," data.oecd.org. "Asl" is Australia; "Aus" is Austria. The lines are linear regression lines.

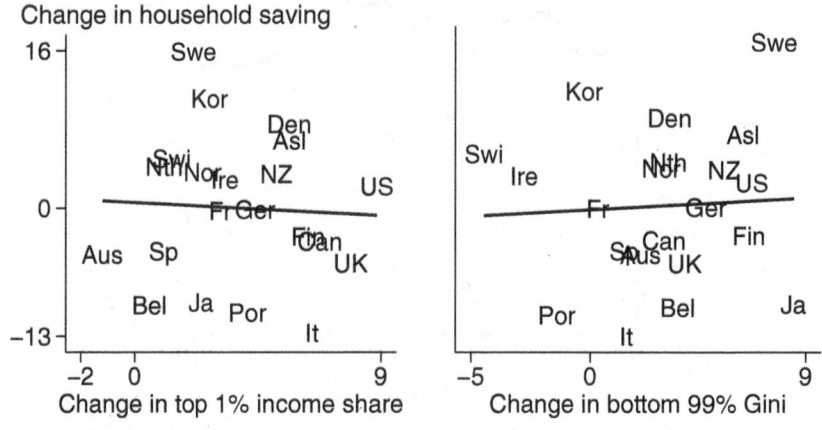

Figure 2.8 Change in income inequality and change in household saving

Change from 1979 to 2019. Horizontal axes: change in income inequality, 1979 to 2019. For data description and sources, see figures 1.1–1.4. Vertical axes: change in net household saving as a share of disposable household income, 1995 to 2019. Data source: OECD, "Household Savings," data.oecd.org. "Asl" is Australia; "Aus" is Austria. The lines are linear regression lines.

Let's look more closely at the US experience. Studies focusing on the 1990s and 2000s, which featured the housing bubble and the 2008–9 financial crisis, have tended to conclude that income inequality contributed to a rise in household borrowing and debt. One study found that from 1995 to 2007 Americans who live in commuting zones with higher income inequality were likely, if they moved, to move to a more expensive home and to take on more debt.[24] Another found that changes in income inequality within the bottom 99 percent between 1990 and 2000 were correlated with changes in the rate of nonbusiness bankruptcy filings.[25] And as income inequality was rising in the United States, average household saving as a share of disposable household income decreased—from 12 percent in the 1970s to 10 percent in the 1980s to 8 percent in the 1990s to 5 percent in the 2000s.[26]

However, other empirical patterns in the United States are inconsistent with the inequality-is-harmful hypothesis. First, in the 1990s and 2000s low-income households in high-inequality regions borrowed relatively less, not more, than their counterparts in low-inequality regions.[27] And second, household saving in the United States rose to 8 percent in the 2010s, the same level as in the 1990s, even though income inequality was much higher in the 2010s than in the 1990s. Indeed, figure 2.9 shows that household debt service payments as a share of household disposable income, which is perhaps the best indicator of the debt position of American households, decreased in the 2010s to their lowest level since 1980.

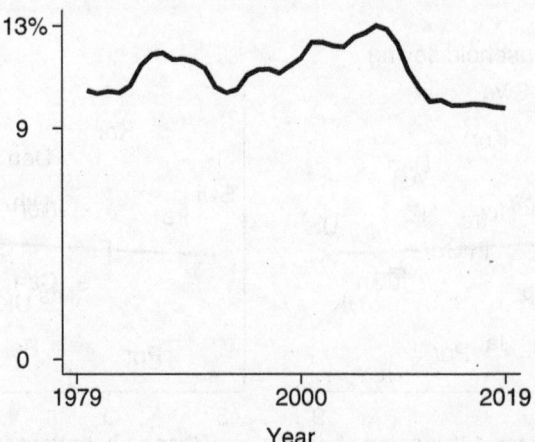

Figure 2.9 Household debt service payments as a share of disposable personal income, United States

Total required household debt payments (for mortgage debt and consumer debt) as a share of total disposable household income. Data source: St. Louis Federal Reserve, FRED database, series TDSP.

If it wasn't income inequality that caused the drop in saving and the rise in debt in the United States in the 1980s, 1990s, and 2000s, what *was* the cause? An alternative hypothesis points to the increase in the supply of available credit. Beginning in the early 1980s, US financial firms became increasingly aggressive in developing new and augmented financial products and marketing them to investors and consumers.[28] This included smaller down payments for mortgage loans, access to home equity loans and lines of credit, and reductions in the stringency of criteria by which borrowers' creditworthiness was assessed. These shifts sharply boosted Americans' access to credit, and in doing so they contributed to a loosening of their attitudes toward borrowing and financial risk.[29]

Is Income Inequality Bad for Living Standards?

There are plausible hypotheses about why income inequality might slow economic growth, reduce income growth for poor and middle-class households, and increase household borrowing and debt. But the comparative experience of the world's rich longstanding-democratic countries in the era of rising inequality suggests little reason to think that inequality has had these effects.

3

Does Income Inequality Degrade Democracy?

Democracy is a system of decision-making in which people have approximately equal opportunity to influence government policy.[1] Economic inequality can make the political system less democratic, because those with more money are likely to be able to exert disproportionate influence over policymaking. How strong is this effect? How much does inequality matter?

I focus in this chapter largely, though not exclusively, on the United States. Although that's due to data limitations, the US case happens to be a useful one to explore. Income inequality between the rich and the nonrich is greater in America than in other countries, and it has increased sharply since the late 1970s, as we saw in chapter 1. The same is true for wealth, as we'll see later in the book. As top-end economic inequality grows, a country like the United States may increasingly get government by the affluent.

The Inequality-Is-Harmful Hypothesis

There are five main ways that people with more income, along with companies they own or control, can deploy money to increase their influence over policymakers' decisions. First, they can donate to politicians and political parties. Election campaigns are expensive, and private donations account for most of the money that campaigns spend. Expenditures in US elections totaled more than $16 billion in 2020 and in 2024, up from $5 billion in 2000.[2] Americans in the top 0.01 percent of incomes account for about 40 percent of campaign contributions.[3] It wouldn't be surprising to find that candidates and elected officials listen most attentively to the policy preferences of their most generous donors.

Second, affluent Americans can run for office themselves. More than half of the 535 members of the Senate and the House of Representatives have a net worth of more than $1 million.[4] A billionaire, Donald Trump, succeeded in getting elected president in 2016 and 2024, and fellow billionaires Michael Bloomberg and Tom Steyer ran for the Democratic Party nomination in 2020, albeit unsuccessfully.

Third, the rich and their companies can spend money to lobby elected policymakers. Lobbying expenditures in the United States total about $3.5 billion each year, and they increased sharply in the 2000s before leveling off in the 2010s.[5]

Fourth, those with money can fund organizations and movements that pressure policymakers in other ways—calling their office, showing up at town hall meetings, generating online petitions, canvassing voters, marching in the streets.

Fifth, affluent Americans can use their money to influence ideas. They can finance research. They can establish and fund think tanks. They can create or buy media outlets. They can sponsor and promote like-minded opinion leaders.

The inequality-is-harmful hypothesis predicts that as income and wealth inequality have increased since the late 1970s, the political influence of those at the top will have risen in tandem.[6] Indeed, the United States could now be stuck in a plutocratic "doom loop"—economic inequality rises, causing an increase political inequality, which leads to policies that further increase economic inequality—from which there is no escape.

Yet money in politics surely is subject to diminishing returns. There was considerable economic inequality in the United States in the late 1970s. In all likelihood, America's affluent already had a good bit more political influence than the rest of the citizenry at that point in time, and it's conceivable that their advantage had reached its maximum. If so, then even though the rich have gotten a rising share of the country's income and wealth during the ensuing four decades, this might not have increased their advantage in influencing policy decisions.

What kinds of things would we expect to observe if the inequality-is-harmful hypothesis is correct? Do we observe them?

Do America's Rich Have Disproportionate Political Influence?

Scholars have been researching the political influence of economic elites since the middle of the twentieth century. Studies have tended to focus on individual policies, or sometimes on a handful of related policies. This is helpful, but to really answer the question we need a more comprehensive analysis. Unfortunately, we have very little.

In one of the few attempts at a comprehensive study, Larry Bartels uses public opinion survey data to identify the policy preferences of Americans in three income groups: low, middle, and high.[7] He then examines the degree to which these opinions correlate with votes by people's elected representatives in the House and the Senate in the early 1990s and early 2010s. Bartels concludes that policymakers' voting tends to correspond much more closely to the desires of people with high incomes than to the wishes of those with middle and low incomes. This kind of study is a big advance, in that it gives us evidence on the influence of different income groups across an array of policies and issues. But legislators' voting may or may not translate into actual policy decisions.

In his book *Affluence and Influence*, Martin Gilens takes this next step.[8] He begins by measuring the policy preferences of high-income, middle-income, and low-income Americans in public opinion surveys from 1981 through 2002. Where the preferences of people at these various income levels differed, Gilens looks to see whether policy changed over the ensuing four years, and if so in what direction. The data include a total of 1,779 policy outcomes. Gilens finds that policy decisions have been more likely to conform to the expressed preferences of high-income Americans than of middle-income or low-income Americans.

So yes, Americans with more income do seem to have more political influence than those with less income, as the inequality-is-harmful hypothesis predicts.

However, there are caveats. First, high-income Americans had a different preference than middle-income Americans on only 10 percent of the policies Gilens studied.[9] So the advantage in political influence held by those with high incomes is relevant for a fairly small number of policy choices.

Second, research has uncovered very little evidence that campaign contributions and lobbying influence policy decisions.[10] There are, as I noted earlier, other pathways through which money can affect policy, but it's surprising that researchers haven't identified a connection via the campaign donation and lobbying routes.

Third, despite the heroic efforts of Gilens and some others, social scientists don't yet have the evidence we really would want for testing the inequality-is-harmful hypothesis. For one thing, much of the discussion of inequality's impact on democracy focuses on top incomes, but the sample sizes in public opinion surveys are too small to get an accurate reading of the views of this group. There aren't enough top-1-percenters in the survey. Thus, "high income" in Gilens's analysis refers to roughly the ninetieth percentile of the income distribution rather than the top.

Also, the policy decisions in Gilens's data are limited to those that public opinion surveys have asked about. This leaves out a lot of policy. An alternative strategy is to begin with the full array of potential policy changes and study a random sample of them. Paul Burstein uses this approach in a recent study.[11] He begins with all of the policy proposals considered by Congress during the 1989–90 legislative session, draws a sample of 60 (manifested in a total of 417 bills), and then tracks their fate. Unfortunately, he, like Gilens, is unable to identify the views of rich Americans. And his data cover only two years.

It probably doesn't make sense to weight all potential policy changes equally, since both affluent and ordinary Americans likely care much more about some than others. In a statistical analysis this can be handled by differentially weighting the cases.

An ideal database probably would be something like Burstein's. However, it would cover many more years. It would cover not just legislation but also executive branch actions such as implementation of laws and regulations and issuance of executive orders. And it would include information about the policy preferences not only of people with high incomes but also those at the very top of the income distribution.

In the absence of this ideal database, I agree with Larry Bartels that "Gilens's work provides the best evidence we have regarding the responsiveness of the American political system to the preferences of its citizens."[12] Gilens's findings suggest, consistent with the inequality-is-harmful hypothesis, that higher-income Americans very likely do have disproportionate influence on policy decisions.

Has the Gap in Political Influence Between the Rich and the Rest Increased as Economic Inequality Has Increased?

Income inequality in the United States has increased sharply since the late 1970s. If the inequality-is-harmful hypothesis is correct, this rise in economic inequality should have led to a rise in inequality of political influence during these past four decades.

But in a study tracing policy wins by rich Americans and by business in recent decades, Jacob Hacker and Paul Pierson don't find a rise in the frequency of such wins.[13] Nor do Gilens's *Affluence and Influence* data suggest an increase in inequality of political influence. In addition to his core period of 1981 to 2002, Gilens examines the correlation between income and political influence for a selection of earlier and later years. He finds that the gap in influence between high-income Americans and those with middle or low incomes was small during the Johnson presidency in the 1960s, larger during the presidencies of Reagan and Clinton in the 1980s and 1990s, but then smaller during George W. Bush's presidency in the 2000s.[14] Christopher Wlezien and Stuart Soroka conduct an analysis similar to Gilens's and covering the years 1972 to 2008, though for a relatively small set of policies. They too find no indication of a rise in policymakers' disproportionate responsiveness to Americans who have higher incomes.[15]

This isn't the final word. It's possible that when someone updates Gilens's analyses through the 2010s (and beyond), or when researchers compile something like the ideal database I outlined in the previous section, the data will reveal that the rich-versus-the-rest gap in political influence has indeed increased in concert with economic inequality. But that isn't what's suggested by the best research we have at the moment.

Is The Gap in Political Influence Between the Rich and the Rest Larger in Nations with More Economic Inequality?

If the inequality-is-harmful hypothesis is correct, we would expect more inequality of political influence in countries with higher levels of income inequality. But that's not what the evidence suggests.

There are single-country studies of the link between preferences of people at different income levels and policy decisions in Germany, the Netherlands, Norway, Spain, Sweden, and Switzerland.[16] With the exception of Norway, these analyses conclude that, as in the United States, when the views of higher-income persons differ from the views of those with lower incomes, policy changes are more likely to reflect the desires of people with more income.

There also are two cross-country analyses that look at the degree to which policy changes tend to correspond to the expressed preferences of people at different income levels in an array of affluent democratic nations. Both find that, contrary to what the inequality-is-harmful hypothesis predicts, the magnitude of the rich-poor disparity in policy responsiveness is quite similar across countries that have very different levels of income inequality.[17]

These findings are consistent with the large research literature on why the United States has perhaps the least expansive and generous social policy among the rich democratic nations. That literature emphasizes culprits other than America's high level of economic inequality, such as its winner-take-all elections and consequent two-party political system, its large number of government veto points, its weak labor unions, its lack of corporatist concertation, its racial and ethnic diversity, and its absence of a feudal history.[18]

Have Top-End Tax Rates, Financial Regulation, and Unionization Decreased More in the United States Than in Countries with Less Economic Inequality?

Top-end income inequality has increased more in the United States than elsewhere. According to the inequality-is-harmful hypothesis, we should therefore expect greater movement toward policy outcomes desired by the well-to-do in America than in other rich democratic nations.

Begin with taxes. The top statutory federal income tax rate was indeed reduced more sharply in the United States than in most other affluent democracies. Yet some other countries where income inequality barely increased at all, such as Japan and Norway, made similar changes to their top statutory tax rates.[19] Just as puzzling, nearly all of the change in the United States occurred at the beginning of the rise in income inequality, in the 1980s, rather than toward the end.

The top statutory tax rate is of limited relevance if there are numerous loopholes and deductions that allow the rich to shield a sizable portion of their income from taxation. What really matters to taxpayers is the "effective" tax rate—taxes paid as a share of pretax income. Estimates of the top effective tax rate in the United States suggest that while it has fluctuated—decreasing under Reagan, increasing under the first Bush and Clinton, decreasing again under the second Bush, increasing again under Obama, and decreasing again under Trump—it was about the same in 2017 as when Reagan entered office.[20] Even with the Trump tax cut, it remains higher than it was after the 1981 Reagan cuts.

What about financial regulation? The United States did reduce regulations on the financial sector, but here too the most significant change occurred at the beginning of the era of rising economic inequality, around 1980. And most of the other rich democratic countries for which data are available have made bigger deregulatory reforms in finance than America did.[21]

Unionization has dropped sharply in the United States. But that decline began in the 1950s, long before income and wealth inequality started to rise. And since the late 1970s, unionization rates have been falling in most affluent nations, at about the same pace as in America.[22]

None of these patterns is consistent with what the inequality-is-harmful hypothesis predicts.

Do Republicans Receive More Campaign Money Than Democrats and Consequently Win More Elections?

Most of the money spent in political campaigns comes from private donations. Although we have limited direct information about the policy preferences of America's rich, a 2011 survey suggests that they tend to have views on core economic policy issues, such as taxes and government spending, that are much closer to those favored by Republicans than to those of Democrats.[23] It's no surprise, therefore, that the affluent have tended to give more money to Republicans and conservative groups than to Democrats and progressive groups.[24]

If the well-to-do favor Republicans, the inequality-is-harmful hypothesis would expect Republican candidates to have enjoyed a steadily rising advantage in campaign spending as income inequality has increased. But they haven't.

Since the late 1990s, when comprehensive and reliable data on campaign expenditures begin, Democrats and their supporters have kept pace with Republicans.[25] That's continued even after the Supreme Court's 2010 *Citizens United* ruling, which made it easier for donors to hide their contributions.

Nor has money led to Republican electoral dominance. Democratic candidates have won the popular vote in seven of the last nine presidential elections. It's true that Republicans have fared better in House and Senate elections than they did in the middle of the twentieth century. But in that earlier era Democrats had a big advantage because of their perceived success in dealing with the Great Depression and World War II and because the legacy of the Civil War and Reconstruction gave them a virtual monopoly in the South. By the 1990s, both of those advantages had evaporated. And in recent decades Democrats have been hurt in House elections by the fact that their voters are highly concentrated in urban areas, in Senate elections by the fact that low-population conservative states such as Wyoming get the same number of seats as high-population liberal states such as California, and in presidential elections by the Electoral College.[26]

Maybe America's plutocrats haven't needed Republicans in order to get their desired policies enacted. If the rich have become much more politically powerful, presumably they're able to sway Democrats as well. The Clinton administration's embrace of financial deregulation seems to fit with this prediction. But the fact that center-left parties in other far-less-economically-unequal countries did the same thing suggests reason for skepticism. And trends in top income tax rates aren't consistent with the notion that America's rich have been effective at getting Democrats to do their bidding. As noted earlier, while top tax rates were reduced under Republican presidents Reagan, George W. Bush, and Trump, under Democrats Clinton and Obama they were increased.

Have Policy Trends over the Long Run of American History Corresponded to Trends in Income Inequality?

In their book *Democracy in America?*, Benjamin Page and Martin Gilens attempt a rough tracing of trends in economic inequality and inequality of political influence over the long arc of American history. They conclude that there is substantial correspondence: "Economic inequality—the concentration of wealth and income in a few hands, with a big gap between rich and poor—has risen and fallen at various times. And democracy—popular control of government—has tended to move in the opposite direction. When citizens are relatively equal, politics has tended to be fairly democratic. When a few individuals hold enormous amounts of wealth, democracy suffers."[27] Specifically, Page and Gilens say the federal government's responsiveness to the policy wishes of ordinary Americans was low in the 1790s, higher in the Jacksonian era, lower in the second half of the 1800s, and higher in the 1950s.

It's worth treating this conclusion with skepticism. Consider the period for which the story seems, on the surface, most clear-cut: the second half of the 1800s. This was the era of industrialization and the Gilded Age. Inequality of income and wealth increased significantly.[28] According to Page and Gilens, this led to a shift in government attentiveness away from commoners and in favor of the affluent. But did key policy choices during the second half of the 1800s tend to go against what ordinary Americans wanted, or at least what was good for most? Slavery was outlawed. Real living standards doubled each generation.[29] As government created and expanded a nationwide public education system, average years of schooling rose steadily from four in 1870 to six in 1900 to eight in 1930. With advances in medical knowledge and public health systems, life expectancy jumped from thirty-nine in 1880 to fifty in 1900 to sixty in 1930.

Does Policy in American States with Greater Income Inequality Conform More to the Preferences of the Rich?

Social scientists have compiled data on top-end income inequality not only for countries but also for the US states.[30] The twelve states in which the top 1 percent's income share is largest include eight—New York, Connecticut, Massachusetts, California, Washington, DC, Illinois, New Jersey, and Washington state—where Republican vote shares tend to be lowest, state tax systems are least regressive, and state public social programs are most expansive and generous.[31] That isn't what the inequality-is-harmful hypothesis would predict.

California is a particularly striking case. Between 1979 and 2015, the share of income going to the top 1 percent of Californians soared from 10 to 24 percent. If the United States is on the road to plutocracy, California ought to be leading the charge. Yet California has the least regressive tax system of any state in the country, in part due to new taxes on high incomes added in recent years. Since 1999 California has enacted paid sick leave, paid parental leave, an automatic-enrollment pension system for people whose employer doesn't offer a plan, a large Medicaid expansion (it now covers one in three Californians), an expansion of Temporary Assistance for Needy Families (TANF) eligibility, a phased-in $15 per hour minimum wage indexed to inflation, a state Earned Income Tax Credit, increased money for K-12 schooling funded by two tax increases on high-income households, an array of services for residents with severe mental illnesses, universal free school breakfast and lunch, low-cost public auto insurance for persons with low income, new funds for roads and high-speed rail, a significant reduction in incarceration, and more. In 2018 California passed a law requiring an end to the use of fossil-fuel-based electricity by 2045, and the governor issued an executive order committing the state to full carbon neutrality by that same year.[32]

Does Income Inequality Degrade Democracy?

The available evidence suggests that economic inequality has an impact on inequality of political influence. America's rich very likely have more influence on policy decisions than the nonrich do. However, because there is a tipping point beyond which this effect diminishes, affluent Americans may have no more political advantage nowadays than they did in the late 1970s. If the United States were to reduce income and/or wealth inequality to where it was in 1979, there is little reason to be confident that this would reduce inequality of political influence.

4
Does Income Inequality Obstruct Opportunity?

True equality of opportunity is unattainable. Equal opportunity requires that each person has equivalent skills, abilities, knowledge, and noncognitive traits upon reaching adulthood, and that's impossible to achieve. Our capabilities are shaped by genetics, developments in utero, parents, siblings, peers, teachers, preachers, sports coaches, tutors, neighborhoods, and a slew of chance events and occurrences. Society can't fully equalize, offset, or compensate for these influences.

In fact, if we think about it carefully, few of us actually want equal opportunity, as it would require massive intervention in home life and probably also genetic engineering. Moreover, if parents knew everyone would end up with the same capabilities at the end of childhood, they would have little incentive to invest effort and money in their children's development, and that would result in a lower absolute level of capabilities for everyone.

What we really want is for each person to have the most opportunity possible. We should aim, in Amartya Sen's helpful formulation, to maximize people's capability to choose, act, and accomplish.[1] If we do that, opportunity will be somewhat unequal but not too much.

There is no straightforward way to measure opportunity, so social scientists tend to infer from outcomes, such as employment or earnings. If we find that a particular group fares worse than others, we suspect a barrier to opportunity. It isn't ironclad proof, but it's the best we can do. To assess equality of opportunity among people from families with more versus less income, we look at relative intergenerational income mobility—a person's position on the income ladder relative to her or his parents' position.[2]

Figure 4.1 shows the degree of equality of opportunity in the United States using this type of measure. It uses data from a large sample of Americans born in the years 1978–83 and their parents. On the horizontal axis is the parents' income rank—their income relative to the incomes of other parents—when the children were in their late teens. On the vertical axis is the average income rank of the children of those parents when the children are in their thirties. The dot farthest to the left, for instance, shows the average income rank of children whose parents were in the lowest income percentile.

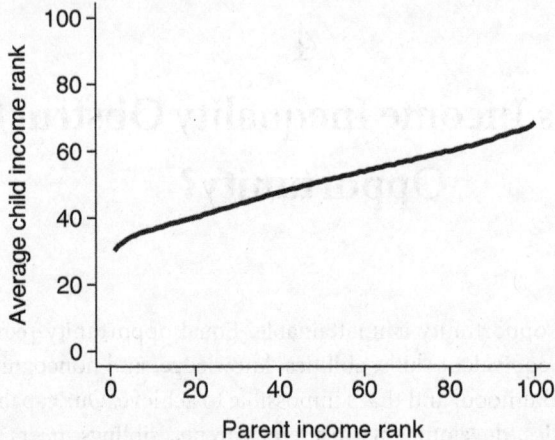

Figure 4.1 Parents' income rank and their children's income rank in adulthood

United States. Horizontal axis: parents' household income rank when the child is in her or his late teens, in 1994–2000. Vertical axis: child's average household income rank at age 31–37, in 2014–15. The sample is children born in the years 1978–83. The income data are from tax filings merged with Social Security records. Data source: Raj Chetty, Nathaniel Hendren, Maggie R. Jones, and Sonya R. Porter, "Race and Economic Opportunity in the United States: An Intergenerational Perspective," Working Paper 24441, National Bureau of Economic Research, 2018, online appendix figure 1.

In a society with perfectly equal opportunity, the data points in this chart would form a flat line—children's income position (rank) in adulthood would, on average, be the same no matter what their parents' income position was. Instead we see a line that slopes upward. Among people whose parents were on the bottom rungs of the income ladder, the average income ranking in young adulthood is relatively low. Among those whose parents were in the middle, the average is in the middle. And persons whose parents' income was at the high end tend to end up toward the high end themselves.

There is some movement up and down from one generation to the next. Among Americans whose parents were in the lowest income percentile, for instance, the average ranking is the thirty-third percentile. This means that among those who start at the bottom, some end up at the bottom, some end up in the middle, and perhaps a few end up even higher. Similarly, among children whose parents were at the top of the income distribution, the average income ranking is around the sixty-eighth percentile, which means many of them don't stay at the very top. Even so, the correlation between parents' income and children's income is fairly strong.

To what degree, and in what ways, is income inequality the cause of this inequality of opportunity?

The Income-Inequality-Is-Harmful Hypothesis

A prominent hypothesis holds that income inequality is a major contributor to inequality of opportunity. In 2013, Alan Krueger popularized this hypothesis with a graph showing that countries with higher levels of income inequality tend to have lower levels of relative intergenerational income mobility. Krueger called this pattern the "Great Gatsby curve."[3]

I'll come back to this, but first let's examine the pathways through which income inequality might affect inequality of opportunity. The income-inequality-is-harmful hypothesis tends to emphasize family structure, parenting, schooling, health, and neighborhoods.[4]

As in chapter 3, I focus here on the United States. It's the nation with the highest level of income inequality and one of the largest increases since the late 1970s. If income inequality is bad for equality of opportunity, we ought to observe the impact in the United States. The United States also is a country for which there are data that allow us to assess the hypothesized causal pathways.[5]

Has Rising Income Inequality Caused an Increase in Inequality of Family Structure?

Children who grow up in a home without both of their original parents tend to fare worse on a host of outcomes, including earnings in adulthood.[6] Does income inequality increase inequality of family structure?[7]

For the United States, figure 4.2 is the best picture we have of developments over time in family structure inequality. It shows the share of American children who aren't living with both of their biological parents at age sixteen (near the end of childhood). The trend is shown for three groups. We don't have good historical data for groups based on parents' income, so the chart uses parents' (mother's) education instead. The share not living with both biological parents has increased for all three groups, but much more for children whose parents have less education.

Is income inequality a key cause of this divergence in family structure? Have Americans who don't get a four-year college degree become more likely to have children out of wedlock or to get divorced because they are stressed by increased income inequality or because they are trying to keep up with the Joneses or because rising income inequality has reduced the number of available jobs that pay decent wages? That isn't likely. The weakening of family began in the 1960s, and it was most pronounced in the 1970s. This preceded the rise in income inequality.

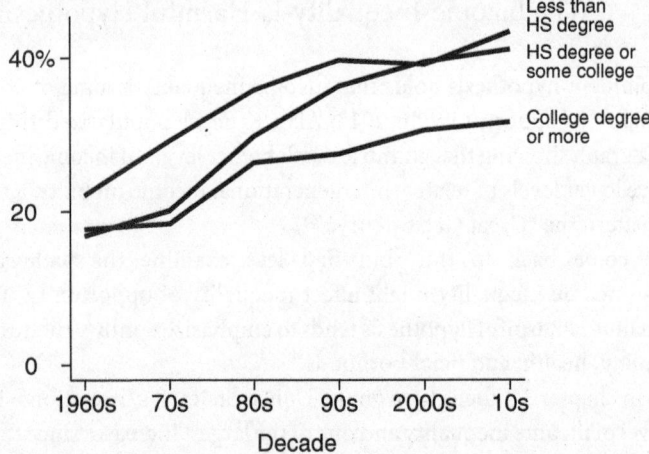

Figure 4.2 Children not living with both biological parents at age sixteen by mother's education

United States. HS = high school. Data source: General Social Survey, sda.berkeley.edu/archive.htm, series family16, maeduc.

Rather than income inequality, the driving force behind changes in family structure has been improved economic conditions for women and a shift in cultural norms. Historically, marriage has been as much a product of economic necessity and social norms as of love and friendship.[8] As societies get richer, economic circumstances and norms tend to change in ways that are likely to reduce the prevalence of marriage. Women become better educated, more likely to be employed, and more likely to earn enough to live independently. In addition, government benefits allow women with limited labor market prospects to survive without dependence on a husband. So for an increasing share of women, getting married, or remaining in an unsatisfying marriage, becomes a choice rather than a financial necessity.

Another change that comes with growing affluence is that people attach greater importance to individual freedom and choice.[9] As a result, norms discouraging divorce, nonmarital cohabitation, and out-of-wedlock childbearing weaken.

The puzzle isn't why family structure has weakened among Americans with less education. It's why family structure hasn't weakened very much for those who get a college degree—those who are higher up the socioeconomic ladder. The main reason is that the latter have shifted toward later childbearing. Among American women who have a college degree, the average age of first childbirth is now around thirty. This enables women and men to establish themselves financially, to figure out what they want in a relationship and what kind of person they'd like to be with, and to find that preferred type of partner.[10] I'm not aware of any research suggesting that this shift is a consequence of rising income inequality.

Has Rising Income Inequality Caused an Increase in Inequality of Parenting?

A second pathway through which income inequality might affect inequality of opportunity is parental attitudes and behaviors. One indicator is spending on (nonschool) goods and services aimed at enriching children—music lessons, other extracurricular activities, travel, summer camp.[11] Figure 4.3 shows this spending by parents' income quintile in the United States. Inequality of parents' spending on their children has increased since the late 1970s, consistent with what the income-inequality-is-harmful hypothesis predicts.

However, the increase in parents' spending inequality consists almost entirely of a separation between those in the top quintile versus everyone else. We don't have good information about whether, and if so how much, this kind of spending matters for children in affluent families compared to children in nonaffluent families.

It also isn't clear to what degree the rise in income inequality has been a cause of this development. This was an era in which there was a cultural shift in parenting—the advent of the modern intensive-parenting culture.[12] Affluent

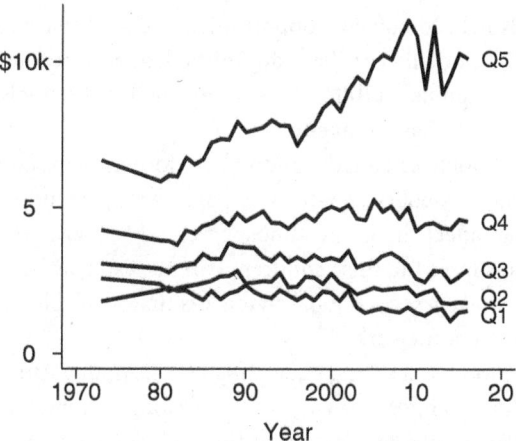

Figure 4.3 Expenditures on children by parents' income

United States. Spending per child. Inflation adjustment is via the CPI-U-RS. Includes expenditures on childcare, education, clothing, toys, games, musical equipment, bicycles, camping equipment, and services and repairs for these items. Q1 is the bottom fifth (quintile) of the income distribution; Q5 is the top fifth. Data source: Sabino Kornrich, "Inequalities in Parental Spending on Young Children," *AERA Open*, 2016, using data from the Consumer Expenditure Survey.

parents might have increased their spending on enriching activities for their children not because income inequality increased but because the cultural shift caused those parents to view such spending as vital for their children's development.

Some other indicators of parental attitudes and behaviors suggest not an increase but instead a reduction in inequality by socioeconomic status. For instance, over the past three decades American parents at the top and bottom of the income distribution have converged in their views about the type of skills they believe are important to instill in their children, prioritizing "thinks for self" and "works hard" over "obeys," "well-liked or popular," and "helps others."[13] There's been a similar convergence in intense parenting time, such as reading to children or playing directly with them, with the gap decreasing over the past two decades from about eight hours per week to three.[14]

Has Rising Income Inequality Caused an Increase in Inequality of Educational Attainment?

A third pathway through which income inequality can increase inequality of opportunity is schooling.[15] The United States has little in the way of public early education, so childcare and preschool are mostly private and often expensive. Children of affluent parents frequently attend high-quality education-oriented preschools, whereas kids of poorer parents are more likely to be left with a neighborhood babysitter who plops them in front of the television.[16] Elementary and secondary schools help to equalize opportunity, and as disparities in funding across public K-12 school districts have diminished, they've become more effective at doing so. Yet significant differences in the quality of schools persist, and poorer areas still tend to have weaker ones.[17]

What happens at home can affect children's performance in school. In a context of high income inequality, low-income parents may be more anxious and stressed, which can affect the home atmosphere and hinder parents' ability to provide emotional support to their children. Parents also may be more likely to work long hours or take a second job, leaving less time available to read to their children or help with homework.[18]

College completion has a strong equalizing effect. Among Americans whose family incomes during childhood were in the bottom fifth but who get a four-year college degree, 53 percent end up in the middle fifth or higher, which is pretty close to the 60 percent chance they would have if there were perfectly equal opportunity.[19] However, children from poor backgrounds are less likely than others to enter and complete college. One reason why is that they lag behind at the end of high school, and income inequality could be partly to blame, in ways I've just described. Another reason is that college can be expensive. Here too income inequality might have contributed, though the cost of public colleges for students from low-income families hasn't actually increased much.[20]

The income-inequality-is-harmful hypothesis predicts that inequality of educational attainment by parental income in the United States will have increased in the era of rising income inequality. Has it?

There are two main measures of educational attainment: how students perform and how many years of school they complete. Figure 4.4 shows the trend in test score inequality among American middle school and high school students. Contrary to what the income-inequality-is-harmful hypothesis predicts, the gap between students whose parents are at the ninetieth percentile of the socioeconomic status distribution and students whose parents are at the tenth percentile was smaller among those growing up in the 1980s, 1990s, and 2000s than among those growing up in the 1950s and 1960s.[21] According to this measure, rising inequality of income hasn't resulted in rising inequality of educational attainment.

For years of schooling completed, our best measure is college completion. Figure 4.5 shows college completion by parents' income for children growing up in the 1960s and 1970s (birth years 1961–64) and children growing up in the 1980s and 1990s (birth years 1979–82). College completion increased among all groups. If we focus on absolute increase, inequality rose. But if we focus on

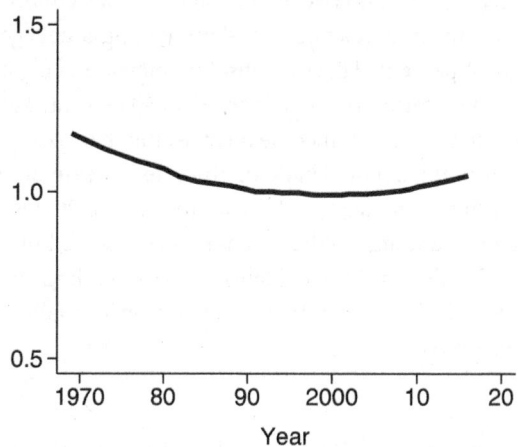

Figure 4.4 Test score gap between students from high-SES families and students from low-SES families

United States. Average difference in test scores between children whose family socioeconomic status (SES) is at the ninetieth percentile of the distribution and students whose family SES is at the tenth percentile. Standard deviation units. 2.7 million students age 14 to 17. Family SES is measured via parents' education and student reports of home items. Test subjects are reading, math, and science. The tests are the Long-Term Trend NAEP, Main NAEP, PISA, and TIMSS. Data source: Eric A. Hanushek, Paul E. Peterson, Laura M. Talpey, and Ludger Woessmann, "The Achievement Gap Fails to Close," *Education Next*, 2019, figure 1.

44 IS INEQUALITY THE PROBLEM?

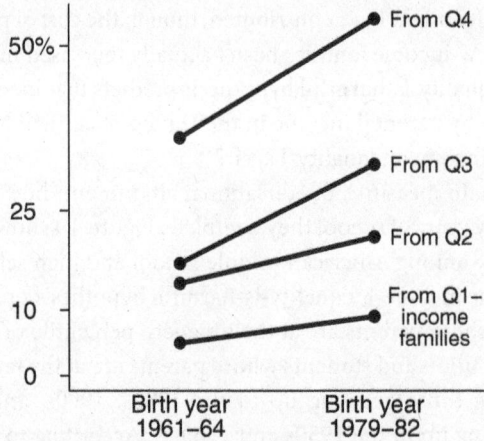

Figure 4.5 College completion by parents' income

United States. College completion: four or more years of college. Q1-income family: the person's family income during childhood was on the lowest quarter of the income ladder. Q2, Q3, and Q4 refer, respectively, to the second, third, and fourth quarters of the income ladder. Data source: Martha Bailey and Susan Dynarski, "Gains and Gaps: A Historical Perspective on Inequality in College Entry and Completion," in *Whither Opportunity? Rising Inequality, Schools, and Children's Life Chances*, edited by Greg J. Duncan and Richard J. Murnane, Russell Sage Foundation, 2011, figure 6.3, using National Longitudinal Survey of Youth data.

percentage increase, there was no rise in inequality. Among children whose parents were in the top income quartile, the share getting a college degree rose from 36 percent to 54 percent. That's an absolute increase of eighteen percentage points. In percentage terms, that's an increase of 50 percent. Among children whose parents were in the bottom income quartile, the share completing college rose from 5 percent to 9 percent. That's an absolute increase of only four percentage points. But in percentage terms, it's an increase of 80 percent, which is larger than the increase among children from higher-income households.[22]

On the whole, then, there is little evidence in US schooling and educational attainment to support the hypothesis that rising income inequality has worsened inequality of opportunity.

Has Rising Income Inequality Caused an Increase in Inequality of Health?

Health affects people's capabilities. And there is a socioeconomic gradient to health; people with less income tend to have worse health outcomes than those with more income. Has the rise in income inequality accentuated this barrier to opportunity?

Using longevity as our indicator of health, in the United States the answer appears to be yes. Since 1980, life expectancy for Americans in the top 60 percent of incomes has increased, but for those in the lower 40 percent of incomes it has been stagnant.[23]

There are a number of contributors to this trend, some of which may be a consequence, at least in part, of rising income inequality.[24] Smoking has decreased less rapidly among lower-income Americans than among those with higher incomes. Opioid addiction and overdose have increased more rapidly among Americans with less education and income. Between 1980 and 2010 the share of Americans without health insurance increased (this has reversed since 2010), and most who lack insurance have low to moderate income, so the income disparity in medical care may have increased. Differences in healthcare provision between more-affluent urban areas and poorer rural areas appear to have widened.

On the other hand, some longevity determinants haven't diverged according to income. For instance, while lower-income Americans are more likely to be overweight or obese than those with higher incomes, the income gap in obesity actually has shrunk in recent decades.[25] And as we'll see in chapter 5, the opioid epidemic in the United States doesn't seem to have been a product of rising income inequality.

What about in other rich democratic nations? In eight European countries for which data are available for the 1990s and 2000s—Finland, France, Italy, Norway, Spain, Sweden, Switzerland, and the United Kingdom—mortality decreased (longevity increased) more among persons with less than a high school education than among those with a college degree. Other findings suggest the same is true in Canada.[26] This isn't what the income-inequality-is-harmful hypothesis predicts.

Has Rising Income Inequality Caused an Increase in Inequality of Neighborhoods?

A fifth pathway through which income inequality may matter for opportunity is neighborhoods. Housing is the most expensive thing people buy, so we would expect more income inequality to cause more inequality of neighborhood quality. Children's capabilities can be affected by a variety of neighborhood features, from crime to adult employment levels to the quantity and quality of institutions and organizations (civic groups, churches, sports leagues).[27]

During the era of rising income inequality in the United States, residential segregation by income has increased, consistent with what the income-inequality-is-harmful hypothesis would predict. This has occurred mainly at the top.

Among families with children, those at the high end of the income distribution have become more residentially segregated from the rest of Americans.[28]

However, we don't know whether this has harmful effects for equality of opportunity. We know that living in a poor neighborhood tends to be worse for children than living in a not-poor neighborhood.[29] But we don't know if living in a rich neighborhood confers any advantage compared to living in, say, an upper-middle-class one.

Has Inequality of Opportunity in the United States Increased as Income Inequality Has Increased?

Let's now turn from potential causal pathways to inequality of opportunity itself. From the mid-1800s to the 1970s, opportunity in the United States almost certainly became more equal.[30] As the farming-based US labor force shifted to manufacturing, many Americans joined the paid economy, allowing an increasing number to move up the income ladder. Elementary education became universal, and secondary education expanded. In the 1960s and 1970s, school desegregation, the outlawing of discrimination in college admissions and hiring, and the introduction of affirmative action further opened economic doors.

What has happened during the era of rising income inequality since the late 1970s? It's probably too soon to draw a conclusion, as most Americans who grew up in the post-1970s period are still fairly young, making it difficult to know where on the income ladder they will end up. Still, some analysts have examined the data we do have. A few studies have concluded that inequality of opportunity in the United States has increased—relative intergenerational income mobility has declined—during the era of rising income inequality.[31] However, a more common conclusion is that there has been no change.[32] This latter conclusion is inconsistent with what the income-inequality-is-harmful hypothesis predicts.

It's conceivable that income inequality has caused inequality of opportunity to worsen but that this impact has been offset by other developments. Racial discrimination has continued to decrease, health insurance coverage for the poor has expanded due to changes in Medicaid in the 1980s and the late 1990s, lead was removed from gasoline beginning in the 1970s, violent crime has decreased sharply since the early 1990s, and in many states the gap in school funding between low-income districts and high-income districts has been reduced.[33] However, at least on the surface the over-time trend in inequality of opportunity in the United States doesn't appear to support the income-inequality-is-harmful hypothesis.

Is Inequality of Opportunity Greater in Countries That Have Greater Income Inequality?

Now let's return to the "Great Gatsby curve." In order to compare across countries, we need a single number to represent relative intergenerational income mobility, rather than the curve shown in figure 4.1 above. The number used in figure 4.6 is the share of persons with parents in the bottom fifth of incomes who remain in the bottom fifth when they are adults. It's an indicator of immobility, and therefore of inequality of opportunity.

The pattern across the countries is consistent with what the income-inequality-is-harmful hypothesis predicts. In nations with greater income inequality, a larger portion of children who grow up in low-income households tend to end up with low incomes themselves. However, it's difficult to have much confidence that this pattern indicates a genuine causal effect. One obvious problem is that there are so few countries. We need comparable data for more.[34]

Just as important, there are other things that could be the true cause of the association we observe in figure 4.6. The three Nordic nations in the chart—Finland, Norway, and Sweden—have low income inequality and high relative intergenerational income mobility. Maybe their low income inequality is the cause of their high mobility. But they also have been providing affordable high-quality early education to a substantial portion of children age one to five

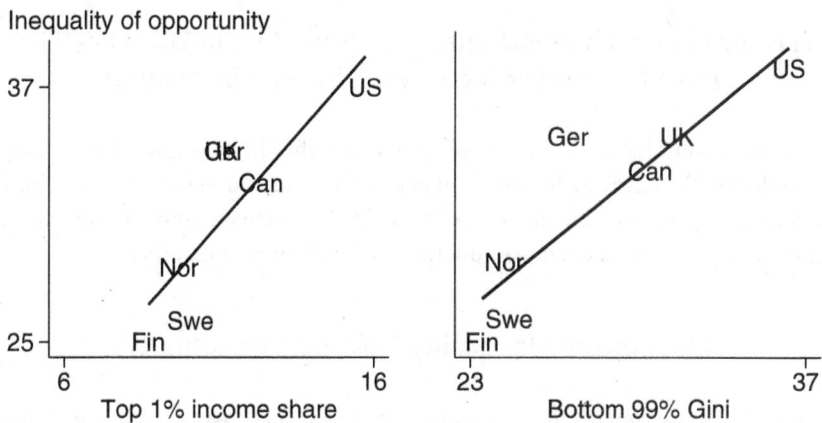

Figure 4.6 Income inequality and inequality of opportunity

Horizontal axes: income inequality. Average for 1979–2019. For data description and sources, see figures 1.1–1.4. Vertical axis: share of persons with parents' income in the bottom fifth who remain in the bottom fifth when they are adults. A larger share indicates less relative intergenerational mobility and hence less equality of opportunity. Data source: Scott Winship, "Economic Mobility in America," part 2: The United States in Comparative Perspective, Archbridge Institute, 2018, figure 3.

for roughly a generation.[35] James Heckman and Gøsta Esping-Andersen, among others, have concluded that early education is perhaps the single most valuable thing a society can do to equalize opportunity.[36] In addition, these countries feature late tracking in K-12 schools and heavy government subsidies to ensure that college is affordable for all. These public services, rather than low income inequality, could be the key to why the Nordic countries have comparatively low inequality of opportunity.[37]

Is Inequality of Opportunity Greater in US Labor Markets That Have Greater Income Inequality?

Data are available for local labor markets ("commuting zones") within the United States. There is little if any correlation between income inequality and relative intergenerational income mobility across these labor markets.[38] That's inconsistent with the income-inequality-is-harmful hypothesis.

Has Inequality of Opportunity Increased More in Countries That Have Had Larger Increases in Income Inequality?

This is an important question. Unfortunately, we don't know the answer, because we don't have over-time data on inequality of opportunity for many countries.

Has Inequality of Opportunity Increased More in US States That Have Had Larger Increases in Income Inequality?

Deirdre Bloome has examined mobility trends in the US states and whether they correlate with trends in income inequality. She finds no evidence of a robust relationship. States in which income inequality has increased more haven't been more likely to suffer a decline in intergenerational income mobility.[39]

Does Income Inequality Obstruct Opportunity?

As with living standards and democracy, there are good reasons to suspect that income inequality might have harmful effects on equality of opportunity. But also as with living standards and democracy, the available evidence gives us little reason to conclude that reducing income inequality would yield a better outcome.

5
Does Income Inequality Lessen Longevity?

Health is a core component of well-being. What does the evidence tell us about the effect of income inequality on health, and particularly on lifespan, in rich longstanding-democratic countries?

The Inequality-Is-Harmful Hypothesis

The notion that income inequality worsens health outcomes—not only for the poor, but for nearly everyone—has been prominent since the early 1990s.[1] There are three pathways through which income inequality is predicted to reduce longevity.[2]

The main one is that larger differences in income within a society increase stress. "Greater inequality," according to Richard Wilkinson and Kate Pickett, "seems to heighten people's social evaluation anxieties by increasing the importance of social status. . . . If inequalities are bigger, so that some people seem to count for almost everything and others for practically nothing, where each one of us is placed becomes more important. Greater inequality is likely to be accompanied by increased status competition and increased status anxiety."[3] Stress is harmful for health on its own, and it may foster behaviors that are bad for longevity, such as smoking, overeating, and alcohol or drug abuse.

Second, income inequality may block economic opportunity, foster a perception of relative deprivation, and up the stakes in the competition for status. In doing so it may encourage people, particularly young males, to turn to criminal activity, including violence.[4]

A third hypothesized causal link is public policy. Greater income inequality may spur opposition by the rich to higher taxes, thereby slowing investment in medical research or expansion of public healthcare services.[5] As a result, the quality and quantity of healthcare might improve less than they otherwise would.

Does Income Inequality Increase Violence?

For longevity, homicide is the most directly relevant type of violence, and it happens to be the only type of violent crime for which comparable country-level longitudinal data are available.

Figure 5.1 shows income inequality levels and homicide levels across the rich democratic nations since 1990, the earliest year for homicide data. The United States, with its high inequality and high homicide rate, is a huge outlier. Across the other countries there is no association.

When we turn to changes over time, a significant problem for the inequality-is-harmful hypothesis is that homicide rates in the rich democratic nations have decreased, not increased, during the era of rising income inequality.[6] Has inequality contributed to variation across the countries in the amount of decrease? Figure 5.2 suggests that the answer is no. There is no indication of the predicted positive association between changes in inequality and changes in homicide. Note, too, that here the United States is an outlier in a way that's inconsistent with the inequality-is-harmful hypothesis. It has had one of the largest increases in income inequality, yet its homicide rate has decreased the most.

Does Income Inequality Increase Smoking?

Cigarette smoking has long been one of the principal ways people have attempted to alleviate stress. Income inequality may therefore tend to increase smoking.[7] If it does, that's bad for longevity, because smoking causes lung disease and heart disease.

Figure 5.3 shows smoking levels by income inequality levels in the rich democratic countries. We don't see the positive association predicted by the inequality-is-harmful hypothesis.

Scientists have known since the middle of the twentieth century that smoking is bad for health. This has prompted public awareness campaigns, increased taxation of cigarettes, and bans on smoking in indoor spaces, leading to a reduction in smoking beginning in the 1960s. If income inequality increases smoking, countries with a bigger rise in income inequality should have had less decline in smoking. But as we see in figure 5.4, that isn't what has happened. Smoking has tended to decrease just as much in nations experiencing a large rise in income inequality as in nations with little or no rise in inequality.

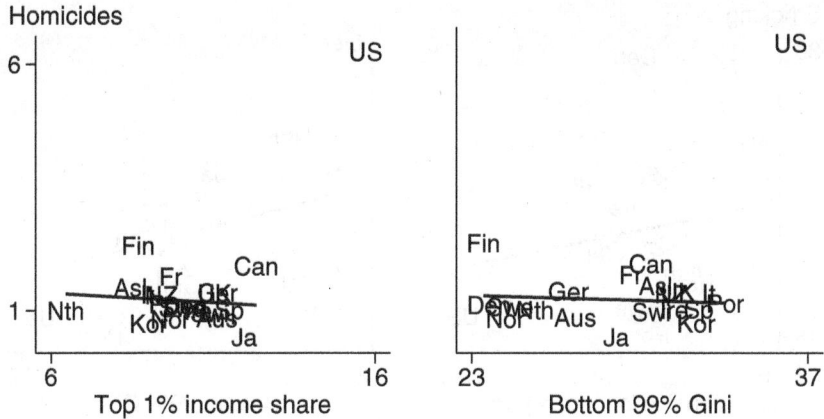

Figure 5.1 Income inequality and homicides

Average for 1990–2019. Horizontal axes: income inequality. For data description and sources, see figures 1.1–1.4. Vertical axes: homicides per 100,000 population. Data source: United Nations Office of Drugs and Crime, "Intentional Homicide," dataunodc.un.org/dp-intentional-homicide-victims. "Asl" is Australia; "Aus" is Austria. The lines are linear regression lines, calculated with the United States omitted.

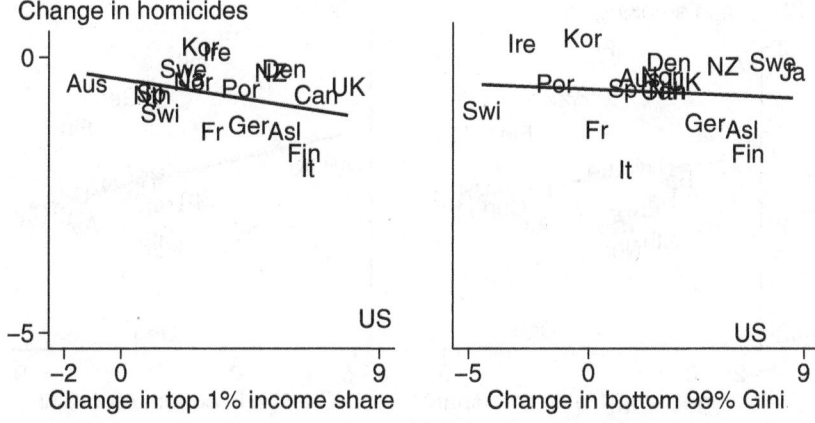

Figure 5.2 Change in income inequality and change in homicides

Change from 1990 to 2019. Horizontal axes: change in income inequality. For data description and sources, see figures 1.1–1.4. Vertical axes: change in homicides per 100,000 population. Data source: United Nations Office of Drugs and Crime, "Intentional Homicide," dataunodc.un.org/dp-intentional-homicide-victims. "Asl" is Australia; "Aus" is Austria. The lines are linear regression lines, calculated with the United States omitted.

Does Income Inequality Increase Obesity?

Income inequality might contribute to obesity. The hypothesized causal path is that inequality increases status competition, which increases stress, which in

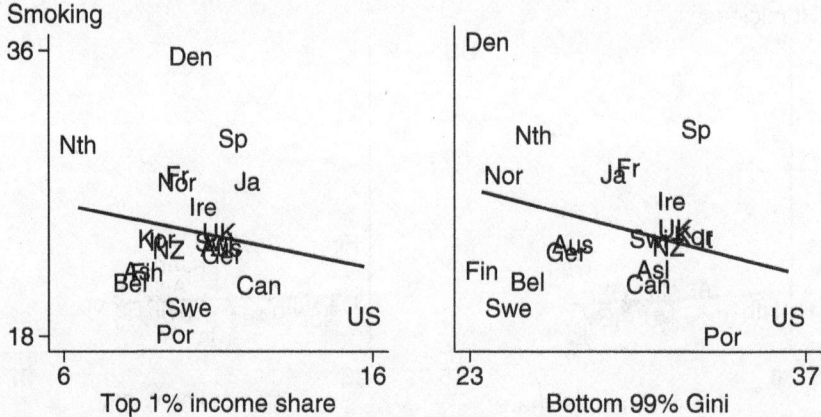

Figure 5.3 Income inequality and smoking

Average for 1979–2019. Horizontal axes: income inequality. For data description and sources, see figures 1.1–1.4. Vertical axes: share of people age 15 and over who say they smoke every day. Data source: OECD, "Daily Smokers," data.oecd.org. "Asl" is Australia; "Aus" is Austria. The lines are linear regression lines.

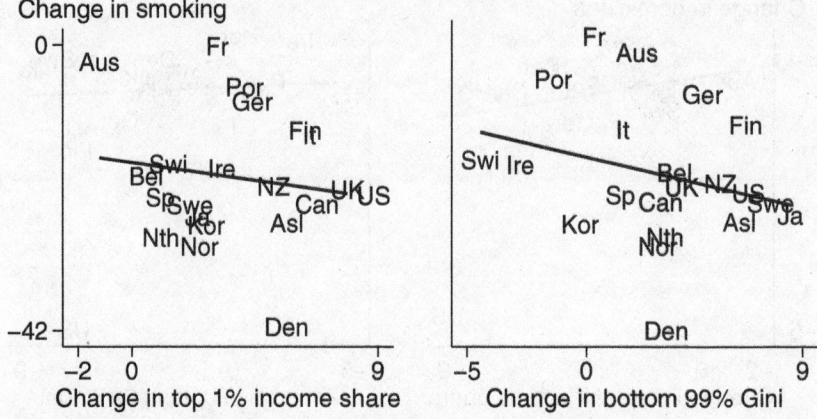

Figure 5.4 Change in income inequality and change in smoking

Change from 1979 to 2019. Horizontal axes: change in income inequality. For data description and sources, see figures 1.1–1.4. Vertical axes: change in the share of people age 15 and over who say they smoke every day. Data source: OECD, "Daily Smokers," data.oecd.org. "Asl" is Australia; "Aus" is Austria. The lines are linear regression lines.

turn prompts overeating.[8] People with obesity are more likely to be depressed and are at greater risk of diabetes, heart disease, stroke, and some types of cancer. Obesity has become one of the most significant health problems in the rich democratic countries.[9]

Figure 5.5 shows levels of income inequality and levels of obesity (the most recent year of data is 2016 rather than 2019). If we set aside the United States, there is no association. Countries with greater income inequality don't tend to have more obesity.

What about changes over time? Figure 5.6 shows changes in income inequality and changes in obesity across the countries. The chart on the right, which uses income inequality within the bottom 99 percent, again suggests no correlation. But the chart on the left, with inequality between the top 1 percent and the bottom 99 percent, shows a positive association, which is what the inequality-is-harmful hypothesis predicts.

Does the pattern in the graph on the left in figure 5.6 reflect a genuine causal effect of income inequality on obesity? Probably not. The positive association in that chart is driven entirely by the position of five countries: the United States, Canada, the United Kingdom, Australia, and New Zealand. These five nations entered the period of rising obesity lacking a preexisting food culture centered around consumption of healthy low-calorie foods, and they experienced a comparatively large increase in the supply of tasty, inexpensive, calorie-dense foods. It is this, rather than rising top-end income inequality, that most likely accounts for these five countries' comparatively large rise in obesity.[10]

Examining differences within the United States—comparing across the US states—also offers no indication that income inequality contributes to obesity.

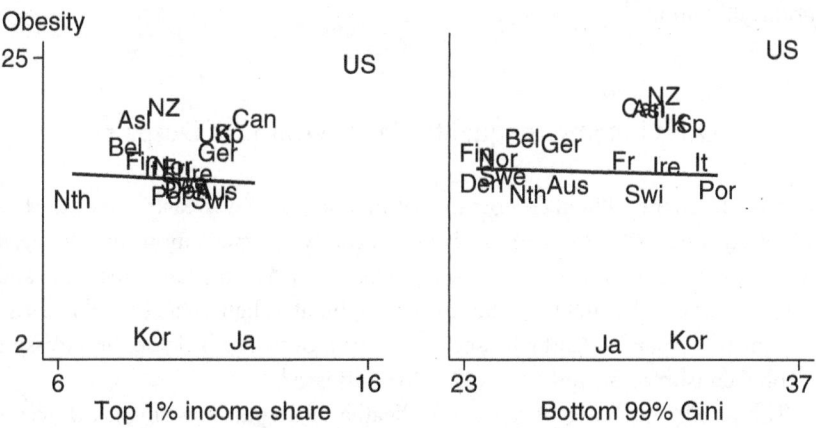

Figure 5.5 Income inequality and obesity

Average for 1979–2016. Horizontal axes: income inequality. For data description and sources, see figures 1.1–1.4. Vertical axes: share of adults with a body mass index (BMI) of 30 or more. These data are age-standardized: They take into account the differences in age structure of the populations across countries and over time. Data source: World Health Organization (WHO), "Prevalence of Obesity Among Adults," who.int/data/gho/data. "Asl" is Australia; "Aus" is Austria. The lines are linear regression lines, calculated with the United States omitted.

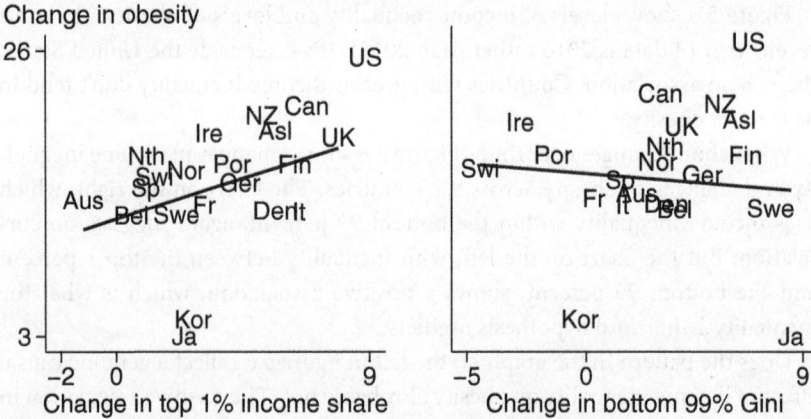

Figure 5.6 Change in income inequality and change in obesity

Change from 1979 to 2016. Horizontal axes: change in income inequality. For data description and sources, see figures 1.1–1.4. Vertical axes: change in the share of adults with a body mass index (BMI) of 30 or more. These data are age-standardized: They take into account the differences in age structure of the populations across countries and over time. Data source: World Health Organization (WHO), "Prevalence of Obesity Among Adults," who.int/data/gho/data. "Asl" is Australia; "Aus" is Austria. The lines are linear regression lines, calculated with the United State omitted.

Here too variation in levels and changes in obesity appear to be mainly a product of eating cultures and the way they've shaped the impact of the rising supply of nonhealthy food.[11]

Does Income Inequality Cause Deaths of Despair?

Death rates in the affluent democratic nations have been decreasing since the late 1800s. Around 1999, however, the fall in mortality reversed among middle-aged whites in the United States. This owed mainly to a rise in what Anne Case and Angus Deaton, who first brought this development to light in a 2015 article, call "deaths of despair"—deaths by accidental drug overdose, suicide, or excessive alcohol consumption and consequent liver disease.[12]

The proximate cause of the rise in deaths of despair was increased access to opioid pain relievers.[13] These pain relievers—oxycodone, hydrocodone, and others—became increasingly available via prescription beginning in the late 1990s. Purdue Pharma, the maker of OxyContin, the most popular of these drugs, aggressively marketed it to physicians and hospitals, encouraging them to prescribe it more frequently and in larger quantities. As opioid pain relievers became more widely available in a nonstigmatized (prescription) form, more Americans began to use them. Because opioids are addictive, more people got hooked and became regular users. Some overdosed on the pain reliever itself, some created a toxic mix by combining it with another drug (such as a sleep aid), and some switched to heroin and eventually overdosed on that. In the 2010s fentanyl use exploded, replacing opioid pain relievers and heroin as the chief cause of overdose deaths.

The rise in accidental poisonings in the United States has been striking. From 1960 to 1999 there were about 2 such deaths per 100,000 Americans each year. That number rose to 8 in 2005, 11 in 2010, 15 in 2015, and 20 in 2017, 2018, and 2019. That's 65,000 Americans dying from accidental poisonings in each of those recent years. Suicides and deaths from chronic liver disease or cirrhosis of the liver add another 90,000.

Some attribute these deaths of despair to income inequality.[14] As with obesity, the main hypothesized causal pathway is status comparison and stress:

> When the gap between those with ample income and those with insufficient income widens in society, those left behind, even those who may not be deprived in an absolute sense (i.e., lacking sufficient food, nutrition, living space, or safe neighborhoods), experience a sense of relative deprivation. This psychosocial deprivation can directly harm mental well-being (feelings of self-worth and hope) and/or increase the risk of harmful coping behaviors in an attempt to alleviate psychological stress.... Therefore, during a period of increasing income inequality, it is plausible to hypothesize an increase in population harms associated with self-destructive health behaviors, such as drug abuse, alcohol poisonings, and suicide.[15]

Case and Deaton have studied the American story most extensively. They are skeptical that income inequality has had much of an impact, noting that "the epidemic of deaths of despair is no worse in less equal states. New Hampshire and Utah, two states with the lowest levels of income inequality, have been much harder hit than New York and California, two states with the highest."[16]

What can we glean from the cross-country evidence? Figure 5.7 shows levels of income inequality and deaths of despair. There is no association.

When we look at changes in income inequality and changes in deaths of despair, in figure 5.8, the story is different. Here we see a positive association in both charts, which is what the inequality-is-harmful hypothesis predicts. This suggests income inequality might indeed have contributed to the deaths-of-despair phenomenon.

Four caveats are worth emphasizing. First, deaths of despair are only one among many sources of mortality. Second, deaths of despair actually decreased in all but three of the countries. So what the data suggest is that in most of

56 IS INEQUALITY THE PROBLEM?

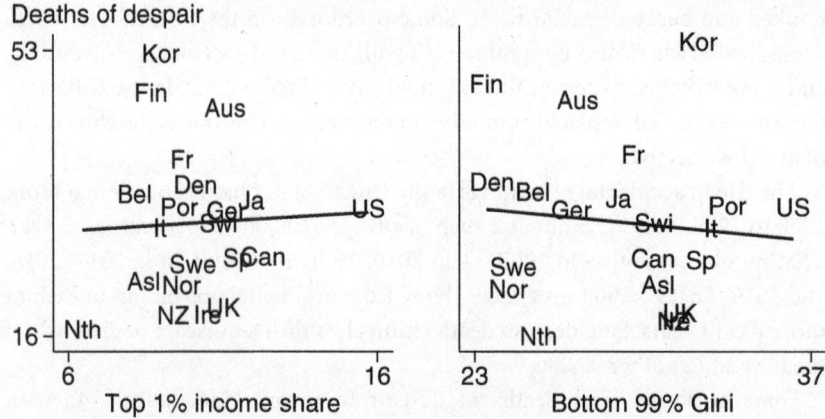

Figure 5.7 Income inequality and deaths of despair

Average for 1979–2019. Horizontal axes: income inequality. For data description and sources, see figures 1.1–1.4. Vertical axes: deaths of despair per 100,000 population. Deaths of despair are calculated as deaths due to accidental poisoning, intentional self-harm, or chronic liver disease/cirrhosis. Data source: OECD, "Causes of Mortality," stats.oecd.org. "Asl" is Australia; "Aus" is Austria. The lines are linear regression lines.

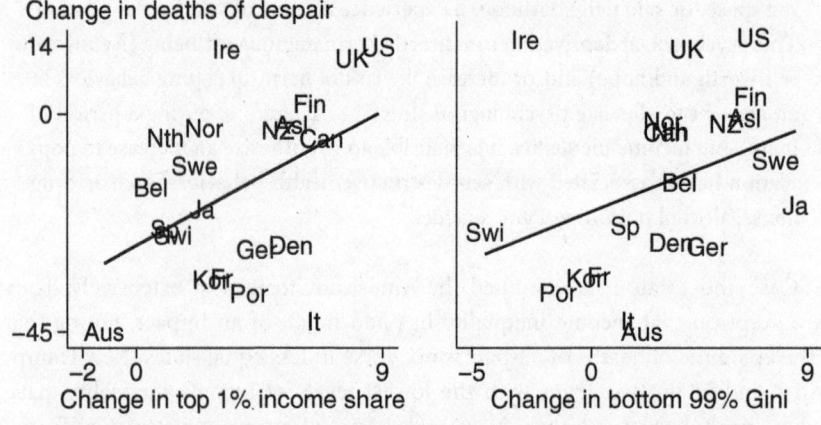

Figure 5.8 Change in income inequality and change in deaths of despair

Change from 1979 to 2019. Horizontal axes: Change in income inequality. For data description and sources, see figures 1.1–1.4. Vertical axes: Change in deaths of despair per 100,000 population. Deaths of despair are calculated as deaths due to accidental poisoning, intentional self-harm, or chronic liver disease/cirrhosis. Data source: OECD, "Causes of Mortality," stats.oecd.org. "Asl" is Australia; "Aus" is Austria. The lines are linear regression lines

these affluent democratic nations, rising income inequality may have slowed what otherwise would have been a faster decline in deaths of despair. Third, in both charts in figure 5.8 the correlation is fairly weak, with the countries spread out far off the best-fit line. This suggests that if income inequality has had an impact, its magnitude likely has been quite limited. Fourth, recall that there is good reason, expressed by Case and Deaton in the quotation above, for skepticism about whether there has been an actual causal effect of income inequality in the US case.

Still, among the hypothesized pathways we've looked at thus far, this is the first for which the country evidence offers indication of an adverse impact of income inequality on longevity.

Does Income Inequality Reduce Life Expectancy?

Let's turn now to a direct measure of longevity: years of life expectancy at birth.[17]

Consistent with the inequality-is-harmful hypothesis, a variety of studies have concluded that income inequality is negatively correlated with life expectancy.[18] Most of these studies are cross-sectional. They examine the association between the level of income inequality and the level of life expectancy across nations, regions, counties, or cities at a particular point in time. But some cross-sectional studies find no association between income inequality and longevity.[19] As we see in figure 5.9, the cross-sectional picture for the rich longstanding-democratic countries over 1979–2019 isn't consistent with the hypothesized life-shortening effect of income inequality.

Studies analyzing cross-country differences in change over time typically haven't found the predicted negative association between changes in income

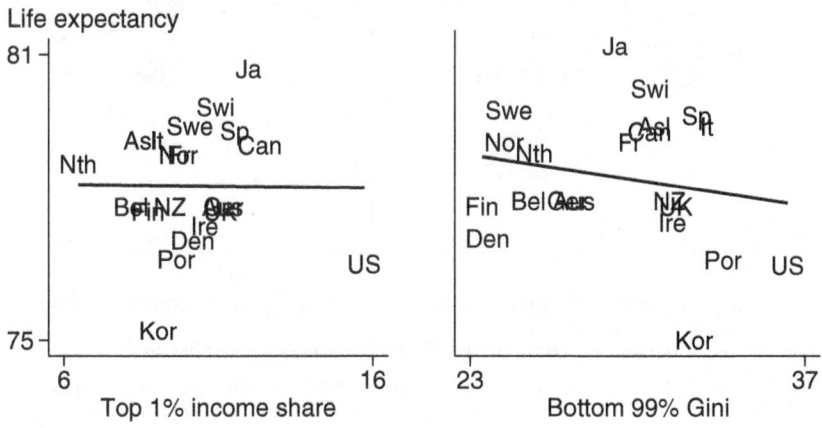

Figure 5.9 Income inequality and life expectancy

Average for 1979–2019. Horizontal axes: income inequality. For data description and sources, see figures 1.1–1.4. Vertical axes: years of life expectancy at birth. Data source: OECD, "Life Expectancy at Birth," data.oecd.org. "Asl" is Australia; "Aus" is Austria. The lines are linear regression lines.

inequality and changes in life expectancy.[20] Comprehensive reviews thus have tended to conclude that the empirical case for an effect of income inequality on life expectancy is very thin.[21] One summarizes this conclusion this way: "A few high-quality studies find that inequality is negatively correlated with population health, but the preponderance of evidence suggests that the relationship between income inequality and health is either non-existent or too fragile to show up in a robustly estimated panel specification. The best cross-national studies now uniformly fail to find a statistically reliable relationship between economic inequality and longevity."[22]

Life expectancy increased in all of the rich democratic countries during the era of rising income inequality. The twenty-one-nation average rose from seventy-four years in 1979 to eighty-two years in 2019. This suggests that if inequality does adversely affect life expectancy, its effect has been weaker than that of whatever has been driving improvements in longevity—less smoking, more exercise, increased access to medical care, improved quality of medical care, and so on. If income inequality has adversely affected longevity, it has done so by slowing the amount of increase over time.

The two charts in figure 5.10 show change in life expectancy by change in income inequality. Change in life expectancy, on the vertical axes, is adjusted for a catch-up process—countries that began the period with lower life expectancy

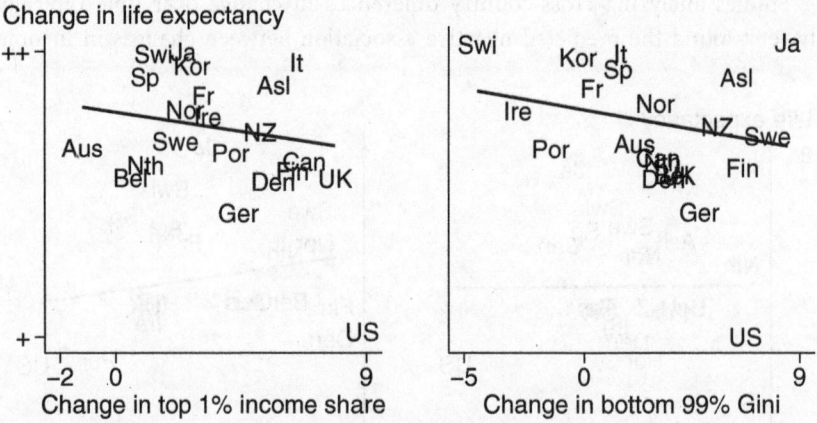

Figure 5.10 Change in income inequality and change in life expectancy

Change from 1979 to 2019. Horizontal axes: change in income inequality. For data description and sources, see figures 1.1–1.4. Vertical axes: change in years of life expectancy at birth. Change in life expectancy is adjusted for starting level of life expectancy; the vertical-axis measure is the residuals from a regression of change in life expectancy on 1979 level of life expectancy. "+" = increase; "++" = larger increase. Data source: OECD, "Life Expectancy at Birth," data.oecd.org. "Asl" is Australia; "Aus" is Austria. The lines are linear regression lines, calculated with the United States omitted.

experienced faster increases than those beginning with high levels, probably because advances in medical devices, pharmaceuticals, nutritional information, public health strategies, and other improvements can be easily borrowed by laggards.[23] Setting aside the United States, neither chart suggests any association. This is consistent with the findings of most previous research. It is not what the inequality-is-harmful hypothesis predicts.

What Does the US Experience Tell Us?

The United States stands apart from the other countries on a number of the longevity-related indicators in this chapter—homicides, obesity, deaths of despair, and overall life expectancy. And in each case except change in homicides, while the pattern across the other nations yields little or no support for the hypothesis that income inequality is bad for longevity, the position of the United States *is* consistent with the hypothesis. Does the US experience tell us something important about income inequality's effect on longevity?

Possibly, but there is reason for skepticism, because for each indicator there is a very plausible alternative explanation for why the United States differs from the other nations.[24] For homicides, it's America's lax government regulation of guns. For obesity, it's the large increase in the supply of tasty, inexpensive, high-calorie foods—in grocery stores, in fast-food restaurants, and in large-portion sit-down restaurants—coupled with the lack of a preexisting food culture that facilitates moderation in calorie consumption. For deaths of despair, it's the increase in supply of opioid pain relievers due to pharmaceutical companies' aggressive marketing in a context of weak government regulation.[25]

Figure 5.11 shows life expectancy in each of the affluent democratic nations since 1960. For much of the 1960s and 1970s, the United States was in the middle of the pack. Around 1980, life expectancy for Americans began to increase at a slower pace than in any other nation.[26] At first glance, that timing seems to fit well with the inequality-is-harmful hypothesis. However, income inequality began rising around 1980, so if it was in fact a key driver of the slowdown in longevity's rise in the United States, its effect had to have kicked in immediately. That seems unlikely, especially given that it wasn't until the early 1990s that many Americans became aware that income inequality was increasing.[27]

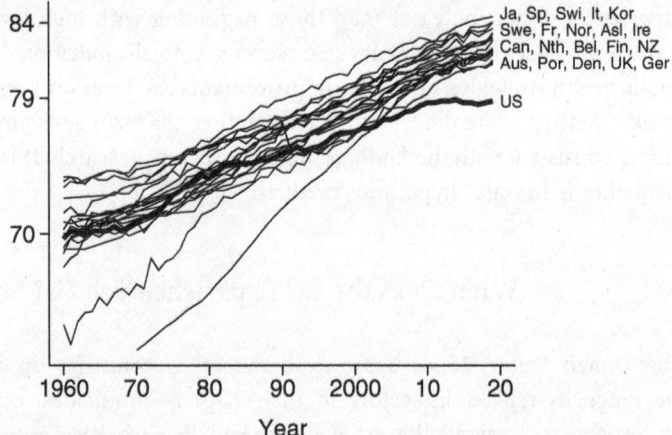

Figure 5.11 Life expectancy

Years of life expectancy at birth. Data source: OECD, "Life Expectancy at Birth," data.oecd.org. Thick line: United States. "Asl" is Australia; "Aus" is Austria.

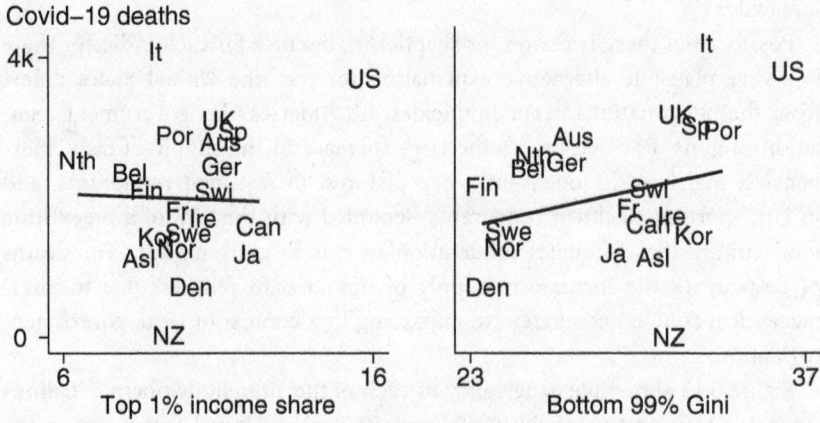

Figure 5.12 Income inequality and Covid-19 pandemic deaths

Horizontal axes: income inequality. Average for 1979-2019. For data description and sources, see figures 1.1–1.4. Vertical axes: estimated deaths caused by Covid-19 per million people. Cumulative difference between the reported number of deaths from January 2020 through May 2023 and the projected number of deaths for the same period based on previous years. "k" = thousand. Data source: Our World in Data, "Excess Mortality: Cumulative Deaths from All Causes Compared to Projection Based on Previous Years, Per Million People." "Asl" is Australia; "Aus" is Austria. The lines are linear regression lines, calculated with the United States omitted.

Given these considerations, I think it's difficult to have much confidence in a conclusion that income inequality has had a significant adverse impact on longevity in the United States.

Did Income Inequality Increase Covid-19 Pandemic Deaths?

The Covid-19 pandemic from March 2020 to May 2023 killed approximately seven million people worldwide. If income inequality increases stress, it may have made people more likely to contract the virus or to die from it if contracted. Inequality-induced concern to "keep up with the Joneses" might have caused more people to continue going to work, increasing their risk of catching the virus.[28] Did income inequality worsen the Covid death toll?

The pandemic period was too brief to expect changes in income inequality to have had an impact, so we should focus on levels. Figure 5.12 shows the cross-country patterns. Because of the Republican Party's embrace of vaccine skepticism during the pandemic, we should discount the United States. Across the other countries, there is little indication of an effect.

Does Income Inequality Lessen Longevity?

There are plausible hypotheses about why income inequality could be bad for longevity. But the evidence from the rich democratic nations offers little reason to think income inequality has in fact tended to have harmful health effects.[29] It might contribute to "deaths of despair"—deaths due to drug and alcohol abuse, overdose, or suicide—though its causal impact on those deaths is questionable. Income inequality doesn't appear to have increased violence or smoking or obesity or Covid deaths. And it doesn't look to have reduced life expectancy.

6
Does Income Inequality Hinder Happiness?

Happiness isn't the only outcome on which a society should be judged. But it clearly matters. And for some it is at the top of the list.[1] Does income inequality hinder happiness?

Subjective well-being used to be ignored by analysts of societal performance because we had little or no data, and hence no way to study it scientifically. Now we do. These data come mainly from public opinion surveys. People are asked a question such as "All things considered, how satisfied are you with your life as a whole these days?" Respondents indicate their satisfaction on a scale of 0 to 10. Eurobarometer has regularly asked this question in many European nations since the 1970s, as has Japan's Life in Nation Survey. The World Values Survey has asked it in the rich democratic countries at five-year intervals since the early 1980s.

This life satisfaction question asks people to appraise the overall condition of their life. There are other components of subjective well-being: positive feelings such as pleasure and joy and negative feelings such as worry, frustration, anger, and sadness. But feelings are more fleeting—more likely to vary from moment to moment, day to day, month to month—and as such are generally considered less useful than life satisfaction as indicators of subjective well-being.

Can we trust this type of measure to accurately tap people's happiness? Yes. Responses tend to correlate strongly with the assessments of friends and family and with clinical assessments. There is no indication of desirability bias in responses. When the same people are asked these survey questions over time, their responses tend to be consistent, with predictable changes in the face of major life shocks such as divorce and unemployment. And when people are asked this life satisfaction question along with a separate question about happiness, their answers are strongly correlated.[2]

The Inequality-Is-Harmful Hypothesis

There are a variety of reasons why income inequality might be bad for subjective well-being.[3] One is that our sense of material well-being affects our happiness.

The higher a person's income, the happier they tend to be. But humans are social creatures; we compare ourselves to others. If my income is less than other people's income, or if it's rising less rapidly, I'm less likely to be satisfied with it.[4] The greater the income inequality, on this view, the larger the share of people who will feel they aren't doing well.

A second path through which income inequality might reduce subjective well-being is status anxiety. This too stems from social comparison, as Richard Wilkinson and Kate Pickett explain:

> The more hierarchical a society is, the stronger the idea that people are ranked according to inherent differences in worth or value, and the greater their insecurities about self-worth.... As greater inequality makes social position more visible, we come to judge each other more by status. With more social evaluation anxieties, problems of self-esteem, self-confidence, and status insecurity become more fraught.... Perhaps the most likely explanation of why inequality increases status anxiety across entire societies is because it increases the sense that people at the top of the social ladder are extremely important and those at the bottom almost worthless, and, as money becomes more entrenched as a measure of people's worth, it makes us all more worried about where we come in the hierarchy.[5]

A third hypothesized pathway is that people dislike too much inequality, perhaps because they see it as unfair. So when income inequality is high and/or rising, it frustrates them, regardless of their own position on the income ladder.[6]

Humans need social connections and support. A fourth hypothesized pathway suggests that income inequality is bad for happiness because it corrodes civic engagement, trust, social cohesion, and community.[7] The evidence on this is mixed. Some studies have found links between inequality and lower civic engagement or trust, while others haven't.[8] In the United States, membership and participation in civic organizations and trust have declined during the era of rising income inequality.[9] However, those declines began in the mid-1960s, when income inequality was at its low point and well before it began its rise.[10]

Life Satisfaction Hasn't Increased During the Era of High and Rising Income Inequality

Since the late 1970s, life satisfaction in the rich democratic nations has been largely flat. Figure 6.1 shows the pattern for each of our twenty-one countries.[11]

This is puzzling. One of the main determinants of life satisfaction is income,[12] and incomes have been rising in these countries, as we saw in chapter 2. Even in

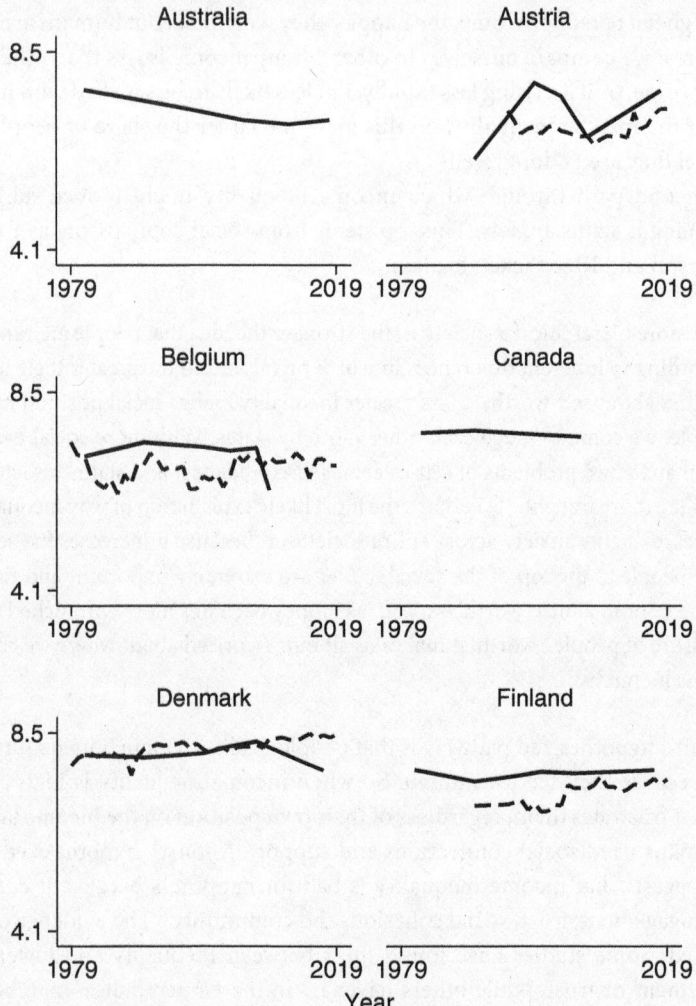

Figure 6.1 Life satisfaction

Scale: 0 to 10. The vertical axis doesn't begin at zero. Solid line: average response to the question "All things considered, how satisfied are you with your life as a whole these days?" Scale of 1 to 10, converted here to a scale of 0 to 10. Data source: World Values Survey. Dashed line: average response to the question "On the whole, how satisfied are you with your life? 1 = not at all satisfied; 2 = not so satisfied; 3 = pretty satisfied; 4 = very satisfied." Converted here to a scale of 0 to 10. Data sources: Eurobarometer and Japan's Life in Nation Survey, via the World Database of Happiness.

the United States, where incomes have been rising less rapidly than the economy would have allowed, the median income for a three-person household increased from about $50,000 in 1979 to just shy of $70,000 in 2019.[13] Why didn't this produce an increase in subjective well-being?

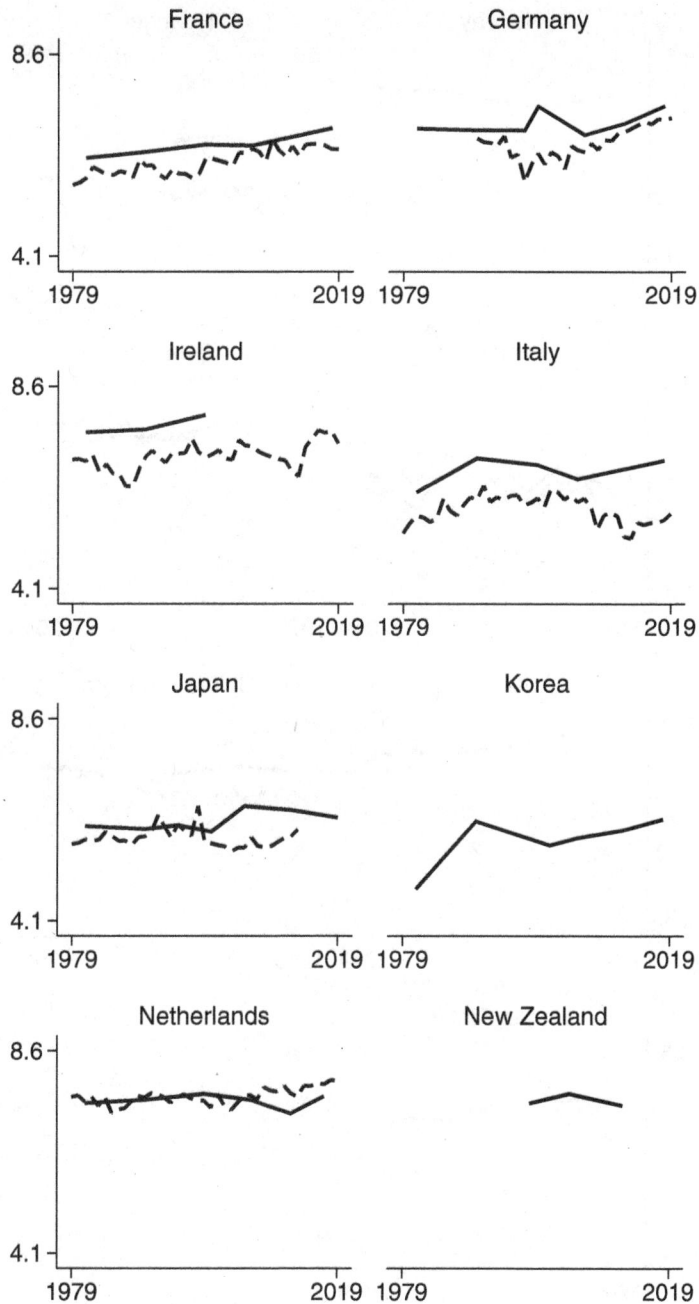

Figure 6.1 Continued

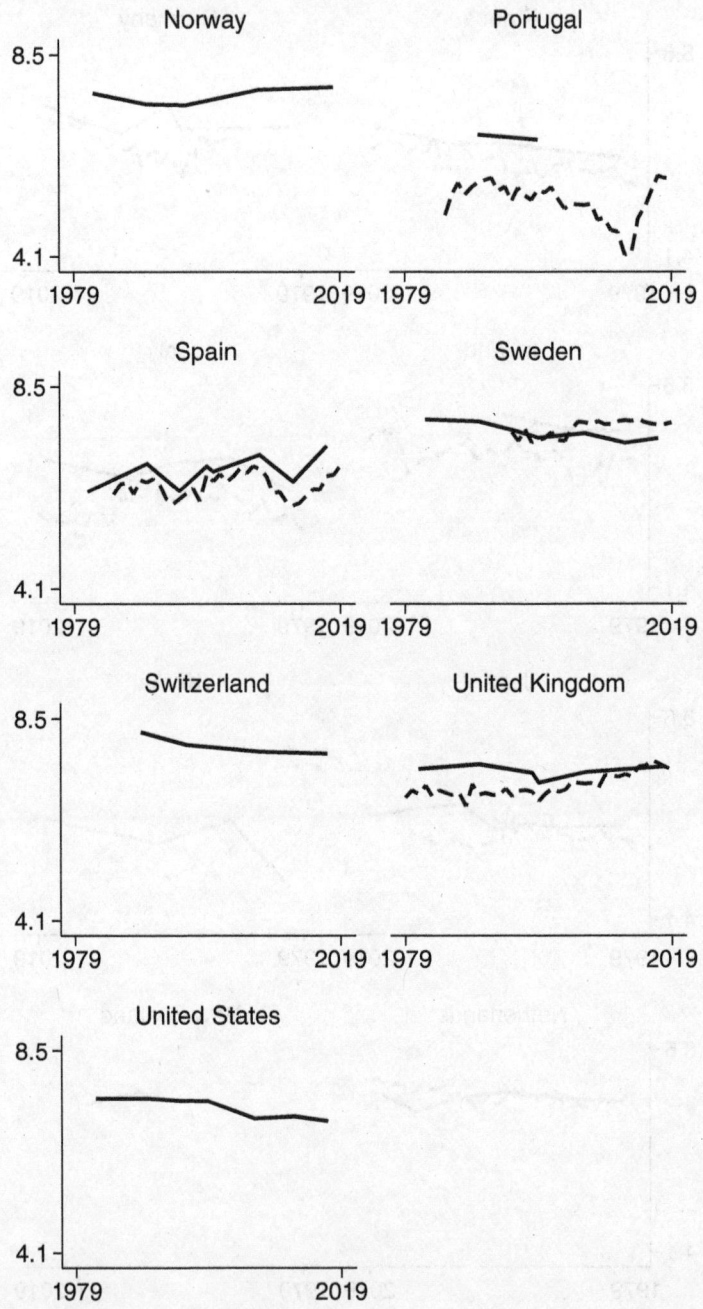

Figure 6.1 Continued

Is stagnant happiness in the rich democratic countries a product of high or rising income inequality?

Have Countries with High or Rising Income Inequality Had Smaller Increases in Life Satisfaction?

If income inequality has contributed to the stagnation in subjective well-being, countries with higher or faster-rising income inequality should have experienced less of an increase (or more of a decrease) in life satisfaction.

Figure 6.2 shows levels of income inequality and changes in life satisfaction over the 1979 to 2019 period. There is no noteworthy association in either of the charts. The best-fit lines do slope down to the right, which is what the inequality-is-harmful hypothesis predicts, but the lines are nearly flat and the countries are spread out all over the chart.

The same is true when we turn to changes in income inequality, in figure 6.3. We see little indication that countries with larger increases in income inequality have done significantly worse in subjective well-being trends.

The Netherlands is illustrative of the lack of association between income inequality and changes in life satisfaction. It's a country in which income inequality is low and has increased by a relatively small amount. Yet life satisfaction has been just as stagnant in the Netherlands as in most of the other rich democratic nations.

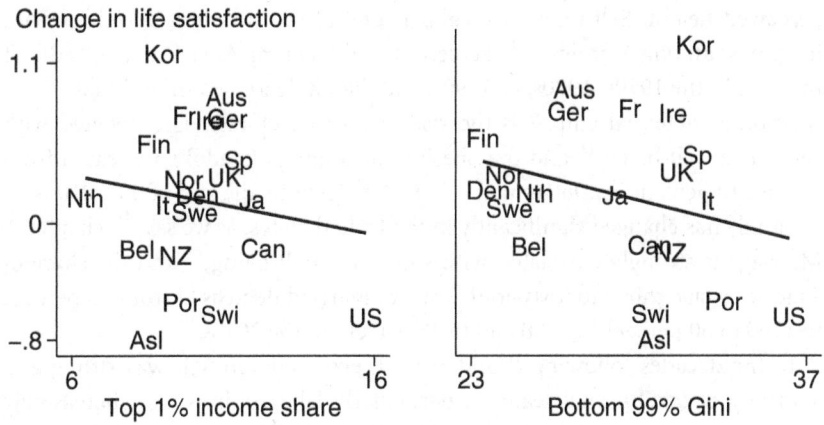

Figure 6.2 Income inequality and change in life satisfaction

Horizontal axes: income inequality. Average for 1979–2019. For data description and sources, see figures 1.1–1.4. Vertical axes: life satisfaction. Change from 1979 to 2019. For data description and source, see figure 6.1. "Asl" is Australia; "Aus" is Austria. The lines are linear regression lines.

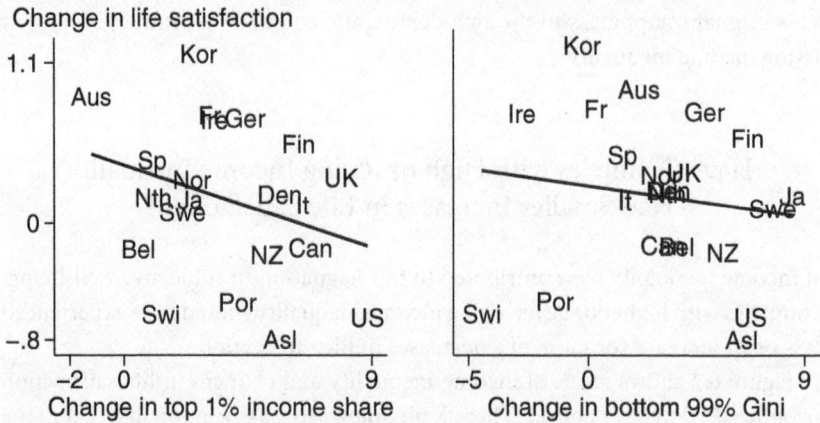

Figure 6.3 Change in income inequality and change in life satisfaction

Change from 1979 to 2019. Horizontal axes: change in income inequality. For data description and sources, see figures 1.1–1.4. Vertical axes: change in life satisfaction. For data description and source, see figure 6.1. "Asl" is Australia; "Aus" is Austria. The lines are linear regression lines.

The US Story

If there is a country that seems to support the inequality-is-harmful hypothesis, it's once again the United States. In each of the charts in figures 6.2 and 6.3, America is in the lower-right corner. Its trend in life satisfaction has been one of the worst. Is its high and rising income inequality the cause?

That's possible, but there are many other plausible culprits. One is people's perceived health. Self-reported health is one of the strongest correlates with happiness among Americans.[14] Perceived health among American adults didn't improve in the 1970s, 1980s, or 1990s, and then it decreased in the 2000s.[15]

Another potential culprit is the rise in obesity. Obesity is correlated with subjective well-being,[16] and the obesity rate among US adults increased from around 10 percent in 1980 to more than 40 percent by the end of the 2010s.

Family has changed significantly in the United States, as we saw in chapter 4. Marriage is strongly correlated with subjective well-being,[17] and the share of Americans age thirty to forty-four who are married decreased from 80 percent in 1960 to 60 percent in 1980 and to 45 percent in the 2010s.[18]

In the decades following World War II, economic growth was strong and a variety of institutional features, particularly labor unions and increasingly generous government transfers, ensured that middle and low-end American households shared in the growing prosperity. Since the 1970s, economic growth has slowed and household incomes have increased less rapidly. For people who had become accustomed to a steady and rapid rate of income growth, this development is likely to have been disappointing.

Worry about finances is the stressor that's most damaging for happiness.[19] Life satisfaction tends to be higher in countries with public services that increase people's ability to find good employment and public insurance programs that cushion economic loss.[20] The United States is one of the rich nations in which public services and public insurance programs are least comprehensive and generous.[21]

Americans likely have come to feel more stressed for time. Weekly hours worked have decreased, but not very much, and not nearly as much as in most other affluent democratic nations. The US offers little government support for childcare costs, even as more women are in paid work. And commute times have increased.[22]

Finally, Americans who are religious tend to be happier than those who aren't, and religiosity has declined significantly since the late 1970s.[23]

Why Has Life Satisfaction Increased So Little in the Other Countries?

So income inequality may have played little or no role in America's stagnant happiness since the late 1970s. But what accounts for the lack of increase in life satisfaction in other rich democratic nations?

While I don't think we have a clear answer, there are a number of possible culprits. For one thing, as in the United States, income growth has slowed.[24]

Family, too, has weakened. Marriage itself has declined, though for some people it has been replaced by long-term cohabitation. Even so, a decreasing share of people are in stable two-adult families.[25]

Another likely contributor is higher unemployment. Being unemployed (wanting a job but unable to get one) decreases happiness. An analysis of European countries in the years 2002–18 found that being unemployed reduces life satisfaction by three-quarters of a point on a 0 to 10 scale, an effect similar in size to that of income and health.[26] Unemployment rates in most western European nations were low in the 1950s and 1960s. They began to increase in the 1970s, and in a number of these countries they have remained high in the ensuing decades.

On many cultural issues, rising affluence has led to replacement of traditional values with more progressive ones. As this has happened, older cohorts have witnessed an erosion of norms and expectations they took for granted. This has contributed to disappointment, frustration, and political backlash.[27]

Does Income Inequality Hinder Happiness?

All of the affluent democratic nations have gotten richer since the late 1970s, with incomes rising even among low-end households. Yet life satisfaction hasn't increased in most of these countries. Given that income is one of the strongest determinants of subjective well-being, this is puzzling. Is income inequality the cause? I don't think we know the answer. But income inequality isn't correlated with trends in life satisfaction across these countries, and there are lots of other plausible culprits. There is little reason to be confident that reducing income inequality would produce an increase in life satisfaction.

7
Is Income Inequality Harmful?

In chapters 2 through 6 I examined country-level evidence on income inequality's consequences for living standards, democracy, opportunity, longevity, and happiness. That evidence offers very little support for inequality-is-harmful hypotheses.

In the affluent longstanding-democratic nations with higher levels or larger increases in income inequality, economic growth hasn't tended to be slower, household incomes in the middle and at the bottom haven't tended to increase less rapidly, and household balance sheets haven't tended to be worse.

Income inequality is bad for democracy in that policy decisions tend to reflect the preferences of people with high incomes more than those of people with middle or low incomes. Yet in the United States, which has experienced a large rise in income inequality since the late 1970s, the magnitude of the gap in political influence hasn't increased. Nor, as best we can tell, does the gap in the United States differ notably from the gap in other nations that have far lower levels of income inequality. This suggests that if we could reduce income inequality in the United States back to its late-1970s level, the lowest it has ever been, there is little reason to expect inequality of political influence would decrease.

Income inequality can potentially impede equality of opportunity through a variety of pathways, from family structure to parenting to educational attainment to health to neighborhoods. Yet evidence that income inequality is a key contributor to unequal opportunity is quite thin.

Higher levels of income inequality encourage us to obsess more about our relative status, which may increase stress. Stress is harmful for health in a direct way, and it might also cause people to turn to a variety of harmful behaviors, from smoking to overeating to drug and alcohol abuse to violence. However, the country evidence offers very little indication that income inequality reduces longevity.

Despite rising incomes and living standards since the 1970s, happiness in the rich democratic nations has been stagnant. Income inequality might be a contributor, but there is good reason for skepticism.

In this chapter I consider some potential objections and caveats to the conclusion that economic inequality has tended to have little in the way of harmful consequences.

Is Country-Level Data the Right Data to Focus On?

I've focused on what the country-level data tell us about the impact of income inequality. As I noted in chapter 1, that's because my chief concern is with policy implications. The main policy levers for affecting inequality are those of the national government. But are there other data that might tell us something helpful?

One possibility, common in research on the rich democratic nations, is to examine country-years. Instead of analyzing cross-country variation in change over the forty-year period from 1979 to 2019, we would analyze cross-country variation in year-to-year changes. This approach significantly increases the number of observations and thereby allows inclusion of more control variables in the statistical analysis. However, as I noted in chapter 2, I do try controlling for some things that might affect these outcomes: change in GDP per capita, change in educational attainment, change in the elderly population share, and change in the immigrant population share. Moreover, analyses with too many control variables are as likely to mislead as analyses with too few, and the ability to throw in lots of controls tends to reduce the thought we put into our choice of statistical models.[1] In any case, analyzing country-years isn't a useful approach in evaluating the impact of income inequality, because the effects of inequality are likely to be slow-moving. If they occur, they'll do so over the long run, rather than from one year to the next.

Another possibility is to look at subnational units. Where data are available, we can examine patterns for regions, states, cities, labor markets, perhaps even neighborhoods. Such data often are available for the United States, and in chapters 2–6 I've highlighted the findings by researchers who utilize those data. For example, I noted in chapter 3 that across the US states income inequality isn't correlated with policies favored by high-income Americans. In chapter 4 I pointed out that comparison across the US states and across US commuting zones finds no association between income inequality and inequality of opportunity. And in chapter 5 I noted that across the US states income inequality isn't associated with obesity or with deaths of despair.

Another alternative is individual-level data. Sometimes studies of individuals provide an abundance of evidence that points in a particular direction. For instance, data from individuals give us strong reason to be confident that smoking reduces life expectancy. Thus, if we were to observe that smoking decreased in a country and yet overall life expectancy didn't increase, we nevertheless could be confident in recommending to policymakers that taking steps to reduce smoking would improve longevity. Income inequality is different. We don't have a large number of individual-level studies with a consensus finding in favor of the hypothesized adverse effects of income inequality.[2]

Should We Look at Other Income Inequality Measures?

The analyses in chapters 2–6 use two measures of income inequality: (1) the share of income that goes to the top 1 percent of households, which is an indicator of inequality between those at the top and everyone else; (2) the Gini coefficient for income inequality within the bottom 99 percent of households. Another candidate for inclusion in these analyses is income inequality within the lower half of the population, commonly measured using the ratio of household income at the fiftieth percentile of the distribution to household income at the tenth percentile ("50/10 ratio").

I haven't included this for two reasons. One is that inequality-is-harmful hypotheses rarely point to income inequality in the lower half. They focus almost exclusively on inequality at the top or on inequality throughout the entire distribution. The second reason is that in many of the rich democracies there hasn't been much change in lower-half income inequality during the era of rising inequality.[3] Even in the United States, where the level of income inequality in the bottom half is comparatively high, there has been virtually no increase in that level since the late 1970s. That makes it difficult to identify a causal effect.

Does the Fact That the United States So Often Stands Apart Imply That Income Inequality Must Have an Adverse Impact?

At first glance, the way in which the United States compares to other rich democratic nations seems to support the view that inequality has harmful consequences. Since the late 1970s the US has had the highest level and one of the largest increases in income inequality, and it has performed worse than all or most other rich democratic countries on more than a few outcomes.

However, as I explained in previous chapters, there are compelling alternative explanations. Income inequality looks unlikely to be the true cause of America's exceptionalism.

Does Income Inequality Have Harmful Effects That Are Context-Specific?

By far the most common hypothesis about adverse consequences of economic inequality is a direct one: income inequality makes a particular outcome worse. Another possibility is that income inequality makes things worse *in a particular context*.

One example has to do with the rise of right-wing populist parties, which has raised concerns about democracy's sustainability. In two European nations where such parties have come to power, Hungary and Poland, the party weakened democracy by taking steps to enhance its ability to remain in power, such as altering electoral rules, reducing the judiciary's authority, and limiting media independence.[4] Although this hasn't yet happened in any of the rich longstanding-democratic nations, it could.

There is little indication that income inequality by itself has spurred a rise in support for right-wing populist parties.[5] But it's possible that rising inequality when coupled with stagnant living standards may have done so.[6] In such a context, citizens might be more receptive to these parties' claim that immigrants or globalization are the cause of their difficulties and thus more willing to vote for these parties.

Figure 7.1 shows one way to assess this hypothesis. On the vertical axis of the two graphs is the increase in the vote share for right-wing populist parties over the period from 1979 to 2019. In some countries, such as Ireland and Spain, the rise has been quite small. In others, like Switzerland, Denmark, and Finland, it has been fairly large. On the horizontal axes is a measure of rising income inequality along with slow growth of median household income. Countries that had both are to the right ("worse"). Countries in which income inequality didn't increase much and in which median income grew fairly rapidly are to the left ("better"). The prediction is that nations to the right in these charts will have had larger increases in voting for right-wing populist parties.

We don't, however, see any such association. Nations with little increase in income inequality and rapid growth of middle-class household income haven't tended to fare any better at fending off the rise of right-wing populism than countries where inequality has soared and median income has stagnated.

Why Doesn't Income Inequality Matter Much?

If income inequality has had little or no impact on the outcomes examined in chapters 2–6, as I've concluded, why is that? Why haven't the hypothesized causal links, many of which are quite plausible in theory, played out in practice?

One possible reason why we observe little indication that income inequality has the hypothesized adverse effects is that it doesn't actually have those effects, or that it has those effects but they are very weak. A second reason is that it does have those effects but also has beneficial effects that offset the damage it does.

A third possibility is that inequality does have significant harmful effects but they don't matter much, if at all, because there are other much more powerful contributors to the outcome. Here it's worth emphasizing that societal affluence

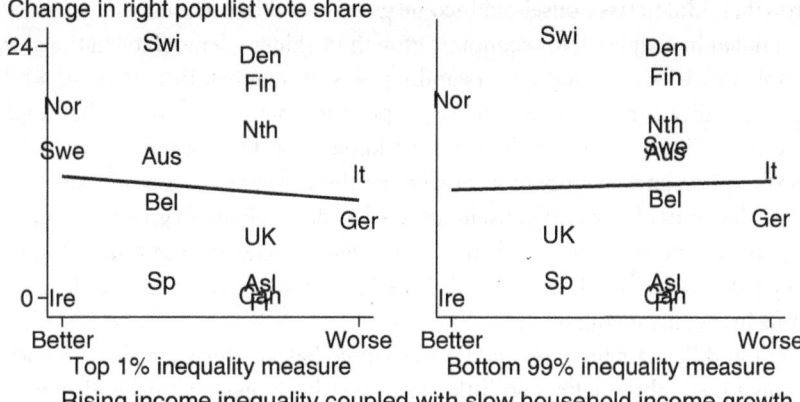

Figure 7.1 Does rising income inequality coupled with slow household income growth increase voter support for right-wing populist parties?

Horizontal axes: combined measure of change in income inequality and change in median household income, 1979–2019. To the left ("better") are countries with less increase in income inequality and faster growth of median household income. To the right ("worse") are countries with more increase in income inequality and slower growth of median household income. For data description and sources, see figure 2.6. Vertical axes: change in vote share of right-wing populist political parties, 1979–2019. Vote share is for elections to parliament (lower house where there are two houses). Data sources: *Wikipedia*; Andreas Bergh and Anders Kärnä, "Explaining the Rise of Populism in European Democracies 1980-2018: The Role of Labor Market Institutions and Inequality," *Social Science Quarterly*, 2022, appendix. Australia: One Nation. Austria: Freedom Party of Austria. Belgium: Flemish Interest. Canada: People's Party of Canada. Denmark: Danish People's Party, New Right. Finland: Finns Party (True Finns). France: National Rally (National Front). Germany: Alternative for Deutschland. Ireland: Irish Freedom Party. Italy: Brothers of Italy, Lega Nord. Netherlands: Forum for Democracy, Party for Freedom. Norway: Progress Party. Spain: Vox. Sweden: Sweden Democrats. Switzerland: Swiss People's Party. United Kingdom: UK Independence Party. Japan, Korea, New Zealand, and Portugal are missing due to lack of data on change in median household income. The United States is missing because it has a two-party winner-take-all electoral system rather than a proportional representation system or a multiparty winner-take-all system. The lines are linear regression lines.

and government provision of extensive public goods, services, and insurance programs almost certainly are a key part of the reason why income inequality matters so little in affluent democratic nations.[7] If there were no universal public K-12 schooling, income inequality across households surely would matter quite a bit in determining opportunity for children. If there were no public provision of health insurance, longevity for people with low incomes, and therefore average life expectancy for their country, surely would be lower. If there were no government transfer programs, income inequality surely would reduce income growth for poor households. And so on.

Let's consider each of the five outcomes in turn. Begin with living standards. I examined four indicators: economic growth, low-end household income growth, middle-class household income growth, and household balance sheets. As I noted in chapter 2, for economic growth in affluent democratic nations, we simply don't have a good understanding of what matters. In particular, while the inequality-is-harmful hypothesis emphasizes that income inequality might lead to too little consumption, we don't know what the optimal mix between consumption and investment is, or whether there is in fact an optimal mix.

For incomes of low-end households, the key determinant of growth over time is government programs. And in the rich democracies in recent decades, the policy decisions that determine this have been largely independent of levels or shifts in income inequality.

For middle-class incomes and for household balance sheets, it isn't clear why income inequality matters so little. The most likely explanation is that other factors—rates of economic growth, employment patterns, labor union strength and strategy, access to credit, and the cost of borrowing—overwhelm any impact of income inequality.

Democracy, which I examined in chapter 3, features equal opportunity to influence policy decisions. Since money can buy political influence in various ways, income inequality seems likely to contribute to inequality of political influence. And the evidence suggests it does. However, in the country for which we have the most research and also a very large rise in income inequality, the United States, inequality of political influence hasn't increased in concert with rising inequality of incomes, as best we can tell from existing studies. Nor, it appears, is inequality of political influence greater in the United States than in lower-income-inequality nations. It could be that this owes to rules that limit the use of money in politics. But in the United States those rules are weak. The main reason probably is that while money buys political influence, it does so only up to a point. Beyond that point, spending additional dollars doesn't matter much, if at all.

For equality of opportunity, the outcome in chapter 4, there are a host of pathways through which income inequality could potentially have adverse effects, including family structure, parenting, education, health, and neighborhoods. The likelihood here is that income inequality matters but that the magnitude of its impact is small enough that it is outweighed by other determinants. For example, while rising income inequality in the United States since the late 1970s might well have widened the gap in children's cognitive development and health, that may have been offset by equalization of school funding or reduction in violent crime or removal of lead from gasoline. Also, for some of the pathways where we do observe a widening of the opportunity gap, including parents' spending on children and neighborhood quality, the widening has occurred mainly at the top of the distribution, and this may have far less impact on capabilities than a widening of the gap between, say, the middle and the bottom.

For longevity, examined in chapter 5, income inequality is predicted to have harmful effects mainly by increasing stress. Stress in turn leads to life-shortening behaviors such as smoking, overeating, drug and alcohol abuse, and violence. For stress itself, we don't have enough data to conduct country comparisons. But there is reason to suspect that income inequality isn't a major contributor to stress. One of the most comprehensive and careful studies of over-time developments—a study cited approvingly by leading proponents of the hypothesis that income inequality harms health by increasing stress[8]—concludes that in the United States anxiety increased steadily in the 1950s, 1960s, 1970s, and 1980s.[9] The 1950s through 1970s were a period of declining income inequality, so a steady rise in anxiety during those decades is the opposite of what we would expect to observe if income inequality is a significant contributor to stress. Also, surveys by Gallup and by the American Psychological Association suggest there was no increase in stress among Americans in the 1990s, 2000s, or 2010s, when inequality was rising.[10]

For happiness, which we considered in chapter 6, I think we simply don't know the reason why income inequality doesn't matter much. We are still in the relatively early stages of understanding the determinants of subjective well-being. But the fact that the stagnation in life satisfaction looks to have begun in the 1970s, prior to the rise in income inequality, suggests that factors other than income inequality have been the key drivers of happiness trends.

Is Income Inequality Harmful?

Income inequality very likely has some harmful effects. But in the world's rich longstanding-democratic nations during the era of rising income inequality since the late 1970s, the magnitude of any such effects seems to have been quite small. There is little evidence to support a conclusion that reducing income inequality in these countries will significantly improve living standards, democracy, opportunity, longevity, or happiness.

This is by no means the final word on the matter. For one thing, it's possible I've drawn the wrong conclusions from the available data. In this chapter I've raised various potential concerns and explained why I suspect my conclusions are correct. But that scarcely guarantees that they are.

In addition, the available data are far from ideal. In considering the effect of income inequality on democracy, for example, we would be in better shape if there were more comprehensive data on the correlation between public opinion and policy changes, if those data spanned lengthier time periods, and if they were available for more countries. Similarly, for opportunity, it would be very helpful to have information about relative intergenerational income mobility for more nations and longer time spans. I've noted a number of other examples in chapters 2–6.

Finally, lessons we draw from the patterns in the rich democratic nations from 1979 to 2019 won't necessarily hold going forward. If, as some project,[11] economic inequality rises to levels even higher than what we see in the contemporary United States, its causal impact might not remain as muted as it seems to have been up to now.

8

People Want Less Inequality, But It's Not a Priority for Them

Chapters 2 through 7 looked at income inequality's effects. In this chapter I consider people's views and preferences. Do people want less income inequality? If so, do they want government to take steps to achieve that?

A Lot of People Think There Is Too Much Income Inequality and Support Efforts to Reduce It

The International Social Survey Programme (ISSP) asks a battery of questions about income inequality and inequality reduction to a representative sample of adults in a number of the affluent democratic countries. One question shows them illustrations of various distributions, as depicted in figure 8.1. It asks "What type of society is your country today—which diagram comes closest?" It then asks "What do you think your country ought to be like—which do you prefer?"

In the most recent ISSP survey, conducted in the late 2010s, the bulk of respondents in every country tended to say their society looked like A or B or C, which depict greater inequality. Smaller shares chose D or E, which depict less inequality.[1] When asked which distribution they prefer, the reverse was true: most people chose D or E. For example, in the United States 80 percent said the country's actual distribution looks like A or B or C, while only 18 percent said this is what the distribution ought to look like. Even in the most egalitarian country, Denmark, 43 percent said the actual distribution looks like A or B or C, but only 17 percent said that is what it ought to look like. This suggests that many people

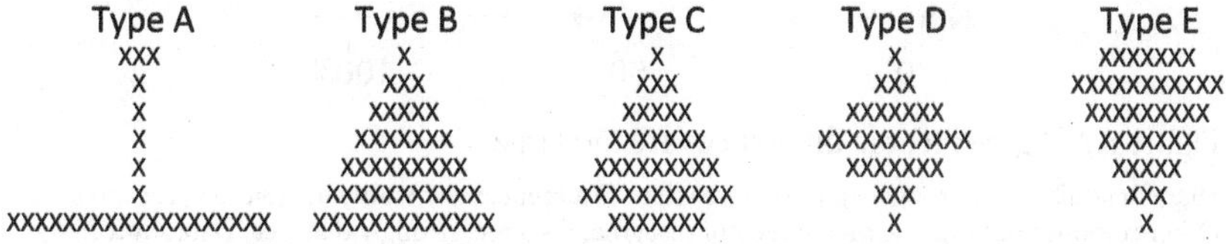

```
      Type A              Type B              Type C              Type D              Type E
       XXX                   X                   X                   X                XXXXXXX
        X                   XXX                 XXX                 XXX              XXXXXXXXXXX
        X                  XXXXX               XXXXX              XXXXXXX             XXXXXXXXX
        X                 XXXXXXX             XXXXXXX          XXXXXXXXXXX             XXXXXXX
        X                XXXXXXXXX           XXXXXXXXX            XXXXXXX               XXXXX
        X               XXXXXXXXXXX         XXXXXXXXXXX            XXX                   XXX
XXXXXXXXXXXXXXXXXXX     XXXXXXXXXXXXX       XXXXXXXXXXXXX           X                     X
```

Figure 8.1 Income distribution in five hypothetical societies
Source: International Social Survey Programme (ISSP), Social Inequality 5, 2019, V48 and V49.

80 IS INEQUALITY THE PROBLEM?

in these countries would prefer there to be less inequality than there currently is.

Other survey questions ask people more directly about whether they favor less inequality. The ISSP asks respondents whether they strongly agree, agree, neither agree nor disagree, disagree, or strongly disagree that "income differences in my country are too large." Figure 8.2 shows that in every rich democratic country a majority, often a strong majority, believes income differences are indeed too large.

These responses are consistent with what most research on this issue has tended to find. When people in the rich longstanding-democratic nations are asked if income differences are too large or if executives are overpaid or if companies ought to reduce pay differences, typically a sizable share say yes.[2]

There also tends to be strong public support for efforts to reduce income inequality. Figure 8.3 shows that a majority or near-majority in every country agree that "it is the responsibility of the government to reduce the differences in income between people with high incomes and those with low incomes." There also is strong support when people are asked if private companies ought to reduce pay differences.[3]

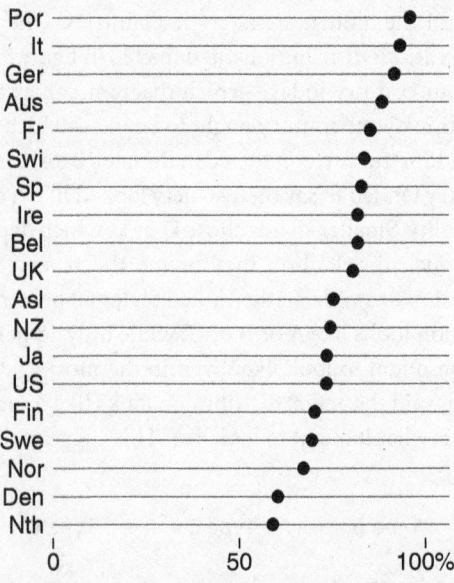

Figure 8.2 Agree income differences are too large

Share of adults who strongly agree or agree that "Differences in income in [country] are too large." Other response options: neither agree nor disagree, disagree, strongly disagree. Data source: International Social Survey Programme (ISSP), Social Inequality 5 Module, 2019, V21. The data for Belgium, Ireland, Netherlands, Portugal, and Spain are from Eurobarometer 2017, via OECD *Does Inequality Matter?*, OECD Publishing, 2021, figure 2.1. "Asl" is Australia; "Aus" is Austria.

PEOPLE WANT LESS INEQUALITY, BUT IT'S NOT A PRIORITY FOR THEM

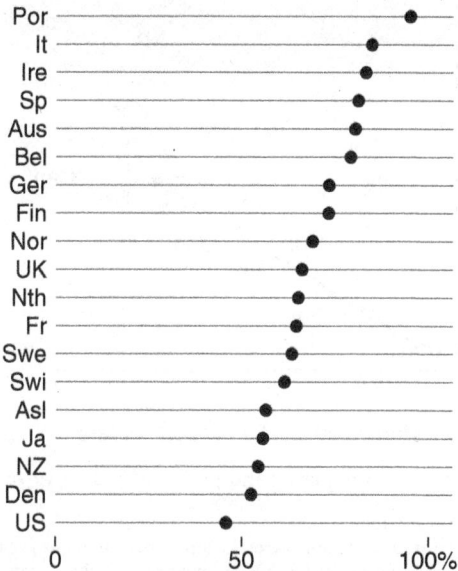

Figure 8.3 Agree government should reduce income differences

Share of adults who strongly agree or agree that "It is the responsibility of the government to reduce the differences in income between people with high incomes and those with low incomes." Other response options: neither agree nor disagree, disagree, strongly disagree. Data source: International Social Survey Programme (ISSP), Social Inequality 5 Module, 2019, V22. The data for Belgium, Ireland, Netherlands, Portugal, and Spain are from Eurobarometer 2017, via OECD *Does Inequality Matter?*, OECD Publishing, 2021, figure 3.1. "Asl" is Australia; "Aus" is Austria.

People's answers in figures 8.1, 8.2, and 8.3 could conceivably owe to social desirability bias—the tendency of respondents in public opinion surveys to give the response they think is the socially acceptable or less controversial one even if they don't actually have an opinion or care about an issue. However, the pattern in figure 8.4 suggests that probably isn't the case. In countries where people perceive there to be greater income inequality, a larger share want government to do more to reduce inequality.[4] This is what we would expect to observe if people genuinely care about this issue.

It's worth emphasizing that the public opinion survey data I've shown here are from the end of the 2010s—not a moment of unusually high or rapidly rising inequality. It's a full decade after the peak of the 2008–9 Great Recession. It's prior to the Covid-19 pandemic. It's at the end of a decade in which income inequality stopped rising or declined a bit in some countries. This too suggests that many people really do believe the level of income inequality in their nation is too high and that it would be good to take steps to reduce it.

Do people favor inequality reduction only or mainly because they think—incorrectly, as we saw in chapters 2–7—that inequality has serious harmful consequences? That seems doubtful. Worry about inequality's effects might well

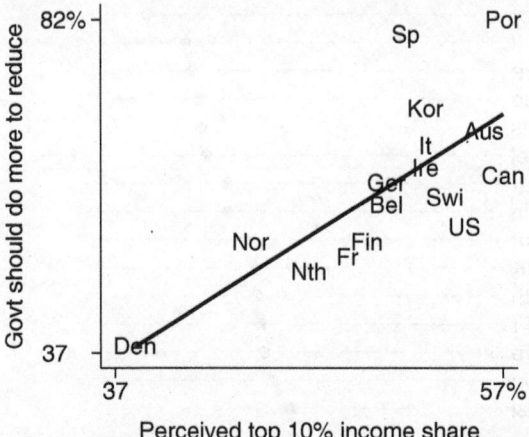

Figure 8.4 Perceived income inequality and preference for government to do more to reduce inequality

2010s. Horizontal axis: perceived income share of the top 10 percent of the population. Vertical axis: share responding "more" to the question "Governments can reduce income differences between the rich and the poor by collecting taxes and providing social benefits. In your country, do you think the government should do more or less to reduce income differences?" Data source: OECD, *Does Inequality Matter?*, OECD Publishing, 2021, figure 1.1, using data from the OECD's 2020 "Risks That Matter" survey. "Aus" is Austria. The line is a linear regression line.

account for some portion of popular sentiment in favor of inequality reduction. But the argument that inequality has harmful consequences has become visible and prominent mainly since 2010, as the quotations in chapter 1 suggest. In the countries for which data are available, large shares of the population already agreed well before 2010 that income differences in their country were too large and should be reduced.[5]

There Is Little Indication That People Think Inequality Reduction Should Be a Priority

While many people believe there is too much income inequality in their country and support efforts to reduce it, the available public opinion data also suggest that most people don't care very strongly about this.

For one thing, research on over-time patterns has tended to find little indication that people respond to a rise in income inequality in their country by favoring an increase in redistribution.[6] When income inequality increases, there often isn't a commensurate increase in the share of people who agree that it is government's responsibility to reduce income differences. This suggests that popular dislike of income inequality and support for efforts to reduce it, while real, are limited in intensity.

Other types of public opinion survey data also suggest that inequality is for many people a secondary concern. For example, Sweden is one of the world's most egalitarian nations. Yet in public opinion surveys since the mid-1980s, the share of Swedes who say equality is very important to them has consistently been much smaller than the share saying freedom or family security is very important.[7]

The United States has the highest income inequality of any affluent democratic nation. And as we saw in figures 8.2 and 8.3, a fairly large share of Americans think the country has too much income inequality and government should do something to reduce it. Yet this doesn't seem to be much of a priority for them. Since 1935, the Gallup organization has frequently asked, as an open-ended question, "What do you think is the most important problem facing this country today?" Only a tiny percentage of Americans have ever given inequality or the gap between rich and poor as their answer, even during the era of rising inequality since the late 1970s.[8]

People Want Less Inequality, But It's Not a Priority for Them

Many people in the rich democratic countries would prefer less income inequality and are supportive of government efforts to achieve that. At the same time, for most people this isn't a high-level concern.

9

Inequality Reduction in Rich Nations May Impede Reduction of Worldwide Inequality

Everything I've said thus far has been about inequality within the world's rich democratic countries. What about the rest of the world?

Most of the World's Poorest People Are Poor Because They Live in a Poor Country

Making progress in reducing worldwide income inequality requires focusing more on low-income countries than on people at the low end of the distribution within rich countries.

Figure 9.1 offers one way to see this. It shows that the income of the poorest Americans (1 on the horizontal axis) situates them at approximately the fifty-fifth percentile of the world's income distribution (vertical axis), meaning their income is higher than that of a bit more than half of the world's population. In China, a person in the middle of the distribution (50 on the horizontal axis) has an income similar to an American at the bottom. In India and Nigeria, 85 to 90 percent of the population have incomes below that of the lowest-income Americans.

Figure 9.2 gives us another way to see it. A widely used measure of poverty is a household income of less than $2,000 a year ($5.50 per day). The share of a country's population that has an income below this amount (vertical axis) is predicted quite well by the country's GDP per capita (horizontal axis).[1] Most of the world's poor people are poor because the country they live in is poor.

Worldwide Income Inequality Has Been Decreasing in Recent Decades

We have no single, unified data source that permits a calculation of the global distribution of income. There is no worldwide survey or income tax database. To

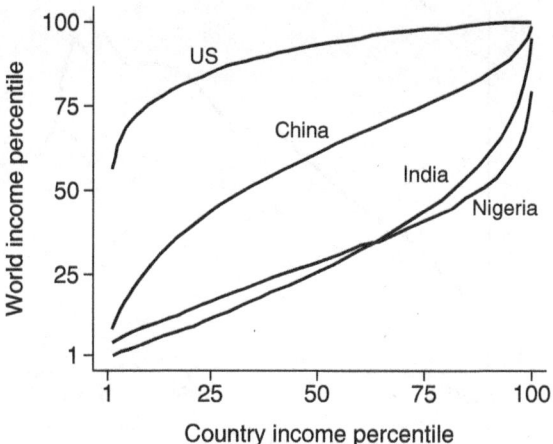

Figure 9.1 Household incomes in the United States and three poorer countries

2018. Horizontal axis: position (rank) in the income distribution within a particular country. Vertical axis: position (rank) in the worldwide income distribution. Posttax income adjusted for household size and converted to a common currency using purchasing power parities. Data source: Branko Milanovic. This updates figure 3 in Milanovic, *The Haves and the Have-Nots*, Basic Books, 2011.

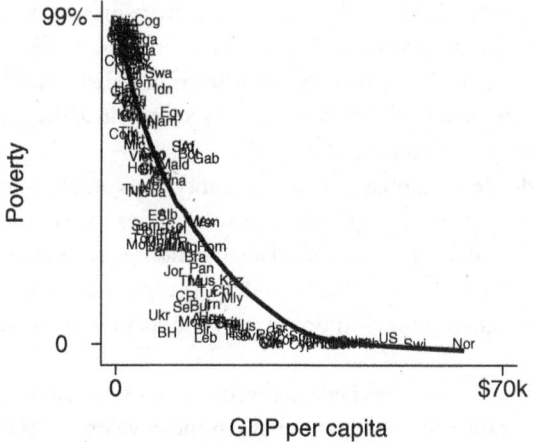

Figure 9.2 GDP per capita and poverty rate

GDP per capita: converted to 2011 US dollars using purchasing power parities. 2010. Data source: UNDP, "Human Development Data." Poverty rate: share of persons living in a household with an income less than $5.50 per day. Incomes adjusted for inflation and converted to 2011 US dollars using purchasing power parities. Average over 2004–15. Data source: World Bank. Three small, rich city-states (Andorra, Luxembourg, and Singapore) are omitted. The line is a loess curve.

estimate income inequality across all of the world's households, researchers combine two sources of information.[2] One source is about the distribution within

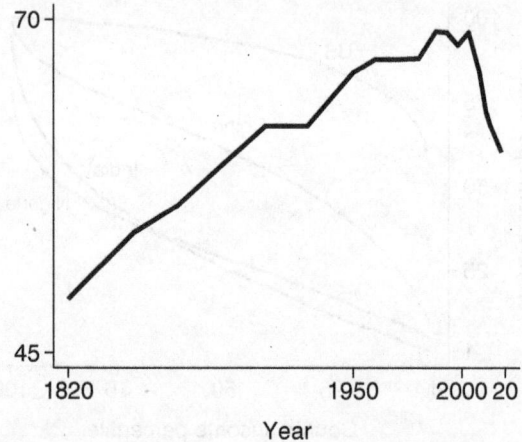

Figure 9.3 Income inequality worldwide

Gini coefficient. Data source: Branko Milanovic, "The Three Eras of Global Inequality, 1820-2020," Working Paper 59, Stone Center on Socio-Economic Inequality, City University of New York, 2022.

each country. Here we use administrative data and/or surveys.[3] The second source of information is about differences in average income across countries.[4]

Figure 9.3 shows the best available estimate of the worldwide income distribution over time. Income inequality rose steadily from the early 1800s until around 1950. It then remained fairly constant for fifty years. Since the early 2000s it has decreased sharply.

The recent decline in global income inequality owes mainly to rapid economic growth and rising incomes in China and some other formerly poor countries, which has narrowed the income gap between nations even as income gaps within many nations have widened.[5] Poor countries getting richer has reduced worldwide income inequality much more than rising income gaps within countries has increased it.

Branko Milanovic, who has been at the forefront of describing and explaining worldwide inequality, summarizes the over-time developments this way:

> The growth of global inequality during the nineteenth century and the first half of the twentieth century was driven both by widening gaps between various countries (measured by the differences in their per capita GDPs) and by greater inequalities within countries (measured by the differences in citizens' incomes in a country).... The second era extends over the latter half of the twentieth century. It featured very high global inequality. Inequality among countries was extremely high. Inequality within countries, however, was falling nearly everywhere.... That era gave way to a new phase at the turn of the twenty-first

century. Global inequality began to dip about two decades ago and continues to do so today. ... This decrease in global inequality, having occurred over the short span of 20 years, is more precipitous than was the increase in global inequality during the nineteenth century. The decrease is driven by the rise of Asia.[6]

This decline in worldwide inequality of income since the turn of the century is consistent with the declines in worldwide inequality in a number of other indicators of well-being, including life expectancy, nutrition, schooling, internet access, and political liberty.[7]

Trade and Migration Have Been Egalitarian Even Though They've Increased Income Inequality Within the Rich Democratic Countries

Economic globalization, which has contributed to rising income inequality within the rich democratic nations, at the same time has facilitated declining income inequality across the world as a whole. Egalitarians thus should think carefully before recommending that policymakers scale back this particular feature of the modern economic landscape.[8]

One element of globalization is trade between poor countries and rich ones. Imports of goods and services from poor countries may reduce jobs and wages for less-skilled workers in affluent nations, thereby contributing to rising income inequality.[9] At the same time, the increase in jobs and incomes in the poorer nations may more than offset this. David Autor has documented the employment and wage losses to ordinary American workers caused by increased trade with China in the 2000s. Yet he emphasizes that "the gains to the people who benefited are so enormous—they were destitute, and now they were brought into the global middle class. The fact that there are adverse consequences in the United States should be taken seriously, but it doesn't tilt the balance."[10] Paul Krugman puts the point in the following way:

> Globalization really did deliver big time. ... I was a grad student in the 1970s and I asked myself, "What should I specialize in?" I said. "Well, what is the most important thing?" The answer was clearly development economics. Nothing was more important than making poor countries less poor. I didn't do it because it was too depressing. In the 1970s, development economics was a very depressing field. It was basically nondevelopment economics. It was all about the reasons why poor countries didn't seem to be able to get rich.

Then all of that changed. Since then, we've seen, in terms of numbers of people, the rise of China, but then a little bit later, the rise of India. You see an enormous expansion of the quality of life for literally billions of people. All of that is clearly closely linked to globalization. All of these are export-oriented success stories.[11]

Another way to help the world's least well-off people is to allow them to migrate to richer countries.[12] This tends to increase income inequality within the rich receiving nations. By the second generation and even more so by the third, immigrants end up looking almost exactly like the native-born population in terms of socioeconomic status (and in other respects). In the short run, though, a large inflow of immigrants, particularly when many have low education and don't speak the language of their new country, almost certainly means economic inequality will increase.[13]

Yet the improvement in well-being for migrants can be huge. The pay of an unskilled worker who moves from Mexico to the United States goes up by 150 percent on average. For an unskilled worker who migrates from Nigeria to the United States, the pay rise is more than 1,000 percent.[14] This gain for immigrants far outweighs any loss to persons in the affluent country to which they migrate.[15] It thus contributes to a reduction in global income inequality.

Inequality Reduction in Rich Nations May Impede Reduction of Worldwide Inequality

If inequality reduction within our own rich nation is high on our priority list, we'll be less likely to embrace imports and immigration from poor nations.[16] That will increase worldwide income inequality and reduce human well-being.

10
What About Wealth?

So far my focus has been on inequality of income. Inequality of wealth may matter too—in fact, it might matter more. We have less data for wealth, and those data have become available only recently, so there is far less research on the impact of wealth inequality. What do we know?

Wealth Inequality

Wealth typically is distributed more unequally than income. In the United States, for instance, the top 1 percent of households get about 15 to 20 percent of the income in any given year, while the top 1 percent of wealth holders have about 35 to 40 percent of the wealth.

Figure 10.1 shows the top 1 percent's wealth share since the early 1900s in four countries for which long-run data are available—France, Sweden, the United

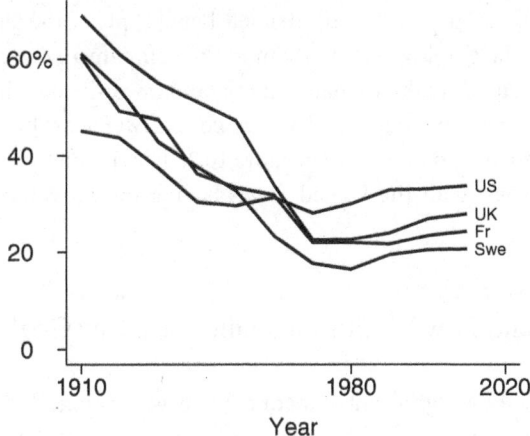

Figure 10.1 Wealth inequality between the top 1 percent and the bottom 99 percent, four countries, 1910ff

Top 1 percent's share of wealth. Wealth = assets minus liabilities. Data sources: Thomas Piketty, *Capital in the Twenty-First Century*, Harvard University Press, 2014, ch. 10; Lucas Chancel, "Ten Facts about Inequality in Advanced Economies," in *Combating Inequality*, edited by Olivier Blanchard and Dani Rodrik, MIT Press, 2021, figure 1.4.

Kingdom, and the United States. In each of the four, wealth inequality decreased from the early 1900s until around 1970 or 1980 and since then has increased a bit.

Here's what that looks like in terms of actual wealth developments, according to a recent study: "The wealth of Western middle classes grew by 2.2 percent per year up to 1950 and by 3.9 percent between 1950 and 1980. The top growth was around zero, 0.2 percent, before 1950 and 2.3 percent between 1950 and 1980. Since 1980, real wealth has grown in the entire population, but at a higher pace at the top."[1]

What accounts for the significant reduction in wealth inequality during the first two-thirds of the twentieth century and the modest increase since then? Five developments appear to have been key.[2] The value of private assets, which are disproportionately owned by those at the top, declined during the two world wars, the Great Depression, and the early post–World War II decades. All of the affluent democracies enacted and expanded new taxes on income, and in some instances on wealth. The 1940s, 1950s, and 1960s featured historically rapid rates of economic growth, coupled with institutions—strong labor unions, in particular—that ensured a significant amount of this growth trickled down to the middle and lower parts of the distribution via rising employment and wages. Homeownership rates increased significantly, particularly after the invention of government-backed long-term fixed-interest-rate mortgage loans in the 1930s, boosting wealth among the middle class. Finally, since around 1970 "funded" (defined-contribution) pensions have become increasingly common. In these types of plans, unlike "pay as you go" (defined-benefit) plans, the pension assets legally belong to the employee rather than to the company or the government, boosting the measured wealth of many middle-and lower-income households.

The OECD has wealth inequality data that cover fewer years but more countries. According to those data, shown in figure 10.2, there is quite a bit of variation across the countries, with the United States having the most top-end wealth inequality.[3]

Should Low Wealth Inequality Be a Key Goal?

Is wealth inequality a significant impediment to well-being? Judging from a comparison across countries, that looks unlikely to be true. Denmark, Norway, and Sweden have comparatively high levels of wealth inequality, as we see in figure 10.2. Yet they are among the best performers when it comes to economic security, equality of opportunity, living standards of the least well-off, and happiness.[4]

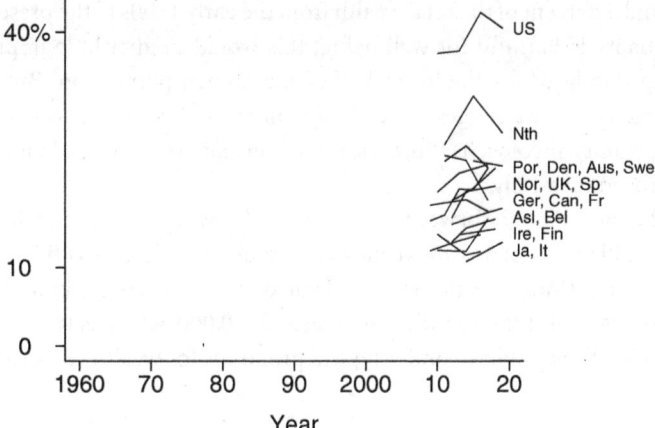

Figure 10.2 Wealth inequality between the top 1 percent and the bottom 99 percent, seventeen countries, 2010ff

Top 1 percent's share of wealth. Wealth = assets minus liabilities. The estimate for Sweden is imputed using top 5 percent wealth share data. Data source: OECD, Wealth Distribution Database, stats.oecd.org. "Asl" = Australia; "Aus" = Austria.

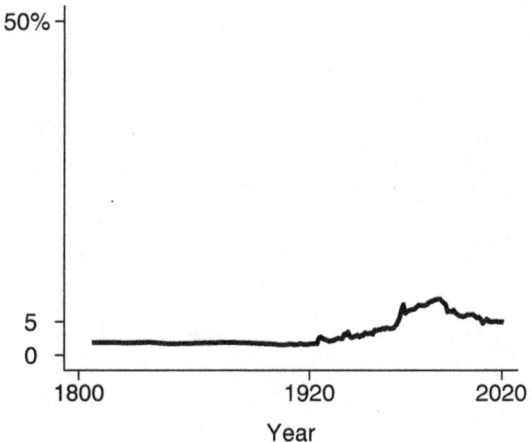

Figure 10.3 Bottom 50 percent's wealth share, France

Share of total net personal wealth held by the bottom 50 percent of the population. Data source: World Inequality Database.

The long-run over-time picture suggests a similar conclusion. France is an informative case here, because we have estimates of wealth and its distribution in France over a very lengthy time period.[5] Figure 10.3 shows the wealth share held by the bottom half of the French population. That share has hovered around 5 percent of the total wealth from the early 1800s to the present. If wealth inequality is harmful for well-being, this would predict little improvement in living standards for the lower half of the French population. But every other indicator we have suggests exactly the opposite. Economic security, economic opportunity, income, health, education, housing, free time, and much more have improved massively.[6]

The most straightforward benefit of wealth would seem to be to help ensure against ill effects of disruptive life events such as job loss, disability, and divorce. Yet a recent study of patterns in the United States finds that a household's wealth only serves this function when it exceeds $200,000, which is far more than most households would have under typical proposals for wealth redistribution.[7]

What About Wealth?

Wealth is distributed quite unequally in the rich democratic countries. But it's not clear that this is a big problem.

11

Inequality Reduction Should Be a Secondary Goal

What should we recommend policymakers in affluent democratic countries do about income inequality and wealth inequality? My answer has five parts: (1) Don't assume that reducing income inequality or wealth inequality will solve other problems. (2) Focus on building the infrastructure for a good society. (3) Recognize that public services and goods reduce inequality of well-being, even though this doesn't show up in measures of income inequality or wealth inequality. (4) Inequality reduction should be a goal. (5) Inequality reduction should be a secondary goal.

Don't Assume That Reducing Income Inequality or Wealth Inequality Will Solve Other Problems

The chief rationale underlying the view that inequality reduction should be a high-level priority is that economic inequality may significantly worsen other things we value, such as living standards, democracy, opportunity, health, and happiness, and that we could therefore improve these by reducing inequality.

As we saw in chapters 2 through 7, empirical support for inequality-is-harmful hypotheses is underwhelming. The experience of the rich democratic countries from 1979 to 2019 suggests little reason to think that reducing income inequality would improve living standards, reduce the disproportionate political influence of people with higher incomes, move us closer to equal opportunity, increase longevity, or boost life satisfaction. While we have less data with which to assess the consequences of wealth inequality, two key facts from the country experience—the success of the Nordic countries in creating a good society despite comparatively high wealth inequality and the massive advance in well-being among the bottom half of the population in France over the past two centuries despite their low and stagnant wealth share—recommend skepticism about wealth inequality's harmful consequences.

Instead of trying to improve living standards, democracy, opportunity, health, and happiness indirectly via reduction in income inequality or wealth inequality, we're more likely to make progress by pursuing these goals directly.[1]

Focus on Building the Infrastructure for a Good Society

In a society where many of life's basic needs and wants—safety, housing, childcare, schooling, medical care, work, time for family and leisure, retirement income, eldercare, and more—are assured, it isn't clear that a moderately high level of income inequality or wealth inequality is especially problematic.[2] Denmark, Norway, and Sweden have some of the highest levels of wealth inequality among the rich democracies, as we saw in chapter 10. And while some egalitarians have argued that there should be no billionaires,[3] Sweden and Norway have more billionaires per capita than the United States.[4] Despite this, in the contemporary Nordic countries there is plenty of economic security, little material hardship, abundant freedom, and most people (including immigrants) say they are quite satisfied with their lives.[5] On the whole, life there is very good.[6] In this kind of context, we may not be bothered by the fact that some persons have a lot of income or wealth, just as most of us aren't too upset that some people are exceptionally intelligent or good looking or socially adept.[7]

Imagine the following life:

During pregnancy your parent or parents regularly visit a doctor who monitors the pregnancy, listens to concerns, and dispenses advice about diet, things to avoid, how to deal with stress, and related matters. The birth occurs in a hospital—or perhaps at home but with access to physician assistance and appropriate technology. Throughout the first year of life, a nurse checks in with you and your parents to promote well-being and supply information about breastfeeding, your sleep patterns, eating, illnesses, and more. All of this is provided free or with a small copayment.

A paid parental leave program gives your parent(s) fourteen months of leave from work, replacing about 80 percent of their former earnings. Parents can split the leave time however they like, though if your father (or other second parent) doesn't take at least two of the months, they get a total of twelve instead of fourteen.

Your parents can enroll you in a high-quality "early education" (childcare) center either part time or full time, depending on how they want to balance their paying jobs with caring for you. The staff in these centers are required to have the same qualifications as elementary school teachers. Many of these centers are run by the government; they are, in effect, extensions of public elementary schools, though they focus more on social activities and play than on education. Others are privately run—some for profit, some not. Private centers may be formed by groups of parents or by companies. They must meet the same quality standards as the public centers. Your parents pay for early education, but the total amount they owe is capped at less than 10 percent of their income.

Throughout your childhood your parents receive a "child allowance" of about $300 per month per child from the government to help defray the cost of childrearing.

Around age six you enter the public school system, where you attend elementary and then secondary school. This costs your parents nothing. There may be some fees for participation in sports or band or the arts, but they are small and families with low income pay less. School provides free, nutritious breakfast and lunch. It also offers free or low-cost after-school activities. If your parents prefer to pay to put you in a private school, they are welcome to do that.

If you have a physical, mental, or emotional disability, you receive support services. When you're young, an aide may come to your home regularly. Once you enter elementary school, much of the service provision may be through the school system. There is no cost to your parents. If your needs persist beyond school age or throughout your life, you will continue to receive appropriate services.

During childhood and beyond, you probably live in either an apartment or a house. Your home has a roof, floors, and walls. There is furniture, some wall decorations, appliances (refrigerator, stove, dishwasher, clothes washer), cooking items, toys.

Your home has running water. Solid waste is collected once or twice a week. Liquid and semisolid waste disappears into sink drains, shower drains, and toilets. A separate system collects and then uses or disposes of rainwater. These services come free or at modest cost.

Your home has electricity to provide light, heat, cooling, and power for devices such as refrigerators and televisions. The energy you use comes entirely (or almost entirely) from non-greenhouse-gas-emitting sources, but that doesn't mean you have access to only a small amount. On average you use about 30,000 kilowatt-hours per year, roughly the same as the current average in Europe.[8]

You're connected. Your home, like everyone's, has access to broadband internet at a small cost. And public Wi-Fi is available in schools, other public buildings, and commercial areas. Coupled with your public library membership, this gives you free or low-cost access to virtually the entire store of human knowledge via books, journal and magazine and newspaper articles, and online content.[9] You can listen to almost any piece of music that's ever been recorded. And you can watch any recorded movie or television show or sports contest or live performance.

Your apartment or house may have a yard or a common area with some grass and trees. If it doesn't, within a ten-minute walk or a five-minute ride there is green space to play or relax in.[10] Access is free. Because you likely live in an area with mixed-use development, you also are within walking distance of one or more stores, restaurants, and cafes, and possibly your workplace.

You are safe. There is violence in your country and perhaps even in your neighborhood, but it isn't common. In a typical year, just one person out of every 100,000 is murdered. Rape, assault, and other types of violence also are rare. Expansive provision of public and near-public goods and services along with widespread economic opportunity reduce the incentive for violence. Safety also is aided by effective policing.[11]

You have health insurance from cradle to grave. There may be copayments, and some elective procedures aren't covered, or are covered only partially, but you are never in danger of dying or suffering a significant deterioration in your quality of life because you lack access to the funds needed to pay for medical care.

You have an array of civil and political protections: freedom from slavery, freedom from torture, the right to a fair trial, the right to be treated with humanity in detention, and more.[12]

As you go through life, institutions and individuals that affect your opportunities and outcomes—schools, businesses, landlords, hospitals, government agencies, and others—aren't permitted to treat you differently because of your sex, race, ethnicity, disability, sexual orientation, gender identity, national origin, or religion. No one is required to like you, your physical features, your beliefs, or your preferences. But they can't discriminate against you on these grounds.

After graduating from high school, you may attend college. If you choose a public university in your state or region, there is no tuition charge. Unless you live at home with your parents, you will owe for the room and board at college, but to pay for this you can take out a government-guaranteed loan. This loan will have a low monthly payment because the interest rate is low and because it can be paid back over twenty (or perhaps thirty) years. And if your wage or salary turns out to be below average, your payments are further reduced.

When you finish college, you may decide to get additional education. Postgraduate schooling isn't free, but again you are eligible for low-interest long-term loans with an income-based repayment plan.

If you aren't interested in college, you may choose to enroll in an apprenticeship program that combines schooling with on-the-job vocational training. These programs run for three or four years and are tightly integrated with local firms and employer organizations to ensure that the skills being produced are needed ones rather than simply ones schools feel competent to provide. The apprenticeship programs are paid for by companies, with a subsidy from the government.

Following school or an apprenticeship, most adults will get a paying job. If you struggle to find employment, or if you lose a job or leave it by choice, you are eligible for government help. Firms must notify a local labor market board in advance when they plan to lay off employees and when they have job openings that have lasted more than a few weeks. Non-employed persons can receive subsidized training. Staff in the labor market boards keep in close communication with firms and with boards in other areas regarding trends in skill needs. The training programs are full time and range in duration from a few weeks to more than a year. The service then helps to place workers in new jobs. If necessary, a subsidy may be used to encourage a private-sector company to hire, or a public-sector job may be created.

If the pay for your job is low, you may receive an earnings subsidy from the government to boost your income.

Throughout your working career you'll receive about 80 percent of your former pay if you can't work due to sickness, injury, or unemployment. Depending on your condition and that of the national and local economy, these payments may last just a short time or as long as a year or more.

Each year you get thirty paid days (six weeks) of vacation or holiday.

If your household's total income is below a level deemed necessary for a minimally decent standard of living and you are neither able to find additional employment income nor eligible for money from various government programs, you will receive cash from a separate public program (typically called "social assistance") to bring your income up to that minimum level.[13]

You can start a business. There are legal requirements, but a government office will help you to navigate them. Competition ("antitrust") law makes it less likely that established firms can impede entry by new start-ups such as yours. You can borrow money to fund your company. Eventually you may decide to get additional financing by selling ownership shares to passive investors. Limited liability rules allow such investors to purchase shares in a company without the risk of losing more than they have invested in the event the company fails. If your business does fail, bankruptcy protections mean you won't spend the rest of your life repaying the debt.

If you're an employee in a medium-size or large firm, you and fellow employees will elect works council representatives who negotiate hiring rules, work conditions, work hours, and firing procedures with management. You also will elect one-third to one-half of the members of the board of directors, which is the firm's main decision-making authority.

While some people in your society own a home, many rent. Government policy ensures there are few barriers to construction of new rental properties, particularly in cities and near them. This increases the likelihood that the supply of rental housing meets or exceeds demand, which helps to keep it affordable. A housing assistance program provides a subsidy to low- and middle-income renters so that rent takes no more than 30 percent of their income. Landlords aren't permitted to discriminate against prospective tenants who receive this assistance. In addition to ensuring that housing is affordable, this gives families genuine choice about where to live, allowing them to escape from problematic neighborhoods if they wish to. Government also provides some rental housing directly ("public housing") and subsidizes additional affordable rental housing owned by nonprofits and communities ("social housing").

You might own a car or multiple cars, but you probably don't need one. Fewer than half of all trips are made in private vehicles.[14] Public transportation, in the form of rail lines, subways, buses, trolleys, and bike- and scooter-sharing, is extensive and affordable. And government provides additional incentives for construction of housing within walking distance of core public transport routes. To get to and from work, there's a good chance you take rail or a speedy bus that travels in a dedicated lane. In a typical day you might use multiple forms of public transport, including a bike or scooter to take you the last half mile or so of your journey or to move around quickly between stores. You pay for this with an integrated app on your phone that automatically tallies your use. If your physical mobility is constrained or you are short on time, you can order just about anything to be delivered to your home, from a new television to a jar of ground cumin for the stew you're making for dinner.

Government is attentive to provision and maintenance of a wide array of public spaces and infrastructure—roads, bridges, bike lanes, walking paths, sidewalks, stoplights, data collection (demographic, health, economic, etc.), enforcement of speed limits, air traffic control, weather forecasts, museums, parks, sports fields, public restrooms, forests, campgrounds, beaches, oceans, lakes, swimming pools, zoos, phone lines, broadband, the internet, public television and radio programming, subsidization of free private television and radio networks, libraries, festivals, and more.

During your working years you have access to the same family-friendly policies used by your parents—paid parental leave, early education, a child allowance, and so on.

You, like every person, are eligible for basic legal services. If you are accused of a crime or your landlord is attempting to evict you, you will receive legal representation at no cost.

You have a free public bank account. In-person banking services are provided by post office branches, and you can use any public or private automatic teller machine (ATM) multiple times per month at no charge.

People tend to enjoy being part of a group. In your society everyone has not only the freedom but also the capability to form groups and to participate actively in them. As a result, there are groups for nearly every interest, belief, and activity imaginable. Some meet in person, some online. Some are local, while others span larger areas. For some, being a "member" means nothing more than signing up or making a small financial contribution. For others, it entails a commitment of substantial time and effort.

If you are religious, you have extensive freedom to practice your faith. You can pray and engage in other religious practices. You can join an existing religious organization or create a new one.

If you are interested in participating in politics, you have multiple options for involvement, particularly at the local level. There are the usual avenues available to citizens in a democracy: you can vote, lobby policymakers, organize in a group, donate money to a campaign, run for office, protest, and more. Beyond this, you may be surveyed regularly by your local government to gauge your opinion on policy issues. You may be randomly selected to participate in a deliberative advisory assembly—similar to a jury but focused on a matter of public policy. You can serve on a user board that oversees the provision of a particular public service such as transportation or job training. You might, as a representative of an interest group such as labor or business, participate in discussions and negotiations over major policy decisions.

When you reach retirement age, you are guaranteed a basic government pension. It's relatively small, but it's enough, when coupled with other public goods and services, to ensure that you can get by. There is a more generous public pension funded by earmarked tax payments throughout your working life, with benefits roughly proportional to your earnings. And many companies offer an additional defined-contribution pension to their employees.

You are eligible to receive public long-term care assistance. You may choose to live in an eldercare institution or to receive eldercare services in your home. In-home assistance can be for several hours, throughout the day, or round-the-clock if needed. There is a copayment, but it is modest—a few hundred dollars per month.

Many of the services, goods, and programs I've described here are paid for and/or provided by government. That's because the government, in a democratic society, is the only mechanism through which we can ensure that people have access to these kinds of goods and services and insurance. There is, unfortunately, no way to guarantee that you'll grow up in a family with two loving, devoted parents, nor that a family member or friend or charitable organization or employer will be there to provide you with food or clothing or money or job training or assistance in caring for your elderly relative.

The total cost of public programs, goods, services, and government operations amounts to about half of your country's GDP. For most people, somewhere between one-third and one-half of household income goes to the government in taxes.[15]

Government provides free tax preparation services for the 80 percent or so of the population who have an uncomplicated tax return. Each person receives a postcard or short letter explaining the government's calculation of the tax you owe or refund you are to receive. If the information is correct, you send a text or email to confirm.

In its provision of goods and services, government is customer friendly. Some of the things it pays for or provides have eligibility requirements, such as age, income, or health. Where such restrictions exist, government's foremost goal isn't to ensure that no one gets a service or benefit for which they aren't genuinely eligible. Preventing cheating is a concern, but the chief aim is to ensure that people are able to access services and other benefits at minimal cost and with little hassle.[16] This is achieved via integrated databases that handle multiple programs, one-stop registration at a website or a physical office, simple sign-up procedures available in multiple languages, one-to-one assistance, and a plentiful supply of service providers.

The array of institutions, policies, and programs I've described here is the infrastructure of a good society. It doesn't guarantee you will find your soulmate and your calling and live blissfully for 115 years. It does ensure that you have much of what's needed for a life that is fulfilling and satisfying.

This good society infrastructure doesn't presuppose low inequality of income or wealth. It's perfectly possible to have these policies and institutions while tolerating high incomes and wealth for some people and fairly low incomes and wealth (even zero wealth) for others.

Recognize That Public Services and Goods Reduce Inequality of Well-Being, Even Though This Doesn't Show Up in Measures of Income Inequality or Wealth Inequality

The public goods and services I outlined in the previous section don't just improve lives. They also reduce inequality. This inequality reduction doesn't show up in most measures of income distribution or wealth distribution, because government provision of childcare and schooling and health insurance and transportation and much more doesn't get counted as part of a household's income or assets. But while they don't reduce inequality of income or wealth, they clearly reduce inequality of living standards and well-being.[17]

How so? For any given type of government service or good, consumption may be progressive, equal, or regressive. That is, the service or good may be used more by poor households than by affluent ones, about the same by each,

INEQUALITY REDUCTION SHOULD BE A SECONDARY GOAL 101

or more by the affluent than by the poor. We have no precise measures of the actual distribution of consumption of public goods and services, but estimates suggest that it tends to be equal across the income scale or slightly progressive.[18] Let's assume, perhaps conservatively, that the distribution is equal rather than progressive.

Public services and goods can be thought of as akin to a cash transfer. If a person receives government-funded healthcare worth $10,000, it is as though she has been given a $10,000 cash transfer that she then uses to pay for those health services. The same holds for schooling, roads, policing, and virtually every other type of public good and service. If the rich, the middle class, and the poor each consume roughly the same total dollars or euros or kroner or yen worth of public goods and services, it is equivalent to the government providing a large flat-rate (equal number of dollars or euros) cash transfer to all households.

In a society in which the market distribution of income is unequal, a flat-rate benefit—one that goes in equal amount to all citizens—is redistributive. It boosts consumption, and hence living standards, for the poor more than it does for the rich. If my market income is $1 million and I receive public services worth $20,000, my consumption has increased by 2 percent. If my market income is $10,000 and I receive government services worth $20,000, my consumption is boosted by 200 percent.

What about the financing of public goods and services? Most rich democratic countries have a tax system that is roughly proportional; people in low-income, middle-income, and high-income households each pay a similar share of their market income in taxes, so the effective tax rate is approximately the same for each group.[19] But because the affluent get so much of the market income, they pay a much larger share of the tax dollars (or euros or pounds) than the poor.

Public goods and services that are consumed equally and financed proportionally are redistributive. Figure 11.1 illustrates this. The tax payment data are estimates for the United States. When all types of taxes are taken into account—income, payroll, consumption, and others—the US tax system is approximately proportional; groups with different levels of pretax income pay about the same share of their income in taxes.[20] But because the distribution of pretax income is quite unequal, those with higher incomes end up paying much more in dollars. The chart assumes that consumption of public goods and services is equal across the income distribution.

In this illustration, households in the bottom income fifth consume about 20 percent of the public goods and services and pay only 3 percent of the taxes that fund those goods and services. Indeed, households all the way up to around

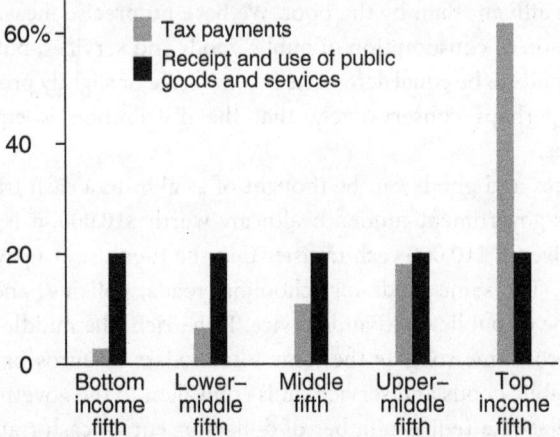

Figure 11.1 Public goods and services are redistributive, even if consumed equally and funded by proportional taxes

Dark bars: share of public goods and services received and used by households in each of the five pretax income quintiles. Lighter bars: share of the tax dollars funding these goods and services that come from households in each pretax income quintile. Both sets of bars total to 100 percent. These shares are hypothetical. They assume all households pay the same effective tax rate (proportional tax system), so each quintile's share of tax payments is the same as its share of the pretax income. And they assume all households receive or use the same quantity (dollar value) of public services. Data source for pretax income shares: Institute on Taxation and Economic Policy (ITEP), "Who Pays Taxes in America in 2019?"

the eightieth percentile of the income distribution are net beneficiaries. Only households in the top quintile pay more in taxes than they receive in public goods and services.

The reduced inequality of living standards and well-being achieved by public goods and services won't show up in a Gini coefficient for income or wealth, but it matters for people's lives.[21]

Inequality Reduction Should Be a Goal

Much of what determines where people end up on the socioeconomic ladder is beyond their control. The amount of income inequality and wealth inequality that exists in at least some, and perhaps all, of the affluent democratic nations is therefore unfair. Less economic inequality would be fairer. And as we saw in chapter 8, lots of people would like there to be less economic inequality. We know it's possible for affluent democratic nations to have lower levels of income and wealth inequality, because they did in the 1960s and 1970s. Moreover, reducing inequality is unlikely to slow economic growth or require other economic or social sacrifices. There surely is some point at which inequality reduction would begin to adversely affect economic growth or some other outcomes, but it's unlikely that any of the rich democracies have reached that point.[22]

Because inequality reduction would enhance fairness, has public support, is achievable, and is likely to come with few if any tradeoffs, policymakers should include it as one of the goals they pursue.

Inequality Reduction Should Be a Secondary Goal

Inequality reduction doesn't need to be a top priority. And where there is a choice between making ordinary people's lives better versus reducing inequality of income or wealth, we should encourage policymakers to opt for the former.

What does this mean in practice? I see four key implications.

Don't Include Income Inequality and Wealth Inequality as Headline Indicators

Gross domestic product and the value of the stock market tend to be the "headline" economic indicators in affluent nations. There ought to be others—ones that tell us more about the well-being of ordinary people.[23] Should the Gini coefficient or the top 1 percent's income share (or some other measure of income or wealth inequality) be one of those headline indicators?[24]

I don't think so. Let's say, arbitrarily, that there should be at most ten headline indicators. (If there are too many, it doesn't make much sense to think of them as "headline.") Here are quite a few more than ten that I would put ahead of income inequality and wealth inequality:

1. Life expectancy (or healthy life expectancy)
2. Perceived health: share of adults reporting their health as good or very good
3. Safety: share of the population not a victim of violent crime (homicide, rape, aggravated assault, robbery) in the past year
4. Perceived safety: share of adults answering no to the question "Is there any area near where you live where you would be afraid to walk alone at night?"
5. Education: average years of schooling completed
6. Affluence: GDP per capita
7. Affluence: median household income
8. Income floor: tenth-percentile household income
9. Housing: share of households not spending more than 30 percent of income on rent

10. Income security: share of households not experiencing a year-to-year income decline of 25 percent or more
11. Perceived freedom to make life choices among youth: share of eighteen- to twenty-nine-year-olds answering satisfied to the question "Are you satisfied or dissatisfied with your freedom to choose what you do with your life?"
12. Equality of economic opportunity: relative intergenerational income mobility
13. Employment: share of the working-age population in paid work
14. Work satisfaction: share of employed persons answering completely satisfied, very satisfied, or fairly satisfied to the question "All things considered, how satisfied are you with your (main) job?"
15. Voice at work: share of employed persons who are self-employed, are employed in a worker cooperative, are employed by a firm with an employee share ownership plan that owns a majority of the firm's stock shares, or are employed in a firm in which workers elect 50 percent or more of the board of directors
16. Work-family-leisure balance: share of employed persons with six weeks or more paid vacation or holiday
17. Connectedness: share of adults answering satisfied to the question "In the city or area where you live, are you satisfied or dissatisfied with the opportunities to meet people and make friends?"
18. Perceived social support: share of adults answering yes to the question "If you were in trouble, do you have relatives or friends you can count on to help you whenever you need them, or not?"
19. Happiness: average response to the question "Please imagine a ladder with steps numbered from 0 at the bottom to 10 at the top. The top of the ladder represents the best possible life for you and the bottom of the ladder represents the worst possible life for you. On which step of the ladder would you say you personally feel you stand at this time?"
20. Happiness: share responding 5 or higher on the life satisfaction ladder question
21. Equality of political opportunity: correlation between policy decisions and expressed preferences of people at different income levels
22. Immigration: share of the population born abroad in a poor or middle-income country
23. Environment: greenhouse gas emissions per capita

What we choose to headline can influence not only where we direct our attention for improvement but also how we understand whether or not we've made progress. For instance, one study that puts economic inequality front and center concludes that in the United States "much of the social progress achieved since the 1920s has been undone."[25] Another goes even further, suggesting that the country has "drifted back to a contemporary version of Grover Cleveland's America" (Cleveland was president in the late 1800s).[26] Given the massive increase in living standards, education, and life expectancy and the very sizable reductions in violence, poverty, and racial discrimination, along with other improvements, these conclusions are at best misleading.[27]

A more nuanced analysis that highlights economic inequality alongside families, civic participation, and political polarization concludes that in the first two-thirds of the twentieth century the United States was on an upswing, but since 1965 the country has been moving in the wrong direction, on a "downswing."[28] That too is unduly pessimistic. Since the mid-1960s living standards have improved considerably, including for Americans at the bottom. Education and life expectancy have risen. Personal freedom, particularly for women, teenagers and young adults, racial and ethnic minorities, gays and lesbians, and assorted other "outgroups," has increased. Openness to less advantaged immigrants is much greater. And access to knowledge and entertainment has skyrocketed.[29]

Eschew Policies That Reduce Inequality but May Get in the Way of Improving Lives

If inequality reduction were a top-level priority, there would be a strong case for choosing the most effective means of achieving it. But some effective strategies wouldn't be particularly desirable. I said earlier in this chapter that, in general, reduction of income inequality or wealth inequality won't require sacrificing other things we want in a good society. But there are some exceptions.

For example, a straightforward mechanism for achieving reduction of income inequality is automatic adjustment of tax rates in response to changes in income inequality. Robert Shiller explains: "While income inequality would be much worse without our current [income] tax system, what we have isn't nearly enough. It's time—past time, actually—to tweak the system so that it can respond effectively if income inequality becomes more extreme.... Taxes should be indexed to income inequality so that they automatically become more progressive—meaning that the marginal tax rate for the highest-income people will rise—if income inequality becomes much worse."[30] In other words, we can set a target goal for posttax income inequality and have an algorithm adjust tax rates until we reach that target level. However, this means tax rates for people will be set retroactively. People with high incomes, in particular, may end up paying a much higher tax rate than they expected to for reasons having nothing to do with their own income—because there were more high earners than in previous years or because those high earners ended up with much larger incomes than they previously got. This uncertainty might lead to much more aggressive efforts to hide income from taxation.

The main thing we need from taxation is money to fund programs that make people's lives better. Revenue considerations should come first, before inequality reduction.

Another potentially effective strategy for reducing economic inequality would be to set a maximum income a person is allowed to receive in a given year or a maximum amount of wealth she can hold.[31] However, debates about where to draw this line, and how to enforce the maximum, are likely to distract from the more important question of how best to tax those at the top. Suppose we set the maximum yearly income at $10 million and the owner of a successful business could, if there weren't such a maximum, receive $50 million. With a statutory maximum, the owner might arrange to have part of the compensation donated to an antitax nonprofit organization. In this scenario, the government loses revenue and quite likely no socially good outcome has been achieved. More than the satisfaction (for some) of seeing restrictions on the income or wealth at the top, what we need is government revenue in order to provide extensive and good-quality public goods, services, and insurance. Better to allow the business owner to receive her $50 million income and tax it.[32]

We could significantly reduce income inequality by replacing a variety of public services with a universal basic income. Giving people money instead of services would instantly reduce income inequality. But it's probably wiser to provide people with services that are critical to capability development and well-being, rather than to give them money and assume they will purchase those services on their own.[33]

Across the affluent democratic countries, the key determinant of the variation in wealth inequality is homeownership. Where more people are homeowners, the middle class has more wealth, and so wealth inequality tends to be lower.[34] The most effective way to reduce wealth inequality in the rich democracies therefore probably is to increase home equity among those in the middle and below. But is that a good policy goal? Not necessarily. There are drawbacks to homeownership. It can impede geographic mobility by tying people to a particular home. It renders wealth vulnerable to swings in housing market prices. And as climate change increases the frequency and unpredictability of weather-related disasters, it can end up costing much more than renting.[35]

Embrace Policies That Improve Lives, Even if They Don't Reduce Inequality
Suppose policymakers have a chance to add or expand a well-being-enhancing public service but only if it is paid for via a proportional tax increase. There are

circumstances in which, due to the balance of political forces, to public opinion, or to electoral precommitments by the party or coalition in power, a proportional tax increase may be more politically salable than a progressive one.[36] But a proportional tax increase won't reduce inequality of income or wealth. Policymakers who prioritize inequality reduction may be tempted to insist that the tax increase be a progressive one. In most instances policymakers shouldn't do that. They should let inequality concerns take a back seat and say yes to a political deal that will improve people's lives.

In the United States, for example, most recent Democratic Party presidential nominees have promised not to increase taxes for Americans in the bottom 95 percent of incomes. If this is dictated by electoral necessity—if it's the only way for the candidate to win election—then okay. But to put in place the good-society infrastructure I outlined earlier in this chapter, the United States would need to increase tax revenues by approximately 10 percent of GDP.[37] Getting that amount of tax revenue from the top 5 percent of households would be nearly impossible.[38]

Prioritize Reduction of Worldwide Inequality over Reduction of Within-Rich-Country Inequality
As I noted in chapter 9, imports and immigration from poor countries very likely increase income inequality and wealth inequality in rich countries. Policymakers in the affluent democratic nations thus face a choice between reducing economic inequality within their country and reducing worldwide inequality. To the extent it is politically feasible, they should lean toward the latter.

Is this ever politically feasible? Migration from poor nations increases ethnic and religious heterogeneity in rich democracies, and a number of studies suggest that this kind of diversity has tended to reduce public support for welfare state generosity.[39] So there might be limited scope for pursuing both openness to the world's less fortunate and the kinds of good-society programs I outlined earlier in this chapter.

Then again, other studies have found little or no evidence that immigration weakens popular sentiment in favor of generous social policy.[40] And in many of the rich democratic nations in recent decades we've seen continued movement toward a Nordic-style welfare state—expansive public insurance and public goods coupled with employment-conducive public services—despite rising immigration.[41]

Sweden is a particularly informative case. Sweden after 1945 demonstrated that it's possible to create and expand a social democratic welfare state and also welcome significant refugee immigration. Beginning in 2015, in the face of an unprecedented immigration surge, Swedish policymakers pulled back, first instituting tougher restrictions on a temporary basis and then making the changes permanent in 2021. However, a careful recent study concludes that the chief cause of Sweden's turn against generous refugee immigration wasn't concern about the welfare state.[42] Instead it was a rise in violent crime. What this suggests is that if a country can do what Sweden did from 1945 to 2015 and also keep a lid on crime, it might be able to persist with this approach.

12

How to Reduce Inequality

This book's main message is that reducing economic inequality shouldn't be a high-level priority. But as I stressed in chapter 11, that doesn't mean we should abandon it altogether. A lot of the existing income and wealth inequality is unfair because it's a product of luck. Many people want less inequality and support government efforts to reduce it. And we could reduce inequality without stifling economic progress. For these reasons, in some contexts—certainly that of the contemporary United States—inequality reduction is a sensible thing to try to achieve.

How to do it? There are four components: earnings from paid work, government transfers, top-end incomes, and wealth.[1]

Earnings

Ideally, earnings up and down the distribution will be not too unequal, and they will remain that way by rising roughly in proportion to growth of the economy. However, capitalism creates incentives for firms to try to minimize labor costs. That is part of its genius, but for ordinary workers and households it's also a drawback. What we need are institutions and policies that reduce companies' incentive and ability to pursue a labor-cost-minimization strategy.

We know this is possible. It's what happened in nearly all of the rich democratic nations in the three decades that followed World War II. And it has continued in some of those countries through the era of rising income inequality since the late 1970s.[2]

Figure 12.1 shows the best picture we have of wage developments in the rich democracies in recent decades. On the horizontal axis is each country's growth rate of GDP per capita, and on the vertical axis is its growth rate of median compensation.[3] The dashed line in the chart is a 45-degree line; a country will be on the line if median compensation has grown at the same pace as the economy. That's roughly what we would hope for in a good economy: ordinary working people see their wages rise in sync with the economy's rate of growth. But it's what has actually happened only in some of these countries. Many lie well below the line, with compensation growth lagging behind economic growth.

110 IS INEQUALITY THE PROBLEM?

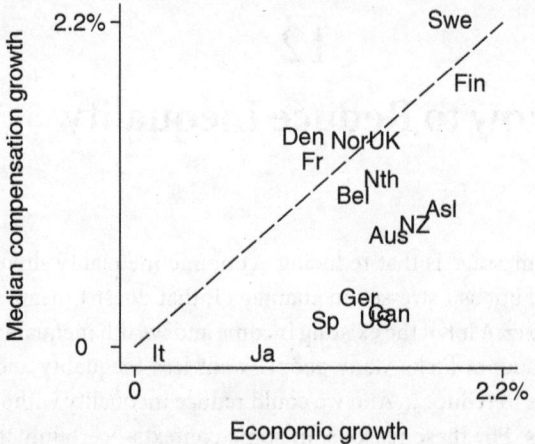

Figure 12.1 Economic growth and median compensation growth

1995-2013 (the earliest and latest years of available data). Median compensation growth: average annual growth rate of median inflation-adjusted compensation (wages plus in-kind compensation plus employees' and employers' social contributions). Data source Cyrille Schwellnus, Andreas Kappeler, and Pierre-Alain Pionnier, "The Decoupling of Median Wages from Productivity in OECD Countries," *International Productivity Monitor*, 2017, table 1. Economic growth: average annual growth rate of inflation-adjusted GDP per capita. Data source: OECD. "Asl" is Australia; "Aus" is Austria. The line is a 45-degree line; a country will lie on this line if its median compensation growth rate is equal to its economic growth rate.

Part of an effective strategy consists of reestablishing things that we know worked in the past. But we'll also need some new approaches, because not everything that worked in earlier eras is likely to be replicable or effective or desirable in today's context.

One example is economic growth. Over the long run, growth of the economy underpins rising earnings. So it would be good to increase the economic growth rate. Unfortunately, we don't know how to do that. When it comes to rich democratic capitalist nations, we have very little clue about what yields faster economic growth over the medium to long run.[4]

Another example is education. Since the late 1800s, rising educational attainment has been a key contributor to rising pay.[5] However, it isn't clear that this can continue. Secondary-school completion has likely reached its ceiling in most of the affluent democracies. And we may not be able to boost the rate of increase in college completion, as it's already been rising rapidly in the post-1970s era.[6]

Jobs in the manufacturing sector were vital to broad pay growth in the rich democratic countries in the twentieth century. But manufacturing employment has been declining steadily in all of the rich democracies since 1970.[7] This owes to technological advance and to firms' increased ability to shift production to low-cost countries. There is little reason to expect this trend to reverse.

In the United States, in some industries or communities a small number of firms account for a large share of the jobs. And some American companies have pressured employees to sign a noncompete clause as a condition of employment, which prevents them from leaving the firm to work for a competitor. These two developments have reduced employees' exit options, and hence their pay leverage.[8] Could increased competition among firms boost pay growth? Possibly, but a reason for skepticism is that excessive monopsony power typically is posited as a phenomenon of the 2000s and 2010s, and yet the pay trend during this period doesn't look different from the trend in the 1980s and 1990s (see figure 12.3 below).[9]

In addition to strategies that we don't know how to achieve or that don't seem especially promising, there is one that we shouldn't want to try: curtailment of imports and immigration from poor countries. These put downward pressure on the earnings of ordinary workers in the rich democratic nations. But as I explained in chapter 9, I don't think it makes sense to try to reduce inequality by blocking trade and/or immigration. For poor countries, exports to rich ones (trade) have been crucial to economic development. And for people in countries that haven't enjoyed much in the way of economic development, migration to a rich nation has been a key route out of poverty.

What, then, should we do?

Labor Unions and Collective Bargaining
Across the rich democratic nations, the degree to which compensation growth has kept up with economic growth is largely a function of labor unions and collective bargaining. The Nordic nations and Belgium have high unionization rates, so it isn't surprising to see them positioned close to the 45-degree line in figure 12.1.[10] France and the Netherlands also are close to the line. In France the unionization rate is low, but the law requires extension of collectively bargained wage agreements to nonunionized workers. In the Netherlands this kind of extension of collectively bargained agreements isn't legally mandated, but it is a strong norm. The countries with the lowest rates of unionization and no compensating mechanism, such as the United States, sit farthest below the line. According to one estimate, if American labor unions today had the same power as they had in the early 1980s, compensation for ordinary workers would be about 25 percent higher than it actually is.[11]

As figure 12.2 makes clear, unionization rates have been falling in most of the affluent democratic nations. Only five countries—Belgium, Denmark, Finland, Norway, and Sweden—still have a rate above 35 percent, and four of those five are helped by the fact that access to unemployment insurance is contingent on union membership. In the United States, unionization peaked around 1950 and

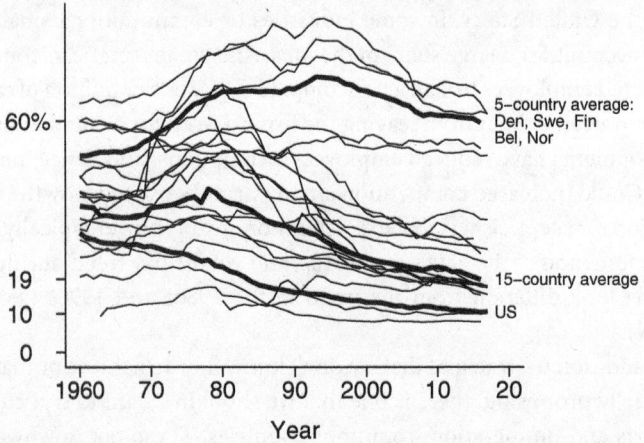

Figure 12.2 Unionization
Share of employees who are union members. Five-country average: Bel, Den, Fin, Nor, Swe. Fifteen-country average: Asl, Aus, Can, Fr, Ger, Ire, It, Ja, Kor, Nth, NZ, Por, Sp, Swi, UK. The thin lines are for individual countries. Data source: Jelle Visser, "ICTWSS: Database on Institutional Characteristics of Trade Unions, Wage Setting, State Intervention, and Social Pacts," Amsterdam Institute for Advanced Labour Studies, version 6.0, 2019, series ud, ud_s.

has been declining ever since, down to just 10 percent today. In the other fifteen countries, the average unionization rate dropped from 42 percent in the late 1970s to just 19 percent in the late 2010s.[12]

The situation isn't as dire when it comes to the share of workers whose pay is determined by collective bargaining, because, as I just noted, extension practices in some countries mean that pay developments for workers who aren't represented by a union are nevertheless determined by a collective agreement. Collective bargaining coverage has remained relatively high in some rich democratic countries despite low unionization. But in a number of these nations bargaining coverage is quite low, and it may decline in others, as it already has to a significant degree in the United Kingdom and Germany.[13]

In the countries where they remain reasonably strong, labor unions will continue to play a vital role in achieving pay growth. They surely would help in others too, but there is little reason to be confident that they can return to their former strength.

Tight Labor Markets

When employers can benefit from hiring more workers but find it difficult to do so, they are more likely to increase wages. The key indicator here is the unemployment rate. A low unemployment rate suggests there are relatively few people

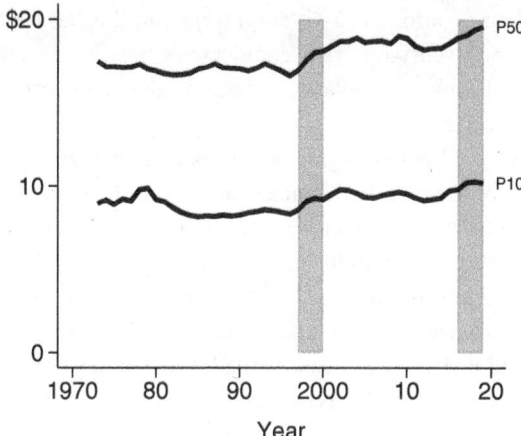

Figure 12.3 Pay in the United States

2020 dollars; inflation adjustment is via the CPI-U-RS. "P10" = tenth percentile; "P50" = fiftieth percentile. Data source: Economic Policy Institute, using Current Population Survey data. The shaded periods are 1997–2000 and 2016–19.

who don't have a job but want one. In this situation, employers will be willing to offer a higher wage in order to attract additional workers and keep the ones they have. Wages will tend to rise.

To create and sustain a tight labor market, the key policy lever is monetary policy. Central banks in the affluent democratic nations are charged with maintaining both price stability and low unemployment. The longer the labor market remains tight, the stronger the pressure on employers to increase wages and salaries. To achieve this, the central bank needs to be willing to resist raising interest rates when the unemployment rate gets low enough to potentially cause a jump in inflation.

In the United States, the central bank's tendency since the inflationary period of the late 1970s and early 1980s has been to increase interest rates quickly and sharply when the unemployment rate falls to 5 or 6 percent. There have been two notable exceptions: 1997–2000 and 2016–19. These are the only post-1979 periods in which the Federal Reserve held the unemployment rate below 5 percent. As we see in figure 12.3, both periods saw significant pay increases.[14] (Early analysis suggests that the low unemployment rates of the post-Covid period have had the same impact.)[15]

Statutory Minimum Wages
In the middle of the twentieth century, during the era of strong labor unions, few of the affluent longstanding-democratic nations had a statutory minimum wage. Unions often didn't want one, fearing that this type of government intervention

would weaken their position vis-à-vis employers. But this has begun to change, and fourteen of the twenty-one rich democracies now have a statutory minimum.[16] Figure 12.4 shows the inflation-adjusted value of the minimum wage in these fourteen countries.

A minimum wage allows policymakers to increase pay via a simple political decision. In some of the rich democracies that's what they have tended to do in recent decades. In France, for example, the minimum wage was increased from $3 per hour in 1960 to $7 in 1980, and then to $11.50 as of 2018. The United Kingdom enacted a minimum wage in 2000 at $6.50 and by 2018 had raised it to $9.60. Ireland too instituted a statutory minimum in 2000, setting it at $7.50, and then increased it steadily to $9.60. Canada's minimum wage also was $9.60 as of 2018, up from $7.60 in 1980. New Zealand's jumped from $6 in 1980 to $10 in 2018.

In other nations, policymakers have decided to limit the degree of increase in the minimum wage, often in an attempt to bring wages more into line with competitor nations. In the Netherlands, the minimum wage was increased steadily from $6.80 in 1961 to $12.60 in 1979. But policymakers then allowed it to fall to $10.50 during the 1980s and have kept it at that level since.[17] Belgium, too,

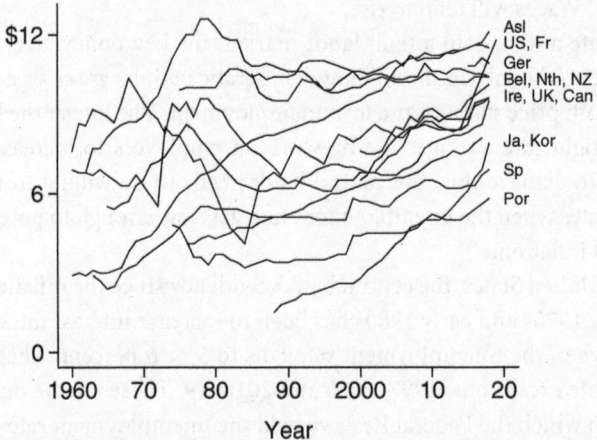

Figure 12.4 Statutory minimum wage

Per hour. 2018 US dollars. Currencies converted using purchasing power parities. The US data are a population-weighted average for the country, taking into account federal, state, and local minimums. Austria, Denmark, Finland, Italy, Norway, Sweden, and Switzerland don't have a statutory minimum wage. Data source: OECD. Data source for US 2000ff: Ernie Tedeschi, "Americans Are Seeing the Highest Minimum Wage in History (Without Federal Help)," *New York Times*, 2019. "Asl" is Australia.

had a comparatively high minimum wage around 1980 but then held it flat in subsequent decades.

The same is true in the United States, at least at the federal government level. The US federal minimum wage was increased steadily and sharply from its inception in the late 1930s until the late 1960s. It then dropped a bit in the 1970s, due mainly to high inflation. Since 1980 it has stayed essentially flat. In the late 1990s, however, some states and cities began adopting a statutory minimum wage above the level of the federal minimum, sometimes also indexing their minimum wage to prices or increasing it regularly. As a result, the average minimum wage across the country has risen, and the rise has been particularly sharp since 2014.

In all of the nations that have a minimum wage, its level is set by elected policymakers (sometimes on the advice of a group of experts, such as the United Kingdom's Low Pay Commission).[18] In principle, this means it can be increased as much as the populace would like it to be. In practice, opponents of a high wage floor, such as business organizations, may be able to exert more influence on policymakers than ordinary citizens and thereby keep the minimum wage below what the majority wants.

Another constraint on the ability of a statutory minimum wage to ensure wage growth is the fact that it will tend to apply to a relatively small number of people. In the United States, for example, the federal minimum wage applies directly to around 2 percent of workers, and the effects of increasing it tend to fade out by around the twentieth percentile of the wage ladder.[19] A rise in the minimum wage doesn't, therefore, guarantee that wages of most ordinary workers will increase.

A way to address this problem is via sector-specific or occupation-specific minimum wages. This enables policymakers to directly affect the wages of a much larger share of the workforce. Australia illustrates how this can work. Each year a Fair Work Commission sets minimum wages for more than one hundred different sectors and occupations, from "Aboriginal Controlled Health Services" to "Wool Storage, Sampling, and Testing," as well as for various pay grades within these categories.[20] These minimum wages ("wage awards") are based on characteristics of the work and required skills. They directly determine the pay of about 20 percent of Australian employees, and indirectly of many more.[21]

The chief worry about a rising minimum wage is that it may reduce employment. However, the best available evidence suggests that modest increases in the statutory minimum in the past haven't done so.[22]

Profit Sharing

Another way to boost earnings is profit sharing, whereby employees receive part of their compensation in the form of a portion of their firm's profit rather than as a guaranteed wage or salary. If profits rise, their pay automatically will too. Over time, their pay will be higher than it would have been without profit sharing.[23]

There is a risk for employees. If profits fall during bad economic times, pay will decrease. Then again, workers will tend to have greater employment security, as the enhanced flexibility in labor costs makes it less likely that firms will need to fire employees during rough times.[24]

Profit sharing isn't common in the rich democratic nations. But it probably could be if it were subsidized.[25]

Earnings Subsidy

A government subsidy to people in paid work but with low earnings is another helpful way to boost incomes in a context of weak labor unions. It typically takes the form of either a cash transfer or a tax credit. The United States and the United Kingdom were the first to do this in the 1970s, and in recent decades many other rich democratic countries have adopted some version of it. These employment-conditional earnings subsidies have proven effective at raising household incomes while also encouraging employment.[26]

The dashed lines in figure 12.5 show the structure of the US Earned Income Tax Credit (EITC). The EITC subsidizes earnings by as much as 45 percent, providing up to $7,400 per year for a household with three or more children, though the average amount recipient households get is $2,500. The benefit level increased sharply between 1987 and 1996, but since then it has been flat.

The solid line in figure 12.5 shows a possible alternative version of the EITC.[27] The alternative version would be paid to individuals rather than households, thereby enhancing work incentives for second earners in households. It also would include workers further up the distribution. The current EITC starts to taper off once earnings reach a certain level and disappears altogether at household earnings of $60,000. The alternative version would give every person who earns at least $17,000 the same amount, say $5,000, and raise the earnings cutoff so that most employed persons qualify. These changes would enhance the degree to which the EITC boosts household incomes.

To enable the EITC to assist with not only income levels but also income *growth*, it could be indexed to GDP per capita (the current EITC is indexed to prices). This would allow the EITC to rise over time in sync with the economy.

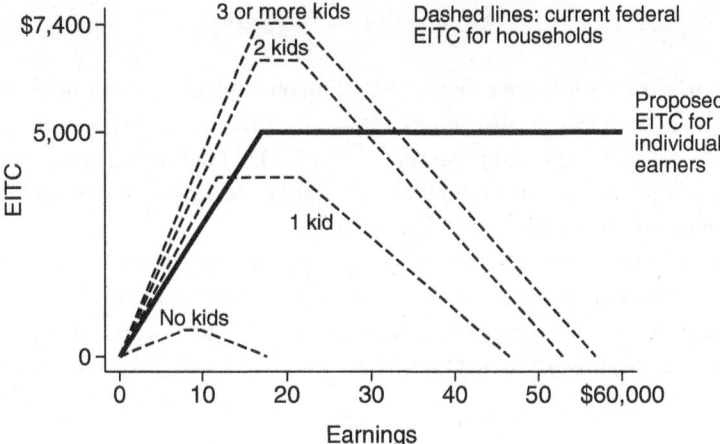

Figure 12.5 US Earned Income Tax Credit benefit structure: actual and proposed
See the text for discussion. Data source for the current federal EITC: Tax Policy Center, "Earned Income Tax Credit Parameters." The data shown for the current EITC are for a single (not married) person.

Some worry that an employment-conditional earnings subsidy will cause wage levels to fall. That's because in the presence of the earnings subsidy, employers may offer a lower wage than they otherwise would, and workers may be willing to accept a lower wage. Also, the earnings subsidy might increase the supply of less-educated people seeking jobs, and without an increase in employer demand for such workers, this rise in supply could push wages down. Studies suggest that the EITC may indeed reduce wages somewhat, but the evidence is thin and the effect is likely fairly small.[28] The best way to address this danger is with a moderate to high minimum wage.

Employment-Friendly Public Policy
Across the rich democratic countries, low household income is more likely to result from lack of employment than from low wages.[29] There are many things government can do to facilitate high employment: services that prepare people to be productive (schooling, training, retraining, healthcare), services that free up people's time to enable them to engage in paid work (childcare, eldercare), policies that connect people with jobs (job placement assistance), policies that encourage people to create a business (modest start-up regulations, assistance with financing a new company, antitrust enforcement), and more.[30]

Government Transfers

Government transfers are a key source of income for many households in the lower half of the income distribution. For some they are *the* key source. I mentioned most of the relevant programs in chapter 11. They include paid parental leave, child allowance, unemployment insurance, sickness insurance, disability assistance, social assistance, and old-age pensions.[31]

The chief task is to establish and maintain a set of generous programs and to structure them so that the benefit levels rise over time—roughly in sync with growth of the economy. Because governments will rightly worry about diminished work incentives if benefit levels exceed wage levels, a key facilitator is a rising minimum wage.[32]

Reducing Top-End Incomes

Inequality between those at the top and everyone else has increased in most of the rich democratic countries. We should focus on bringing up the incomes of households at the bottom and in the middle, but if we aim to reduce inequality we probably also need to reduce the incomes of those at the top.

The United States is the country with the highest level and the most rapid rise in top-end income inequality. It's also the country in which top-end inequality has been studied most extensively. So I'll focus here on what we know about the causes of rising top-end income inequality in America[33] and how to combat them.

Some potential fixes wouldn't be desirable. For instance, one reason why executive pay in the United States was moderate in the decades following World War II was the widespread fear of the threat communism and fascism. CEOs and other high-level executives were willing to sacrifice income to ensure the survivability of capitalism and democracy.[34] Few, however, would want to achieve a reduction in top incomes by promoting a return to Stalinism or to Nazi Germany.

By expanding the size of product markets, technological advance and globalization have produced large increases in firm revenues. This has translated into big payoffs for superstar athletes, entertainers, and CEOs.[35] In the financial sector, computerization and modern communications technology have enabled a large rise in the volume of trades, as well as creation of new financial tools and instruments. These have increased the fees earned by large financial firms, making it possible for these companies to handsomely reward their top creators, analysts, dealmakers, and traders. But we shouldn't aim to limit product market size.

We could reduce top incomes by setting a maximum allowable limit. But as I suggested in chapter 11, that would likely cause all manner of income-hiding strategies and end up reducing the tax base that is critical to our ability to fund public goods, services, and insurance programs.

Some other proposed strategies likely wouldn't have much impact. For example, some prominent observers have suggested that a key cause of high and rising top-end income inequality in the United States is growing market power of large firms.[36] Firms with a dominant position in their product market can deter potential entrants, weaken existing competitors, and extract more revenue from customers. They then pass on the resulting above-market profits, or "rents," to their top executives. But it isn't clear how much this actually matters. According to proponents of this hypothesis, this is a story mainly of the 2000s and 2010s, yet much of the rise in the top 1 percent's income share occurred earlier, in the 1980s and 1990s.

Some other potential strategies might be desirable and helpful but not feasible. Several recent quantitative studies that examine developments over the past generation in the United States alone or in the United States along with other affluent democracies have found unionization to be one of the best predictors of variation in the top-end income inequality.[37] So strengthening labor unions could help a lot. But as we saw earlier in this chapter, the likelihood of union strengthening isn't great.

There are, however, some things we could do that would be desirable, effective, and feasible.

Corporate Governance, Executive Pay, and Employee Board-Level Representation

During the "golden age" of post–World War II capitalism, boards of directors of large publicly owned corporations saw the firm's mission as increasing market share, revenues, and profits. Profits were invested in research or equipment, passed on to employees in the form of wage increases and new hires, or distributed to shareholders as dividends. Beginning in the late 1970s, this orientation came to be replaced by the notion that the principal aim should be to maximize "shareholder value" by increasing the firm's stock price.

Aiming to maximize gains for shareholders doesn't automatically entail offering large compensation to high-level executives, but it just so happened that around the same time corporate boards began to view top executives, and in particular the CEO, as the key to lifting the firm's share price.

Prior to the 1980s it was common for large American firms to hire for top executive positions mainly from within. This meant budding executives had both a financial incentive to stay put and limited opportunity to move to a different company. In the 1980s that norm evaporated, probably pushed along by a similar development in sports (baseball free agency began in 1976) and entertainment. The ability of top executives to move from one firm to another increased their leverage in negotiating salaries, bonuses, and stock options.

As firms increasingly hired CEOs and other high-level executives from a pool that included outsiders, and as large compensation packages became the norm, boards of directors turned to compensation consultants for information about whom to hire and how much to pay them. This has created a benchmarking and leapfrogging process whereby newly hired executives insist on compensation slightly above most of their peers, some are granted this demand, and that shifts the norm steadily upward.[38]

An additional piece of the corporate governance story is the coziness between top executives and the board of directors who decide on their compensation packages. Many members of these boards are in effect handpicked by the CEO and then approved by shareholders who have little information and limited interest in the details of a company's governance. Some board members are executives within the firm itself, and others are top executives at other publicly owned companies. They thus have a direct interest in seeing executive compensation levels rise. In addition, some know each other personally and hence are more likely to vote for a generous pay package.

In an attempt to discourage exorbitant CEO pay, in 1993 the Clinton administration and Congress ruled that a publicly traded corporation can deduct executive compensation from its taxable income only if that compensation is tied to the firm's performance. An unanticipated consequence was that firms increasingly included stock options—shares in the firm that can be sold after a specified number of years—as a component of executive compensation. As the stock market soared, the payoff from those stock options turned out to be enormous.[39]

Executives also discovered a way to help temporarily boost their company's stock price when it came time to cash in their stock options: stock buybacks. Purchasing shares of the firm's own stock drives up the price of the stock. It also increases the firm's earnings per share (by reducing the denominator), a metric investment analysts use in judging a firm's performance. Between 2003 and 2012, firms listed on the Standard & Poor's (S&P) 500 index used an average of 54 percent of their earnings to buy back their own stock.[40]

What should we do here? One option is to hope for change to come from within the business community. In 2019 the Business Roundtable, an organization representing large corporations in the United States, issued a "Statement on the Purpose of a Corporation." This statement said that whereas previously the Roundtable members had believed "corporations exist principally to serve their shareholders," now the signatories were committed to better serving a broad array of stakeholders—employees, suppliers, communities, customers.[41] It's too soon to tell whether these firms will follow through on their new commitment and whether it will have much impact if they do.

Trying to limit the rise in stock values is probably a nonstarter. We don't have a good strategy for how to do it, and it isn't likely to garner much public support. It's not even clear that it would help. There is a strong over-time correlation between stock prices and top-end income inequality in the United States. But when we turn to other rich nations, the story is mixed. In a handful of countries, the over-time correlation is as strong as in the United States. In others, though, it is weak or nonexistent.[42]

Probably the best strategy here is to institute a requirement of board-level employee representation (sometimes called codetermination), whereby employees elect a portion of their company's board of directors. In Germany, workers have been able to elect 50 percent of the directors in firms with two thousand or more employees since the early 1950s and 33 percent of the directors in firms with five hundred to two thousand employees since the mid-1970s. Similar rules exist in Austria, Denmark, Finland, France, Ireland, the Netherlands, Norway, and Sweden.[43] Given the continued weakening of labor unions, this might be the most effective way to discourage or prevent corporate boards from issuing huge executive compensation packages.[44]

Critics of board-level employee representation often suggest it will weaken firms' performance. However, it appears to have had no such adverse effect in the European countries where large firms operate under a codetermination requirement.[45]

Financial Transaction Tax

Finance has contributed to America's top-heavy increase in income inequality.[46] Over the past century, the financial sector's share of US GDP has correlated fairly strongly with the top 1 percent's share of income; it was high in the 1920s, then lower for about fifty years, then high again since the late 1970s. Financial firms' revenues have grown in recent decades, and the salaries and bonuses of top financial managers, traders, and analysts have risen sharply. The amounts for some, such as hedge fund managers, are staggering.

The expansion of finance has multiple causes. Globalization, the emergence of large institutional investors, advances in computing and telecommunications, the creation of new financial instruments, and reductions in regulatory constraints have allowed financial companies to draw on larger pools of funds and to channel those funds into a wider array of investments. The growing size of large financial firms has allowed them to seek more risky investments. This has been accentuated by the expectation of a government bailout should too many of those bets go sour, on the grounds that a bankruptcy by one or more such firms would create too much uncertainty in global financial markets. Nonfinancial companies, struggling in a more competitive global economy and facing investor demands for strong short-term profit performance, have turned to financial operations such as loans and credit cards to shore up revenues and profits.

One common proposal is heavier regulation of finance. However, nearly all affluent nations had deregulated their financial sectors as much as the United States by the early 1990s, with many experiencing nothing like America's surge in top-end income inequality.[47] So it isn't clear that heavier regulation would help to reduce the top 1 percent's income share.

A tax on financial transactions, such as sales and purchases of stock shares, is probably a better choice.[48] Every rich democratic nation other than the United States has one. A small tax along these lines would reduce trading somewhat, thereby reducing revenues and incomes in the financial sector. There is no evidence that this has devastating effects on the financial sector or the broader economy. And it will yield some revenue—on average about 0.5 percent of GDP[49]—that could be used for well-being-enhancing and/or inequality-reducing programs.

Taxation of Top Incomes

A progressive tax system reduces income inequality by taking a larger percentage of income from the rich than from others. It also can influence the pretax distribution of income; when top income tax rates are higher, people and households at the top have less incentive to try to maximize their income.[50]

In the United States, the top statutory federal income tax rate and the top 1 percent's share of pretax income have tended to move in opposite directions over time, as we would expect. In the 1920s the top tax rate decreased and the top 1 percent's income share shot up. The top tax rate rose sharply between 1929 and 1945, and the top 1 percent's income share fell sharply. From 1979 to 2007, the top tax rate decreased a good bit and the top 1 percent's income share increased.[51]

However, there are notable exceptions. The 1963 Kennedy tax reform reduced the top statutory federal income tax rate from 90 percent to 70 percent, yet the top 1 percent's pretax income share continued its slow, steady post–World War II decline. In the early 1990s the (first) Bush administration and the Clinton administration increased the top statutory tax rate from 28 percent to 40 percent, yet the top 1 percent's income share continued its sharp post-1979 rise. Carola Frydman and Raven Molloy have looked closely at whether compensation for top executives in large US firms changes in response to shifts in top statutory tax rates. Drawing on data going back to the 1940s, they find no noteworthy correlation between top tax rates and executive compensation.[52]

What does the experience of other countries suggest? Data are available for most of the rich longstanding democracies since the mid-1970s. In some of them—Australia, Canada, Ireland, New Zealand, Norway, Portugal, and the United Kingdom, along with the United States—we observe the predicted increase in the top 1 percent's income share when the top statutory tax rate decreases. But in others—Denmark, France, Italy, Japan, the Netherlands, Spain, and Sweden—we don't.[53]

All of these countries reduced top income tax rates during this period, but they differed significantly in the degree of reduction. Did the nations with larger decreases in top tax rates experience larger increases in their top 1 percent's income share? Yes, but the correlation isn't especially strong.[54] Particularly noteworthy is that four English-speaking countries—the United States, the United Kingdom, Canada, and Australia—are among those with largest increase in the top 1 percent's income share even though only one of them, the United States, enacted very large top tax rate reductions.

Why isn't the association between top tax rates and top-end income inequality stronger? Part of the reason is that hiding behind statutory tax rates are an assortment of loopholes, deductions, and "tax expenditures." These reduce the effective tax rate on persons or households with high incomes by shielding some, potentially much, of their pretax income from taxation. Warren Buffett's famous discovery that he paid a lower effective federal income tax rate than his office staff illustrates the point. Moreover, different parts of high incomes—salary, business income, capital gains—may be taxed at different rates.[55]

Figure 12.6 gives a sense of this for the US case. It shows the top statutory federal income tax rate along with the effective federal tax rate paid (on average) by the top 1 percent of taxpayers. The top statutory rate dropped sharply in the early 1960s and in the 1980s. The top 1 percent's effective rate fell too, but far less.

A concern with raising taxes on the rich is that it will cause them to flee, or at least to move their money elsewhere. The best available evidence suggests that while high earners are indeed responsive to changes in tax rates, the magnitude of this effect tends to be small.[56]

In the United States, we certainly could increase income tax rates for those in the top 1 percent. As of 2019, the effective tax rate on the top 1 percent—including all types of taxes at all levels of government—was about 34 percent.[57] Raising that to 40 percent or 45 percent would be well within the bounds of the historical pattern we see in figure 12.6.[58] While this wouldn't be a panacea in terms of reducing top-end income inequality, it would help.

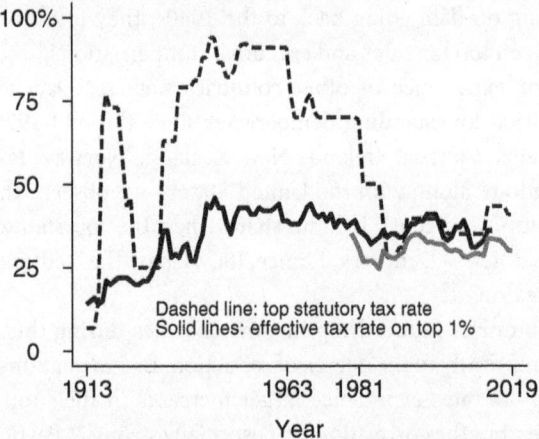

Figure 12.6 Top statutory federal income tax rate and effective federal tax rate on the top 1 percent, United States

Effective tax rate on top 1 percent: tax payments as a share of pretax income for the top 1 percent of taxpayers. Federal taxes include personal income, corporate income, payroll, and excise. Data source for the top (black) effective tax rate line: Thomas Piketty, Emmanuel Saez, and Gabriel Zucman, "Distributional National Accounts," *Quarterly Journal of Economics*, 2018, figure 9. Data source for the lower (gray) effective tax rate line: Congressional Budget Office "The Distribution of Household Income, 2019," 2022, Data Underlying Exhibits, exhibit 11.

Wealth

If we want to reduce wealth inequality, one seemingly obvious path would be by reducing income inequality. However, figure 12.7 shows that when we look across the rich democratic nations, the association between top-end income inequality and top-end wealth inequality is quite weak. The top 1 percent's income share is on the graph's horizontal axis, and the top 1 percent's wealth share is on the vertical. The position of the United States is consistent with what we might expect; it has the most income inequality and the most wealth inequality. But across the other nations there is no correlation at all.[59] So even if a country is able to reduce income inequality, that may have little or no impact on wealth inequality.

If we look across countries, the key determinant of the variation in wealth inequality is homeownership. The horizontal axis in figure 12.8 shows the share of the population that owns a home outright—that is, without a mortgage loan. This is strongly correlated with the top 1 percent's wealth share. Where more people are homeowners and have paid off their mortgage, the middle class has more wealth, and so wealth inequality tends to be lower.[60] The most effective way to reduce wealth inequality in the rich democracies therefore probably is to

HOW TO REDUCE INEQUALITY 125

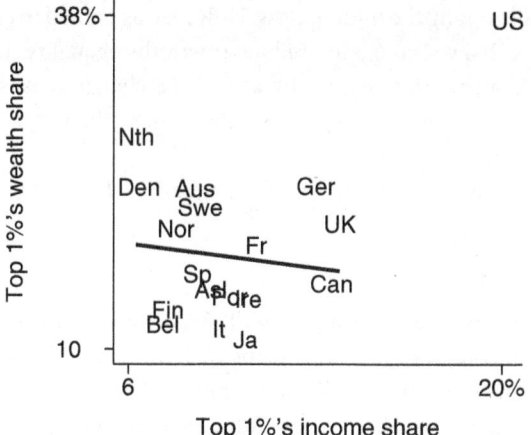

Figure 12.7 Income inequality and wealth inequality

2019 or nearest available year. Income inequality: income share of the top 1 percent. Pretax income. Excludes capital gains. Data source: World Inequality Database. Wealth inequality: wealth share of the top 1 percent. Wealth = assets minus liabilities. The estimate for Sweden is imputed using top 5 percent wealth share data. Data source: OECD, Wealth Distribution Database, stats.oecd.org. "Asl" = Australia. The line is a linear regression line, calculated with the United States excluded.

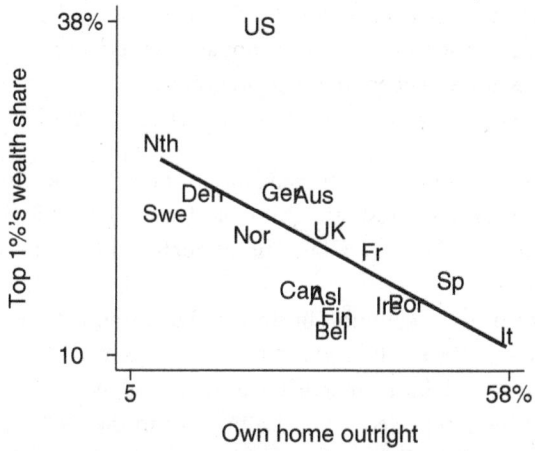

Figure 12.8 Homeownership and wealth inequality

2019 or nearest available year. Homeownership: share of the population that owns a home outright (without a mortgage loan). Data source: OECD, Affordable Housing Database. Wealth inequality: top 1 percent's wealth share. Wealth = assets minus liabilities. The estimate for Sweden is imputed using top 5 percent wealth share data. Data source: OECD, Wealth Distribution Database, stats.oecd.org. "Asl" = Australia; "Aus" = Austria. The line is a linear regression line. The correlation is −.62.

increase home equity among the middle class. However, as I noted in chapter 11, homeownership is a risky strategy for reducing wealth inequality. It can cost significantly more than renting, especially as climate change makes disasters more likely. And it concentrates assets in an investment than can depreciate significantly and be difficult to sell.

Are there better ways to reduce wealth inequality? I see two principal strategies.

Asset-Building Assistance
Government can provide assistance in asset building to middle- and low-income households. Some recommend a government match for saving by the poor, others a government grant at birth ("baby bond") that can grow in a tax-exempt savings account throughout the childhood years, others a lump sum ("stakeholder grant") of, say, $100,000 to be given to each person on reaching adulthood.[61]

This isn't always effective. If the assets are liquid—in a savings account, for example, or a retirement account that can be accessed early—people with low incomes will be tempted to spend them. We see this in the tendency of Americans with a defined-contribution pension (401k) to cash it out when switching jobs. Assets invested in stocks or in housing are vulnerable to market swings. For these reasons, I recommend using asset-building assistance as a supplement to other strategies for reducing economic inequality, not as a centerpiece. We shouldn't allocate funds to this at the expense of other programs.

Taxation of Wealth
As with income, we can reduce wealth inequality by taxing the wealth of those at the top more heavily. The most straightforward way to do this is via what is commonly called a "wealth tax," a tax paid annually on the total value of a household's net assets.

This type of tax was once common in western European nations, but most have now done away with it. "In 1990, there were twelve OECD countries, all in Europe, that levied individual net wealth taxes," notes Sarah Perret. "However, most of them repealed their wealth taxes in the 1990s and 2000s, including Austria (in 1994), Denmark and Germany (in 1997), the Netherlands (in 2001), Finland, Iceland, and Luxembourg (in 2006), and Sweden (in 2007).... France was the last country to repeal its wealth tax in 2018, replacing it with a tax on high-value immovable property. In 2020, Norway, Spain, and Switzerland were the only OECD countries that still levied individual net wealth taxes."[62]

The retreat from wealth taxes has several causes.[63] One is that this type of tax has tended to provoke significant backlash while not raising very much revenue. A second is that it taxes assets each year even if the value of one's assets has decreased. A third is that it may discourage economically productive behavior. Timothy Taylor explains:

> To understand the incentives of a wealth tax, return to the point made earlier that a wealth tax applies every year, whether wealth rises or not. Imagine that an annual wealth tax is 2% of wealth (for those above some threshold amount of wealth). Thus, if the value of your wealth increased by 5% in given year, and the wealth tax takes 2%, then the after-tax gain on your wealth would be 3%. If the value of your wealth fell by 10% in a given year (say, the stock market declines), then the wealth tax still takes 2% and your after-tax loss would be 12%. In this situation, imagine a person with wealth is invested in a low-risk, low-return activity (like government bonds). Especially in a setting of low interest rates, that person could end up paying all of the return to the wealth tax. Do we want to give the wealthy a strong disincentive to choose low-risk, low-return investments? Conversely, imagine a person investing in a high-risk entrepreneurial activity that might have either high or low returns. Say that the entrepreneurial attempt fails, and the investment loses half its value. The wealth tax still applies! Do we want to tax failed entrepreneurs? Or imagine that the entrepreneurial attempt succeeds, and the entrepreneur wants to use the additional wealth to build and expand a company. Do we want to impose an additional tax, above existing income and capital gains taxes, on successful entrepreneurs?[64]

Another reason for the retreat from wealth taxes is that there are alternative ways to tax wealth that generate less opposition and more revenue. One is a property tax. This is an annual tax on the value of owned property—mainly land and buildings (houses and commercial buildings). A second is a capital gains tax. This is a one-time tax on the net gains from sale of an asset, such as land, housing, or stock shares. While technically a tax on income rather than wealth, the effect of a capital gains tax is functionally equivalent to taxing assets.[65] A third is a gift tax, which is a one-time tax on assets that are transferred from one adult to another (non-spouse). A fourth is an inheritance (estate) tax. This is a one-time tax on the value of assets of a person who dies.

Countries use these taxes in different combinations and in varying ways. The United States has a property tax, capital gains tax, gift tax, and inheritance tax, but it doesn't have a wealth tax. (If a wealth tax were enacted in the United States, it might be ruled unconstitutional by the Supreme Court.)[66] Switzerland, by contrast, has a wealth tax but no capital gains tax, and most of its cantons have no gift tax or inheritance tax.

Policymakers face two key challenges in taxing wealth. The first is to figure out the best combination of taxes and the greatest degree of progressivity that are economically workable and politically feasible.[67] Part of the difficulty here is that citizens often are receptive to a wealth tax, but only if they don't have to pay it.[68] So in order to secure passage of a tax on wealth or of an increase in the tax rate, policymakers increase the number or type of exemptions. But that weakens both the tax's revenue generation and its inequality reduction.

The other challenge is to forge greater harmonization of enforcement across countries. That will make it more difficult for the rich to escape taxation by moving money to low-tax jurisdictions.[69]

How to Reduce Inequality

To reduce income inequality in the rich democratic nations, our best bets are strong labor unions and collective bargaining, employment-friendly public services, generous public transfers that rise in sync with the economy, employee board-level representation, a financial transactions tax, and heavier taxation of top incomes. Countries that have weak labor unions will need some combination of tight labor markets, statutory (industry-and occupation-specific) minimum wages, profit sharing, and an employment-conditional earnings subsidy. For reducing wealth inequality, the best strategies are supports for asset building and taxation of wealth.

All of these policies and institutions are already in use in one or more existing rich democratic nations. None of them risk inflicting significant damage to other things we want. Many will contribute to the infrastructure of a good society that I outlined in the previous chapter. And moving in this direction would help bring us closer to the not-too-unequal society that many of us would like to live in.

Acknowledgments

I began writing a version of this book in 2010. Soon after, I discovered that Sandy (Christopher) Jencks had been thinking along similar lines,[1] and he and I hatched a tentative plan for a jointly written book. Within a few years we had abandoned that plan, largely because new empirical research on income inequality's effects was appearing at a rapid clip and we didn't feel we could draw confident conclusions. In 2013 Tim Smeeding and I wrote a report that offered a partial assessment of income inequality's consequences in the United States,[2] and the following year I wrote a different version and included it as a chapter in an online book, *The Good Society*.[3] Both of these laid out evidence but refrained from drawing strong conclusions. I then set this question aside to work on other projects. A couple of years ago I decided it was a good time to return to it. The result—this book—is entirely new, though it draws from some of the earlier iterations.

I've presented my thinking on this question at the Amsterdam Centre for Inequality Studies at the University of Amsterdam in 2010, the University of Arizona Department of Sociology in 2010, the Indiana University Department of Sociology in 2010, the Foundation for International Studies on Social Security (FISS) annual meeting in 2011, the Clark Lecture at the University of Kansas in 2011, the Successful Societies conference in Toronto in 2011, the Ohio State University Department of Sociology in 2012, the Next Centre-Left Century conference at Oxford University in 2012, the New Directions for Research on the Effects of Inequality conference at the Harvard Kennedy School in 2013, the Improving Poverty Reduction in Europe conference in Brussels in 2013, the Harvard Club of Southern Arizona in 2014, the Political Economy Project at Dartmouth University in 2014, the University of California–San Diego Department of Sociology in 2014, the Emory University Department of Sociology in 2014, the Center for Advanced Social Science Research at New York University in 2014, the North Jersey Public Policy Network in 2014, the Central European University in Vienna in 2024, the University of Konstanz in 2024, the Institute for Policy Research at the University of Bath in 2024, and the Oxford University Department of Social Policy and Intervention in 2024. I thank the numerous participants, commentors, and organizers.

My thinking about economic inequality and its consequences has been particularly influenced over the years by Tony Atkinson, Larry Bartels, Gøsta Esping-Andersen, Robert Frank, Martin Gilens, Alex Hicks, John Hills, Evelyne Huber, Sandy Jencks, Paul Krugman, Brian Nolan, Thomas Piketty, Tim Smeeding, and John Stephens. I'm especially grateful to Sandy—not just for helping me to grapple with this issue, but more generally for modeling how to ask big, important questions and attempt to answer them in a context of limited and imperfect evidence.

I want to thank David McBride at Oxford University Press for his continued interest and support.

As ever, I appreciate and treasure my family—immediate and extended.

Appendix

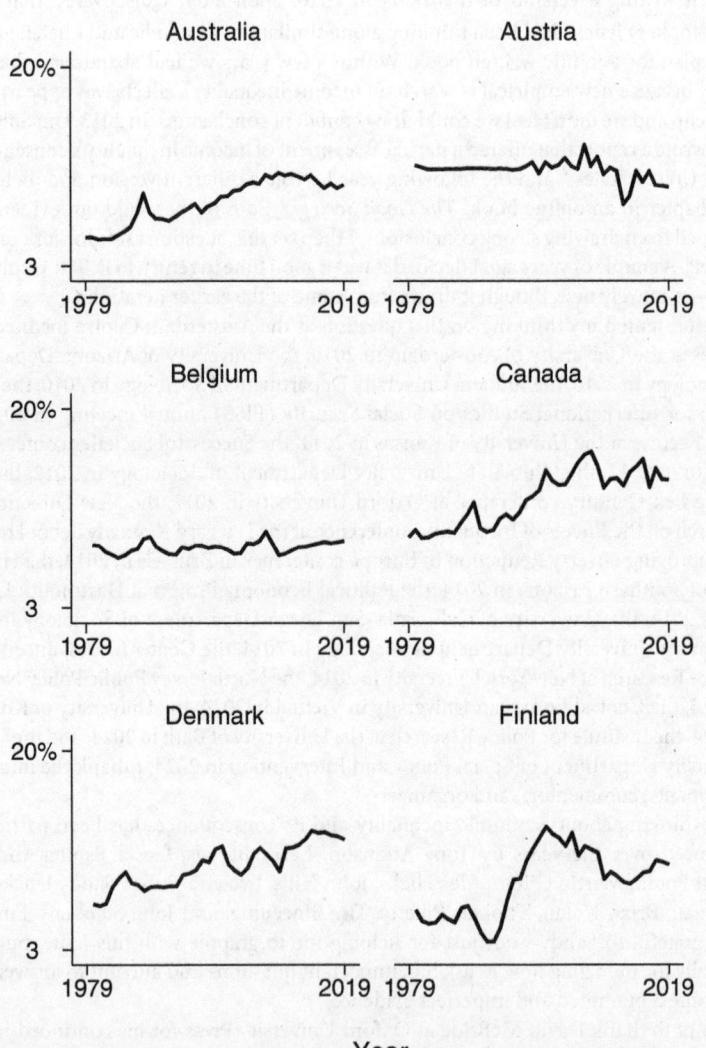

Figure A.1 Income inequality between the top 1 percent and the bottom 99 percent
Top 1 percent's share of income. Pretax income. Excludes capital gains. The vertical axes don't begin at zero. Data source: World Inequality Database.

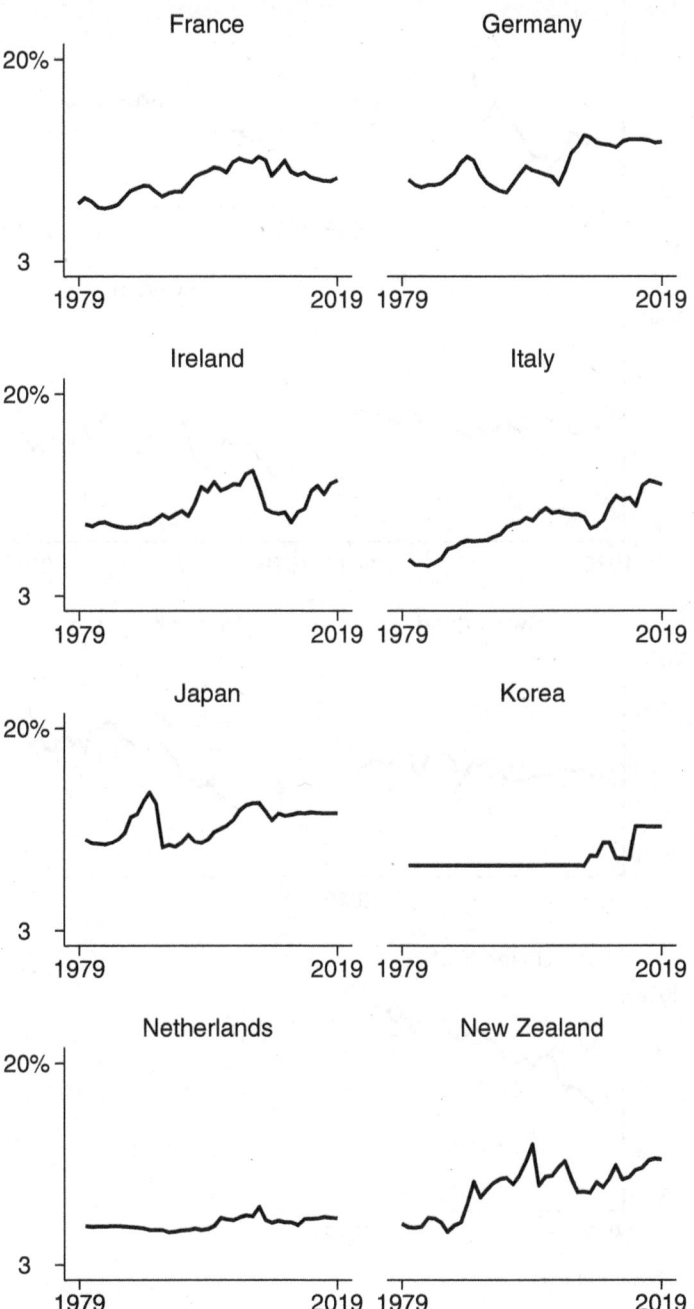

Figure A.1 Continued

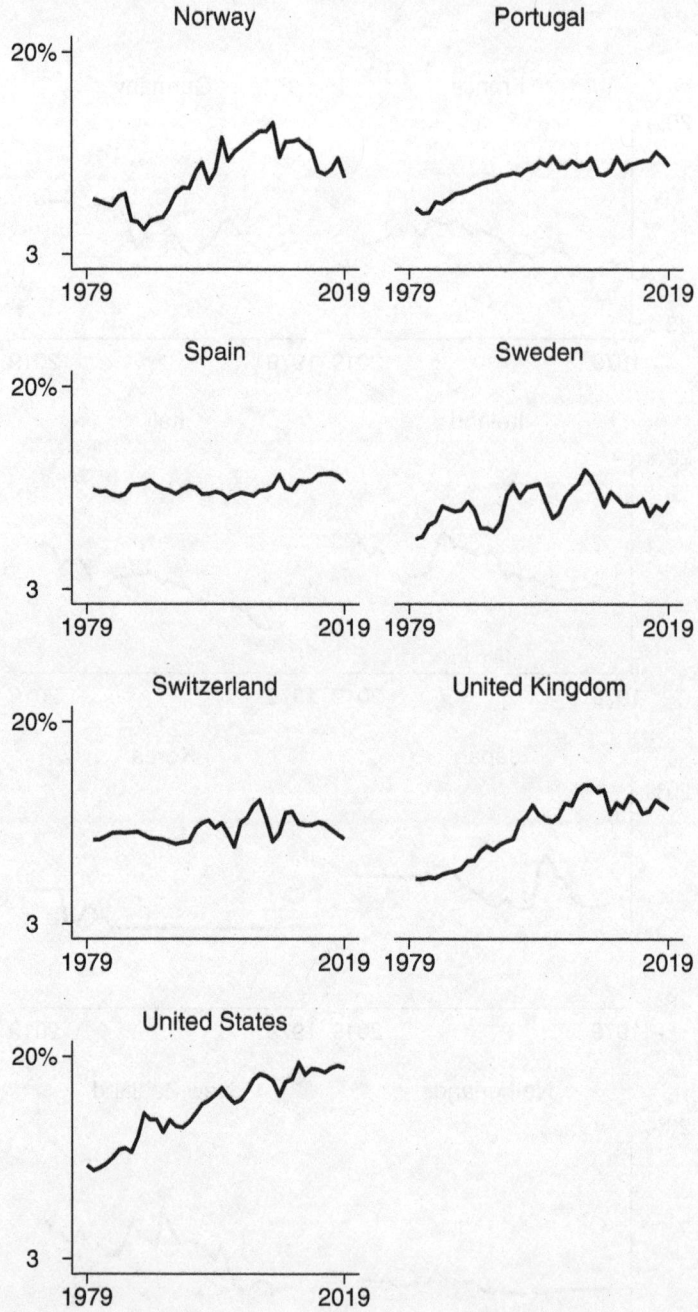

Figure A.1 Continued

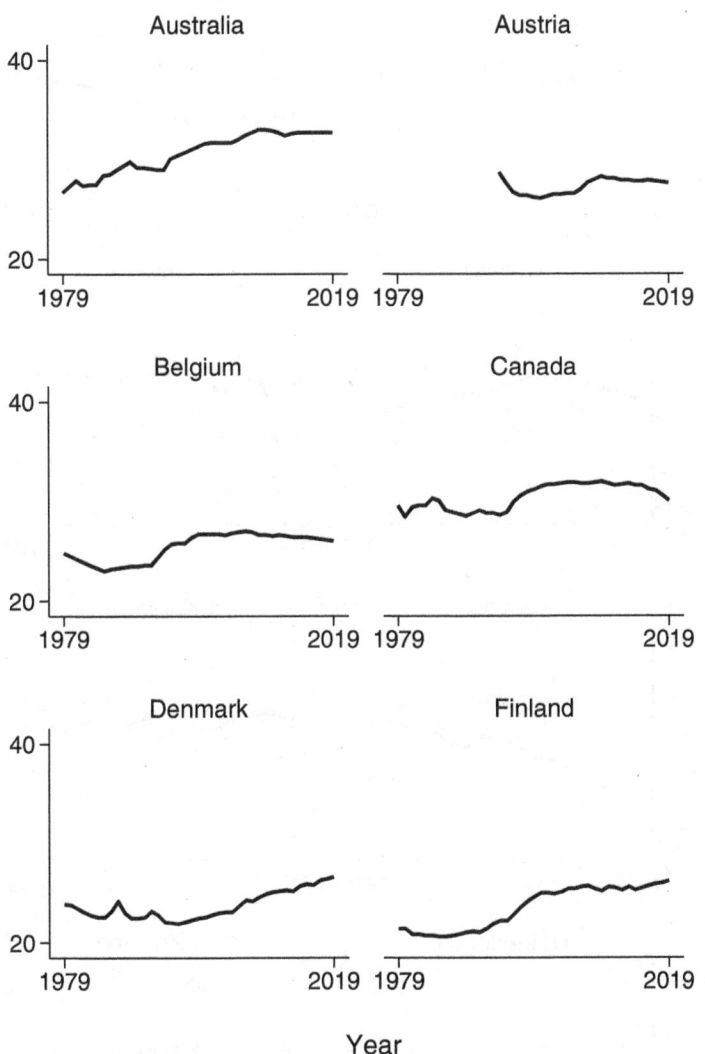

Figure A.2 Income inequality within the bottom 99 percent

Gini coefficient. Posttransfer-posttax income, adjusted for household size. The vertical axes don't begin at zero. Data source: Frederick Solt, Standardized World Income Inequality Database, version 9.5, using data from the Luxembourg Income Study, the OECD, and other sources.

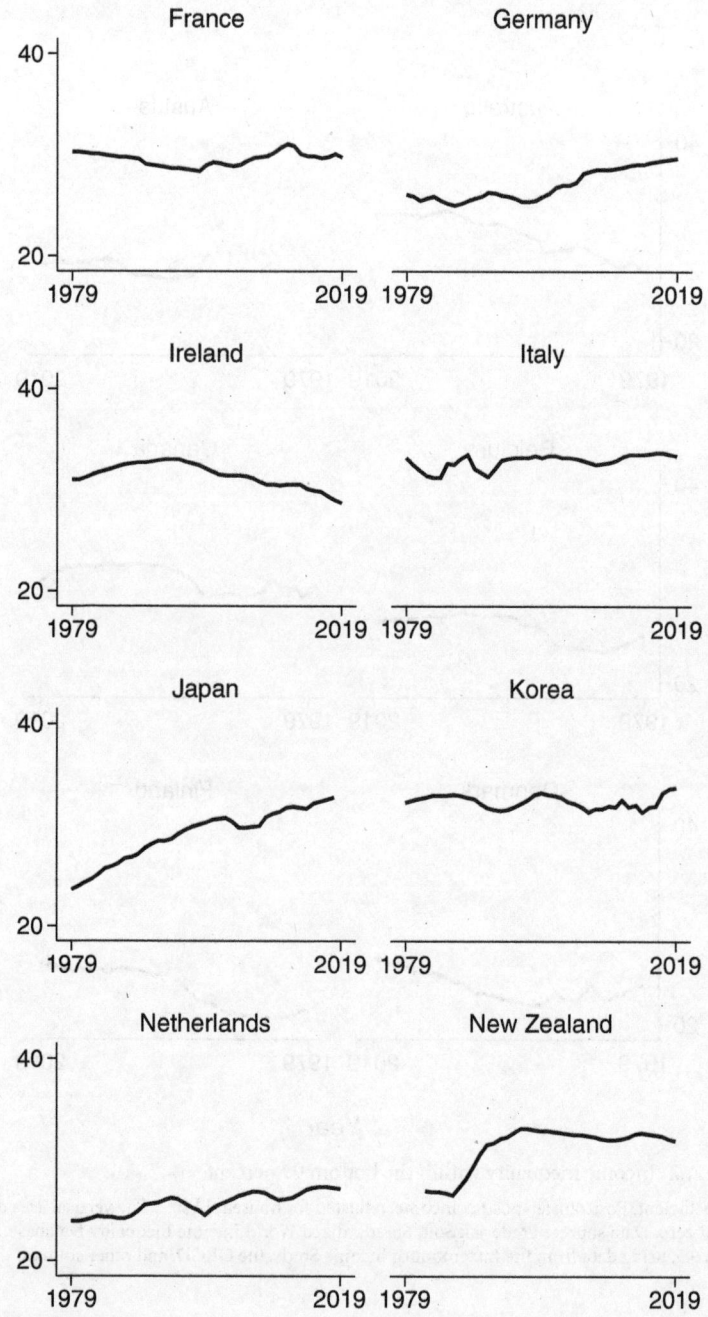

Figure A.2 Continued

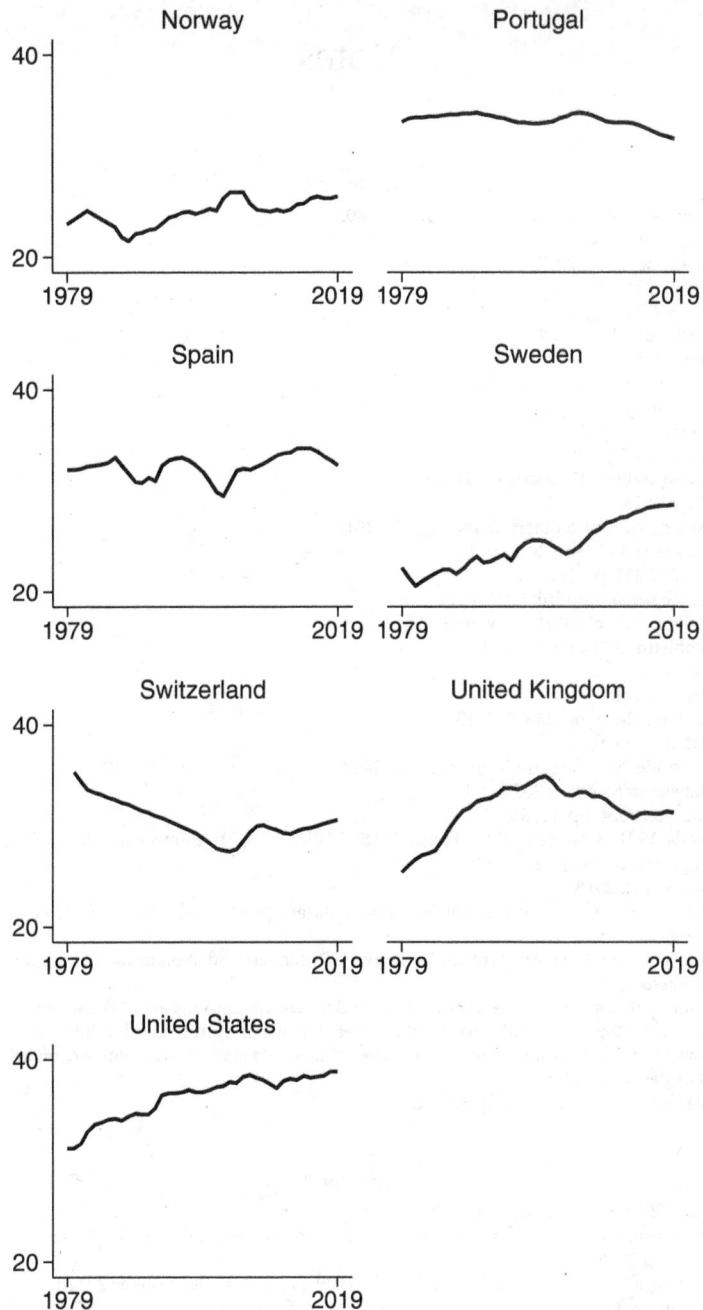

Figure A.2 Continued

Notes

Chapter 1

1. Wilkinson and Pickett 2009, pp. 25, 233, 240.
2. Krugman 2011.
3. Packer 2011, pp. 29, 31.
4. Stiglitz 2012, p. 177.
5. Hayes 2012, p. 16.
6. Freeland 2012, pp. 285–86.
7. Reich 2013.
8. Twitter, @Pontifex, April 28, 2014.
9. Klein and Posner 2014.
10. Cowie 2016, p. 31.
11. Payne 2017, p. 206.
12. Jensen and van Kersbergen 2017, p. 30.
13. Moyn 2018.
14. Twitter, @BernieSanders, September 24, 2019.
15. Hacker and Pierson 2020, p. 1.
16. OECD 2021, p. 156.
17. Blanchard and Rodrik 2021, pp. xi–xii.
18. Twitter, @PikettyWIL, November 22, 2023.
19. Leonhardt 2023, pp. 377–78.
20. Basu 2023.
21. Stiglitz 2023.
22. Malleson 2023, pp. 248, 258, 13.
23. Oxfam 2023, p. 9.
24. Kamande 2024. See also Kamande et al. 2024.
25. Huber and Stephens 2024, p. 1.
26. Robeyns 2024, pp. 15, 36.
27. Rawls 1971; Gladwell 2008; Frank 2016; Malleson 2023; Kenworthy 2025, "Equality of Opportunity" chapter.
28. Bakija et al. 2016.
29. For comparability across countries, these data are pretax and don't include capital gains income.
30. For more detail, see Atkinson and Piketty 2007; Lindert and Williamson 2016; Aaberge and Bengtsson 2023.
31. Some analyses of the United States come to different conclusions about the magnitude of the rise in the top 1 percent's income share. See, for instance, Auten and Splinter 2023. None, however, provide estimates for other nations that would allow cross-country comparison.
32. Blanchet et al. 2022.
33. See, for instance, Kenworthy 2004, 2008a.

Chapter 2

1. Barro 2008; Ostry et al. 2014.
2. For a similar finding with respect to the effect of income inequality on health, see Curran and Mahutga 2018.
3. Firebaugh 2008, ch. 5; Angrist and Pischke 2009, pp. 227–43; Kenworthy 2011b.
4. Change in GDP per capita: Average rate of growth of GDP per capita, 1979 to 2019. Data source: OECD. Change in education: Average per-year change in the share of persons age 25 to 34 with a bachelor's degree or more. Data for 1989, 1999, and 2009 are estimated using the share of those age 55–64, 45–54, and 35–44, respectively, with a bachelor's degree or more as of

2019. Data for 1979 are estimated using the share of those age 55–64 with a bachelor's degree or more as of 2009. Data source: OECD, via National Center for Education Statistics, *Digest of Education Statistics 2011*, table 421 and *Digest of Education Statistics 2020*, table 603.30. Change in elderly population share: Average per-year change in the share of the population age 65 and older. Data source: OECD. Change in immigrant population share: Average per-year change in the share of the population that is foreign born. Data source: OECD. The analyses with control variables are regressions using all possible combinations of change in income inequality and one or two of the controls.
5. Kenworthy 2025, "Affluence and Progress" chapter.
6. Boushey and Hersh 2012; Stiglitz 2012; Boushey and Price 2014; OECD 2015, ch. 2.
7. Kenworthy 2004; Milanovic 2009; Stiglitz 2009; Voitchovsky 2009; Rajan 2010; Reich 2010; Stiglitz 2012; Thaker and Williamson 2012; Cynamon and Fazzari 2014; Kumhof et al. 2015; Palley 2015; Payne 2017, ch. 8; Boushey 2019.
8. Payne 2017, ch. 8; Peters et al. 2024.
9. Atkinson and Morelli 2010; Morelli and Atkinson 2015. See also Bordo and Meissner 2012.
10. Glaeser 2010; Bordo and Meissner 2012; Mian and Sufi 2014.
11. Kenworthy 2004; Barro 2008; Voitchovsky 2009; Castelló-Climent 2010; Andrews et al. 2011; Herzer and Vollmer 2012; Bernstein 2013; Cingano 2014; OECD 2015, ch. 2; El-Shagi and Shao 2017; Berg et al. 2018.
12. Across the countries, 1979-to-2019 growth of GDP per capita correlates at –.72 with 1979 level of GDP per capita.
13. Okun 1975; Lindbeck 1986.
14. Meltzer and Richard 1981.
15. Vohs 2006; Miller 2012; Page and Gilens 2017.
16. The same seems to be true across the US states. See Thompson and Leight 2012.
17. Kenworthy 2011a.
18. Moffitt and Scholz 2009; Scholz et al. 2009; Hills et al. 2009; Waldfogel 2010; Kenworthy 2011a, ch. 2; Kelly 2023; Kenworthy 2025, "A Decent and Rising Income Floor" chapter.
19. In the United States, the over-time story is broadly consistent with this hypothesis. Between the mid-1940s and the late 1970s, with income inequality at its low point, middle-class incomes increased rapidly. Since 1979 inequality has been higher, and in this period the incomes of middle-class households have risen more slowly. Mishel et al. Shierholz 2012; Thompson and Leight 2012; Chetty et al. 2017; Kenworthy 2018.
20. Kenworthy 2013; Thewissen et al. 2018.
21. Hacker 2006; Leicht and Fitzgerald 2007; Reich 2010; Cynamon and Fazzari 2014.
22. Frank 2005, 2007; Frank et al. 2013; Bertrand and Morse 2016; Wilkinson and Pickett 2019.
23. Consider a hypothetical scenario, Robert Frank says, in which you must choose "between world A, in which you will live in a 4,000-square-foot house and others will live in 6,000-square-foot houses; and world B, in which you will live in a 3,000-square-foot house and others will live in 2,000-square-foot houses. Once you choose, your position on the local housing scale will persist. If only absolute consumption mattered, A would clearly be better. Yet most people say they would pick B, where their absolute house size is smaller but their relative house size is larger." Frank 2005, p. 137.
24. Fligstein et al. 2017.
25. Frank et al. 2013.
26. My calculations using data from OECD, "Household Savings," data.oecd.org.
27. Coibion et al. 2014.
28. Lewis 1989; Dynan and Kohn 2007; Tett 2009.
29. Fligstein and Goldstein 2015; Goldstein 2012.

Chapter 3

1. Dahl 1989, 2006; Rawls 2001; Cohen 2009.
2. Center for Responsive Politics, "Cost of Election."
3. Bonica et al. 2014.
4. Evers-Hillstrom 2020.
5. Center for Responsive Politics, "Lobbying Data Summary."

6. See, for example, the quotations in chapter 1. See also Page and Gilens 2017; Reich 2020; Young et al. 2020.
7. Bartels 2016.
8. Gilens 2012.
9. Branham et al. 2017.
10. Ansolabehere et al. 2003; Jacobs et al. 2004; Baumgartner et al. 2009; Burstein 2014; Drutman 2015; Bartels 2016, pp. 263–65; Cao et al. 2018.
11. Burstein 2014.
12. Bartels 2016, p. 253.
13. Hacker and Pierson 2010.
14. Gilens 2012, ch. 7.
15. Wlezien and Soroka 2011.
16. Rosset 2016; Elsasser et al. 2021; Schakel 2021; Mathisen 2022; Lupu and Castro 2023; Persson 2023.
17. Bartels 2017; Persson and Sundell 2023. For an analysis of a much larger set of countries and a less reliable (expert-coded) measure of inequality of political influence, see Leipziger et al. 2023.
18. Hicks 1999; Huber and Stephens 2001; Alesina and Glaeser 2004.
19. Piketty et al. 2014; OECD, "Top Statutory Personal Income Tax Rates," stats.oecd.org, table I.7; Kenworthy 2025, "Taxes" chapter.
20. Piketty et al. 2018, figure 9; US Congressional Budget Office 2022, exhibit 11.
21. Philippon and Reshef 2013; Tooze 2018; Kenworthy 2025, "Finance: Additional Data" appendix.
22. Kenworthy 2025, "Employee Voice" chapter.
23. Page et al. 2013.
24. Page et al. 2019, p. 2.
25. Center for Responsive Politics, "Cost of Election."
26. Rodden 2019; Kenworthy 2025, "Democracy" chapter.
27. Page and Gilens, 2017, p. 19.
28. Lindert and Williamson 2016.
29. Gordon 2016.
30. Sommeiller and Price 2018.
31. Kenworthy 2025, "Democracy" chapter, "Finance: Additional Data" appendix, and "Taxes: Additional Data" appendix.
32. Perry 2017; Pastor 2018; Kenworthy 2025, "Taxes: Additional Data" appendix.

Chapter 4

1. Sen 1999; Nussbaum 2011.
2. There are other types of mobility. See Kenworthy 2008b.
3. Corak 2016.
4. Reeves 2017; Jacobs and Hipple 2018; DiPrete 2020; Durlauf et al. 2021; National Academies of Science, Engineering, and Medicine 2023; Haroon and Harrison 2024.
5. Kiernan et al. 2024 examine the United Kingdom, but they don't explicitly address the question of income inequality's effects.
6. McLanahan et al. 2013; McLanahan and Jencks 2015; Kearney 2023.
7. Some studies have examined the association between income inequality and overall trends in family structure (as opposed to inequality of family structure). They've yielded mixed findings. Several studies have found an association between income inequality and the teen birth rate across countries at a single point in time. Wilkinson and Pickett 2009; Calvert and Fahey 2013. But changes in income inequality aren't correlated with changes in teen births across countries (my analyses). The same is true across the US states. Kearney and Levine 2012. One study finds that county-level income inequality in the United States is positively associated with having a child out of wedlock. Cherlin et al. 2016. Yet there seems to be no such association for early marriage, divorce, or single parenthood. Wilkinson and Pickett 2009; Calvert and Fahey 2013.
8. Coontz 1992; Cherlin 2014.
9. Welzel 2013; Inglehart 2018.
10. Edin and Kefalas 2005; Cherlin 2014; Sawhill 2014; Secura et al. 2014.

11. Duncan et al. 2010; Kaushal et al. 2011; Cooper and Stewart 2013; Schneider et al. 2018.
12. Lareau 2003; Putnam 2015, ch. 3.
13. Ryan et al. 2020.
14. Flood et al. 2022, figure 1, using data from the American Time Use Survey. See also Cha and Park 2021; Prickett and Augustine 2021.
15. Jerrim and Macmillan 2015.
16. Vandell and Wolfe 2000; Waldfogel 2006; Chaudry et al. 2017; Kenworthy 2025, "Early Education" chapter.
17. Jacob and Ludwig 2008; Altonji and Mansfield 2011.
18. Mayer 1999; Lareau 2003; Phillips 2011; Kalil 2015; Cooper and Stewart 2021.
19. Economic Mobility Project 2012.
20. Jencks 2009; Bailey and Dynarski 2011; Kenworthy 2025, "College Education" chapter. A third reason is that many colleges don't have adequate supports in place for students who are less prepared. This is unlikely to have much to do with societal income inequality.
21. The same is true for the p75-to-p25 gap. Hanushek et al. 2019. In addition, the gap at kindergarten entry in reading and math test scores between students whose parents' income is at the ninetieth percentile of the income distribution and students whose parents' income is at the tenth percentile was smaller among children born in the 2000s than among those born in the late 1990s. See Reardon and Portilla 2016.
22. Voss et al. 2024 conclude similarly that there has been little if any increase in inequality of college completion by parents' income.
23. Lee et al. 2015, figure 3-2.
24. Truesdale and Jencks 2016. See also US Congressional Budget Office 2008; Olshansky et al. 2012; Lowrey 2014; Kenworthy 2025, "Longevity" chapter.
25. Kenworthy 2025, "Weight Moderation" chapter.
26. Mackenbach 2016. See also Marmot et al. 2010.
27. Wilson 1987, 1996; Jencks and Mayer 1990; Sampson 2012; Sharkey 2013.
28. Among American families with children, residential segregation by income increased in the 1980s and the 2000s, though not in the 1990s. Across large metro areas, residential segregation by income is higher where income inequality is higher. And metro areas in which income inequality increased more tended to have larger increases in residential segregation by income. This income-based residential segregation consists of the affluent separating from everyone else. It isn't a separation between the middle and the bottom. Watson 2009; Reardon and Bischoff 2011; Fry and Taylor 2012; Bischoff and Reardon 2013; Owens et al. 2016; Reardon et al. 2018.
29. Chetty, Hendren, and Katz 2016; Chetty and Hendren 2018.
30. Ganzeboom et al. 1989; Hauser et al. 2000.
31. Aaronson and Mazumder 2008; Bloome and Western 2011; Davis and Mazumder 2017.
32. Harding et al. 2005; Hertz 2007; Lee and Solon 2009; Winship 2013; Chetty et al. 2014; Bloome et al. 2018; Hout 2018; DiPrete 2020.
33. Bloome et al. 2018; DiPrete 2020; Chetty et al. 2024.
34. Jäntti and Jenkins 2015; Jacobs and Hipple 2018; DiPrete 2020.
35. OECD 2006; Kenworthy 2025, "Early Education" chapter.
36. Esping-Andersen 2008; Heckman 2008.
37. Andersen et al. 2015, ch. 7.
38. Winship and Schneider 2013; Bloome 2014.
39. Bloome 2014.

Chapter 5

1. Wilkinson 1992.
2. Another is that the marginal utility of income in improving health declines as income rises. Life expectancy rises with income, but as we move up the income ladder the degree of improvement per extra unit of income declines. Thus, taking some money from a poor person and giving it to a rich person should increase the life expectancy of the rich person by less than it reduces the life expectancy of the poor person.
3. Wilkinson and Pickett 2009, pp. 39, 43–44, 85. See also Marmot 2004; Paskov et al. 2013; Layte and Whelan 2014 Pickett and Wilkinson 2015; Wilkinson and Pickett 2019.

4. Merton 1968; Freeman 1996; Wilkinson and Pickett 2009; Daly 2016; Santos et al. 2018; Wilkinson and Pickett 2019. Evidence on the link between income inequality and crime is mixed. At the individual level, the propensity to commit crime is higher among those with lower incomes. Cross-sectional studies across US states or localities have sometimes yielded findings of a positive association. Some types of crime that seem likely to be encouraged by inequality, such as theft, do not correlate with inequality across countries. Over time, the association between inequality and crime in the United States is not particularly strong. See Burtless and Jencks 2003; Western et al. 2004; Pazzona 2024.
5. Clarkwest 2008.
6. Kenworthy 2025, "Safety" chapter.
7. Lynch et al. 2004.
8. Kim et al. 2008; Wilkinson and Pickett 2009, ch. 7.
9. US Centers for Disease Control 2012; Dobbs et al. 2014; Hogstrom et al. 2015; Maralani and McKee 2015; Aune et al. 2016; Global Burden of Disease (GBD) 2015 Obesity Collaborators 2017; Waters and Graf 2018; OECD 2019.
10. Smith 2012; Warner 2012; Lăcătus et al. 2019; Bittman and Katz 2020; Dao et al. 2021; Kenworthy 2025, "Weight Moderation" chapter.
11. Kenworthy 2025, "Weight Moderation" chapter.
12. Case and Deaton 2015; Case and Deaton 2020.
13. Ruhm 2018; Cutler and Glaeser 2021; Feldmeyer et al. 2022; Kenworthy 2025, "Longevity" chapter.
14. Payne 2017, ch. 5; Wilkinson and Pickett 2019, p. 207; Thombs et al. 2020; Kuo and Kawachi 2023.
15. Kuo and Kawachi 2023, p. 2.
16. Case and Deaton 2020, p. 134. See also Currie 2024.
17. A better measure of health outcomes, arguably, is healthy life expectancy, but we have very limited over-time data for this.
18. Kondo et al. 2009; Wilkinson and Pickett 2009; University of Wisconsin Population Health Institute 2015.
19. A recent example is Chetty, Stepner, et al. 2016.
20. Judge et al. 1998; Burtless and Jencks 2003; Beckfield 2004; Leigh and Jencks 2007; Leigh et al. 2009; Daly and Wilson 2013; Alexiou and Trachanas 2021; Varbanova et al. 2023.
21. Deaton 2003; Lynch et al. 2004; Mullahy et al. 2004; Leigh et al. 2009; Truesdale and Jencks 2016.
22. Leigh et al. 2009, p. 386.
23. Across the countries, 1979-to-2019 change in life expectancy correlates at −.87 with 1979 level of life expectancy.
24. The US stands out similarly on some other sources of early death, including infant mortality and deaths from vehicle accidents. These too appear to have determinants other than high or rising income inequality. Lundberg et al. 2008; Kenworthy 2025, "Safety" chapter.
25. Achenbach et al. 2023; Burn-Murdoch 2023; Kenworthy 2025, "Guns" chapter, "Weight Moderation" chapter, and "Longevity" chapter.
26. National Research Council and Institute of Medicine 2013.
27. Krugman 1992; McCall and Kenworthy 2009.
28. Fisher and Bubola 2020; Sepulveda and Brooker 2021; Tan et al. 2021; Su et al. 2022; Amate-Fortes et al. 2023.
29. See also Snowdon 2011.

Chapter 6

1. Bentham 1843; Layard 2005; Murray 2012.
2. Diener et al. 2009; Bok 2010, ch. 2; Radcliff 2013, ch. 4; Easterlin 2021, ch. 2; Layard and De Neve 2023.
3. Alesina et al. 2004; Firebaugh and Tach 2012; Layard et al. 2009; Layard et al. 2012; Ferrer-i-Carbonell and Ramos 2014; Clark et al. 2017; Kelley and Evans 2017; Schneider 2019; Hajdu 2021.
4. Easterlin 2021.
5. Wilkinson and Pickett 2019, pp. 25–26, 34, 42–43. See also Wilkinson and Pickett 2009.

6. Alesina et al. 2004; McCall 2013.
7. Uslaner 2002; Stiglitz 2013; Wilkinson and Pickett 2009; Larsen, 2013; Payne 2017, ch. 9.
8. Rothstein and Uslaner 2005; Bjørnskov 2008; Lancee and Van de Werfhorst 2012; Delhey and Dragolov 2013; Fairbrother and Martin 2013; Hastings 2018; Schroeder and Neumayr 2023.
9. Putnam and Romney Garrett 2020.
10. A fifth pathway through which income inequality might reduce happiness is political polarization and oppositional identity. This is specific to the United States. In recent decades, Americans have sorted themselves more cleanly into the two dominant political parties, and those parties have become more distinct in their policy stances. Some attribute this polarization to the rise in income inequality. See McCarty et al. 2008. In addition, political party has become a more prominent identity, influencing not only people's position on political issues but where they decide to live and even what they choose to eat and drink. See Bishop with Cushing 2008; Cho et al. 2013; Iyengar and Westwood 2015; Taub 2017; Mason 2018; Sides et al. 2018; Dyck and Pearson-Merkowitz 2023. As political partisanship has become more all-encompassing, it also has become more oppositional and negative, heightening frustration and anger.
11. See also Easterlin 2021; Veenhoven and Kegel 2023, table 2.
12. Kenworthy 2025, "Happiness" chapter.
13. My calculations using household income data from the Luxembourg Income Study and inflation data from the OECD.
14. From the 1970s through the 2010s, Americans who said their health is poor had an average happiness score of 4 on a scale of 0 to 10, while those who said their health is excellent had an average happiness score of 7. My calculations using General Social Survey data.
15. General Social Survey, series health. It isn't clear why this happened. Perhaps better diagnosis increased our awareness of ailments and diseases. While it's conceivable that income inequality is a cause of perceived health, studies have tended to find no link between them. Qi 2012; Van de Werfhorst and Salverda 2012.
16. Katsaiti 2012.
17. Layard 2005 ch. 5; Layard et al. 2012; Helliwell et al. 2017.
18. Putnam and Romney Garrett 2020, figure 4.10.
19. Buettner 2017, p. 203.
20. Radcliff 2013; Anderson and Hecht 2015; O'Connor 2017; Easterlin 2021.
21. Kenworthy 2025, "Social Programs" chapter.
22. Kenworthy 2025, "Work-Family-Leisure Balance" chapter.
23. Kenworthy 2025, "Religion" chapter.
24. Kenworthy 2025, "Shared Prosperity" and "A Decent and Rising Income Floor" chapters.
25. OECD, OECD Family Database; Our World in Data, "Share of Households That Are Single-Parent," using data from the UN Population Division.
26. Layard 2005, ch. 5; Diener et al. 2009, pp. 160–65; Layard et al. 2012; Helliwell et al. 2020, p. 34.
27. Norris and Inglehart 2019.

Chapter 7

1. Lieberson 1985; Achen 2002, 2005.
2. In many instances it won't be possible to generate such findings. Many of the hypotheses rely on how a person experiences income inequality. But we seldom have good information about how much income inequality a person has encountered, about the extent to which they were aware of inequality, and about how it influenced their lived experience.
3. Kenworthy 2025, "Income Distribution" chapter.
4. Bartels 2022, ch. 7.
5. Some studies examining individuals have found a link between economic inequality and preferences or voting for right-wing populist parties: Engler and Weisstanner 2021; Stoetzer et al. 2023. But others haven't: Brännlund and Szulkin 2023. And when examining countries, there appears to be no link between income inequality and vote share for right-wing populist parties: Bergh and Kärnä 2022.
6. Dal Bo et al. 2019; Acemoglu et al. 2023; Burgoon et al. 2023; Lukk 2024.
7. Currie 2024.
8. Wilkinson and Pickett 2019, p. 15.

9. Twenge 2000.
10. Drum 2024; Fioroni and Foy 2024.
11. Piketty 2014.

Chapter 8

1. The amount of inequality depicted in E actually is the same as in C, but many people are likely to recognize C as more unequal because it shows few people at the top and many at the bottom.
2. Osberg and Smeeding 2006; McCall 2013; Horowitz et al. 2020; Mijs 2021; OECD 2021; Lindh and McCall 2023.
3. ISSP, Social Inequality 5 module, 2019, v24: "It is the responsibility of private companies to reduce the differences in pay between their employees with high pay and those with low pay." See also OECD 2021; Lindh and McCall 2023.
4. See also Finseraas 2009.
5. Kenworthy and McCall 2008.
6. Kenworthy and McCall 2008; McCall and Kenworthy 2009; Barth et al. 2015; Ashok et al. 2016; Breznau and Hommerich 2019; Mijs 2021; Lupu and Pontusson 2024. But see also OECD 2021, section 3.2; Rosset et al. 2024.
7. Martinsson et al. 2018, p. 18.
8. Aisch and Parlapiano 2017; Gallup, "Most Important Problem," gallup.com. See also Harris et al. 2025, table 3, p. 131.

Chapter 9

1. The same is true for life expectancy. Kenworthy 2025, "Affluence and Progress" chapter; Deaton 2013; Dollar et al. 2016; Jetter et al. 2019; Pritchett 2020.
2. We don't have comparable data for the global distribution of wealth. Chancel et al. 2022, ch. 4.
3. In many poorer nations a large share of the population has little or no income because they are subsistence farmers—they grow most of their own food and neither receive nor spend any money. For these countries surveys typically ask about consumption rather than income.
4. Milanovic 2016, 2022; Alderson and Pandian 2018.
5. Kenworthy 2025, "Income Distribution" chapter.
6. Milanovic 2023, pp. 80–82.
7. Follett and Geloso 2023.
8. Stiglitz 2006; Clausing 2019; Aiyar 2024; Furman 2024; Rogoff 2024; Kenworthy 2025, "Migration" and "Trade" chapters. See also Wade 2001, p. 72: "Anybody interested in the wealth and poverty of nations must be interested in what is happening to the global distribution of income, one would suppose. A lot turns on the question. If the world's income distribution has become more equal in the past few decades, this would be powerful evidence that globalisation works to the benefit of all."
9. Dorn and Levell 2024.
10. Quoted in Popper 2016.
11. Krugman 2021.
12. Caplan and Weinersmith 2019.
13. Huber and Stephens 2024.
14. Clemens et al. 2008.
15. Caplan et al. 2019.
16. Van Parijs 2021 makes a similar point.

Chapter 10

1. Waldenström 2024, p. 129.
2. Piketty 2014; Waldenström 2024.
3. A different data source suggests Sweden is similar to the United States or perhaps more unequal: Shorrocks et al. 2022, tables 3-1 and 4-5. Another suggests that is true of Switzerland: Atkinson and Morelli 2014.
4. Kenworthy 2025, "Social Democratic Capitalism" chapter.
5. For other rich democratic nations, these data are available only since 1960.
6. Pinker 2018; Max Roser, *Our World in Data*, https://ourworldindata.org.
7. Rodems and Pfeffer 2021.

Chapter 11

1. This echoes the conclusion of Gary Burtless and Christopher Jencks from two decades ago: "If you care mainly about growth, health, or equal opportunity, changing the distribution of income is not the best strategy for promoting these goals. Redistribution is a hard sell politically and normally consumes a lot of government resources. Those who care about growth, health, and equal opportunity are likely to achieve more if they focus on more proximate determinants of these outcomes, such as encouraging public and private investment in innovation, ensuring good health care and early education for children, reducing smoking and obesity, and making public universities affordable for all talented youngsters." Burtless and Jencks 2003, pp. 101–2. See also Corak 2017, p. 62.
2. See also Baker 2021; Becker 2024.
3. Malleson 2023; Sanders 2023; Robeyns 2024.
4. Andersen et al. 2015, ch. 11; Barth et al. 2021.
5. Partanen 2016; Kenworthy 2020.
6. Even skeptics tend to reach this conclusion. See, for example, The Economist 2013; Booth 2014.
7. Harry Frankfurt puts this point as follows: "Mere differences in the amounts of money people have are not in themselves distressing. We tend to be quite unmoved, after all, by inequalities between those who are very well-to-do and those who are extremely rich. Our awareness that the latter are substantially better off than the former arouses in us no moral uneasiness at all. If we believe of some person that his life is richly fulfilling, that he himself is genuinely content with his economic situation, and that he is not troubled by any resentments or sorrows that more money could assuage, we are not ordinarily much interested—at least, from a moral point of view—in a comparison of the amount of money he has with the amounts possessed by others. Economic discrepancies in cases of this sort do not impress us in the least as matters of significant moral concern. The fact that some people have much less than others is not at all morally disturbing when it is clear that the worse off have plenty" Frankfurt 2015, pp. 41–42.
8. Hannah Ritchie and Max Roser, "Energy Use Per Person," *Our World in Data*, https://ourworldindata.org/grapher/per-capita-energy-use.
9. Articles in academic journals will no longer be behind a paywall.
10. Trust for Public Land, "ParkScore Ratings," www.tpl.org.
11. There is both more and less policing than the current norm in a country like the United States. In high-crime areas, police create a large and highly visible presence, as this tends to reduce violence. At the same time, other matters that currently are under police purview, such as emergency mental health calls, are handled initially by mental health specialists, with police called in only if there is an identifiable threat of violence.
12. Kenworthy 2025, "Human Rights" chapter.
13. Marchal and Marx 2024.
14. This is true in more than a few urban areas today, including London, Amsterdam, and Singapore. See Derrible 2025.
15. Kenworthy 2025, "Taxes" chapter.
16. Marchal and Marx 2024.
17. Esping-Andersen and Myles 2009; Verbist et al. 2012. The top 1% share income inequality data used in chapters 1-7 do include an estimated value of public goods and services in incomes, but this value is assumed to be distributed not equally but instead "in proportion to post-tax disposable income." Alvaredo et al 2021, p. 64.
18. OECD 2008, ch. 9; Garfinkel et al. 2010, table 4.1; Paulus et al. 2010; Verbist et al. 2012; Ogden and Phillips 2024. This is true even though some services, such as early education, are used more by households with higher income than by households with lower income ("Matthew effect").
19. Kenworthy 2025, "Taxes" chapter.
20. The US tax system actually is slightly progressive, so figure 11.1 somewhat understates the redistributive effect of public goods and services.
21. How large is the redistributive impact of public goods and services? Estimates suggest that if receipt of services were counted as household income, they would reduce measured income inequality by one-fifth to one-third, depending on the country and the inequality measure used. And they would reduce relative poverty rates (income inequality in the lower half of the distribution) by approximately half. Verbist et al. 2012.
22. Kenworthy 2004, 2008a, 2011a; Bakija et al. 2016; Kenworthy 2025, "Employment" and "Is Big Government Bad for the Economy" chapters.

23. Atkinson et al. 2002; Stiglitz et al. 2009.
24. Piketty 2022, ch. 1.
25. Wilkinson and Pickett 2019, p. 252.
26. Cowie 2016, p. 29.
27. Pinker 2018; Kenworthy 2025.
28. Putnam and Romney Garrett 2020.
29. Pinker 2018; Kenworthy 2025.
30. Shiller 2014; Ayres et al. 2023.
31. Malleson 2023, ch. 7; Robeyns 2024.
32. Saez and Zucman 2019.
33. Kenworthy 2025, "Universal Basic Income" chapter.
34. Balestra and Tonkin 2018; Causa et al. 2019; Pfeffer and Waitkus 2021; Waldenström 2024.
35. Baker 2011, ch. 9; Blanchflower and Oswald 2013; Causa et al. 2019; Demsas 2022; Keys 2024; Kenworthy 2025, "Climate Stability" chapter.
36. Beramendi and Rehm 2016.
37. Kenworthy 2025, "What America Needs" chapter.
38. Kenworthy 2025, "What America Needs" chapter.
39. Danielson 2016; Yakter 2018; Alesina et al. 2023; Eick 2024.
40. Brady and Finnigan 2013; Burgoon and Rooduijn 2021; Breznau et al. 2022.
41. Palier 2010; Hemerijck 2013, 2017; Birnbaum et al. 2017; Diamantopoulou et al. 2023; Kenworthy 2025, "Social Programs" chapter.
42. Sofocleous 2025.

Chapter 12

1. For a different—and very good—set of recommendations, see Atkinson 2015.
2. Kenworthy 2025, "A Decent and Rising Income Floor" and "Shared Prosperity" chapters.
3. Compensation includes wages plus benefits paid by employers, such as contributions to pensions and workers' health insurance.
4. Krugman 1994, p. 24; Deaton 2013, p. 237; Krugman 2013; Avent 2018.
5. Goldin and Katz 2008.
6. Ashworth and Ransom 2018; Kenworthy 2025, "College Education" chapter.
7. Kenworthy 2025, "Trade" chapter.
8. Sanchez Cumming 2022.
9. See also Manning and Petrongolo 2024.
10. Income inequality within the bottom 99 percent has increased in the Nordic countries, particularly in Sweden and Finland, but that isn't because of slow wage growth in the middle or at the bottom. See Backman and Nelson 2018.
11. Kristal 2017.
12. See also OECD 2019a, section 2.2.
13. Bosch and Weinkopf 2008; Kelly and Tomlinson 2017; IPPR Commission on Economic Justice 2018.
14. Pollin 2011; Baker and Bernstein 2013; Bernstein 2015; Bernstein et al. 2017; Bernstein 2019; Bernstein and Bentele 2019; Newman and Jacobs 2023; Autor et al. 2024.
15. Autor et al. 2024.
16. Marchal and Marx 2024.
17. Gautie and Schmitt 2010.
18. In some countries the statutory minimum wage is indexed to prices or wages, so in practice policymakers tend to have limited influence. See Arpaia et al. 2017.
19. Dube 2019, p. 5.
20. Australian Government, Fair Work Ombudsman, "Minimum Wages" and "List of Awards"; Australian Government, Fair Work Commission, "Annual Wage Reviews."
21. Australian Bureau of Statistics, "Employee Hours and Earnings, Australia, May 2018." The United States has experience with something similar. In the 1940s, "wage boards" determined pay levels for particular occupations and sectors. They exist today in a few states, including California and New York, though they play a small role in overall wage setting. See Madland 2018; Andrias 2019; Dube 2019.

22. The best test, because it is closest to an experimental design, is a "difference in differences" approach. The fact that many of the US states have set minimum wages higher than the federal minimum, in varying degrees and at different times, is helpful for analytical purposes. In the early 1990s David Card and Alan Krueger compared employment changes in fast food restaurants on either side of the New Jersey–Pennsylvania border after one state increased its minimum wage while the other didn't. Arindrajit Dube and colleagues pursued this strategy for every pair of adjacent counties straddling state borders in which one increased its minimum wage between 1990 and 2006. They, like Card and Krueger, found no adverse employment effect of minimum wage increases. Card and Krueger 1995; Dube et al. 2010; Schmitt 2013; Cengiz et al. 2019; Dube and Zipperer 2024.
23. Kruse et al. 2008.
24. Weitzman 1984.
25. Hillary Clinton's 2016 presidential campaign in the United States proposed offering firms that implement profit sharing a two-year tax credit equal to 15 percent of the amount they share (higher for small businesses). The credit would apply to shared profits up to 10 percent of a worker's salary or wage. For instance, if a new profit share program in a firm added $5,000 to the pay of someone making $50,000 a year, the firm would receive a subsidy of $750. See Chozick 2015.
26. Kenworthy 2015; Nichols and Rothstein 2016; Schanzenbach and Strain 2020.
27. This alternative is modeled on an earnings subsidy used in Sweden. Kenworthy 2020, ch. 7.
28. Kenworthy 2015.
29. Lohmann and Marx 2018.
30. Kenworthy 2020.
31. Huber and Stephens 2024; Marchal and Marx 2024; Kenworthy 2025, "Social Programs" and "What America Needs" chapters.
32. Cantillon et al. 2020; Marchal and Marx 2024.
33. Kenworthy 2025, "Income Distribution" chapter.
34. Krugman 2007.
35. Frank and Cook 1995.
36. Reich 2015; Stiglitz 2015.
37. Volscho and Kelley 2012; Jaumotte and Buitron 2015; Huber et al. 2015.
38. DiPrete et al. 2010.
39. Murphy 2013.
40. Lazonick 2014.
41. Business Roundtable 2019.
42. The data are for stock market capitalization as a share of GDP. They are from Huber et al. 2015.
43. Markey et al. 2010; Conchon et al. 2015.
44. Some hope that employee board-level employee representation also would increase pay growth. Holmberg 2017; Warren 2018; Yglesias 2018. But available evidence isn't especially supportive. Blandhol et al. 2020; Jäger et al. 2020.
45. Vitols 2010; Forcillo 2017; Fox 2018; Jäger et al. 2020.
46. Philippon and Reshef 2013; Tomaskovic-Devey and Lin 2013; Flaherty 2015.
47. Philippon and Reshef 2013, appendix data set.
48. Baker 2011, ch. 9.
49. Data source: OECD, Revenue Statistics Database.
50. Piketty et al. 2014; Roine and Waldenström 2014.
51. Kenworthy 2025, "Taxes" chapter.
52. Frydman and Molloy 2011.
53. Kenworthy 2025, "Taxes: Additional Data" appendix.
54. Kenworthy 2025, "Taxes" chapter.
55. Buffett 2011; Förster et al. 2014; Auten et al. 2016; Reid 2017.
56. Young 2017.
57. Wamhoff and Gardner 2019.
58. Some think we could raise it much higher, to around 60 percent. Saez and Zucman 2019, ch. 7.
59. Pfeffer and Waitkus 2021.
60. Balestra and Tonkin 2018; Causa et al. 2019; Pfeffer and Waitkus 2021; Waldenström 2024, ch. 6.
61. Ackerman and Alstott 1999; Sherraden 2007; Boshara 2009; Cramer and Newville 2009; Atkinson 2015; Elliott and Lewis 2018; Piketty 2022, ch. 7.

62. Perret 2020, p. 5.
63. OECD 2018; Perrett 2020; Summers 2021.
64. Taylor 2021.
65. Perret 2020, p. 11.
66. Hemel and Kysar 2019.
67. OECD 2018; Perrett 2020; Summers 2021; Taylor 2021; Waldenström 2024.
68. Schechtl and Tisch 2024.
69. Saez and Zucman 2019; Piketty 2022.

Acknowledgments

1. Jencks 2002; Burtless and Jencks 2003.
2. Kenworthy and Smeeding 2013, 2014.
3. Kenworthy 2025, "Is Income Inequality Harmful?" chapter. This book supersedes that chapter.

References

Aaberge, Rolf and Erik Bengtsson. 2023. "Long-Run Evolution of Income Inequality in the Nordic Countries." *Scandinavian Economic History Review*, https://doi.org/10.1080/03585522.2023.2268624.

Aaronson, Daniel and Bhashkar Mazumder. 2008. "Intergenerational Economic Mobility in the U.S., 1940 to 2000." *Journal of Human Resources* 43, 139–72.

Abt, Thomas. 2019. *Bleeding Out: The Devastating Consequences of Urban Violence—and a Bold New Plan for Peace in the Streets*. Hachette.

Acemoglu, Daron, Nicolas Ajzenman, Cevat Giray Aksoy, Martin Fiszbein, and Carlos Molina. 2024. "Successful Democracies Breed Their Own Support." *Review of Economic Studies*, https://doi.org/10.1093/restud/rdae051.

Achen, Christopher H. 2002. "Toward a New Political Methodology: Microfoundations and ART." *Annual Review of Political Science* 5, 423–50.

Achen, Christopher H. 2005. "Let's Put Garbage-Can Regressions and Garbage-Can Probits Where They Belong." *Conflict Management and Peace Science* 22, 327–39.

Achenbach, Joel, Dan Keating, Laurie McGinley, Akilah Johnson, and Jahi Chikwendiu. 2023. "Dying Early: America's Life Expectancy Crisis." *Washington Post*, October 3.

Ackerman, Bruce and Anne Alstott. 1999. *The Stakeholder Society*. Yale University Press.

Aisch, Gregor and Alicia Parlapiano. 2017. "What Do You Think Is the Most Important Problem Facing This Country Today?" *New York Times*, February 27.

Aiyar, Shekhar. 2024. "Income Inequality and the Liberal Economic Order: A Not Entirely Western Perspective." Bruegel Essay and Lecture Series.

Alderson, Arthur S. and Roshan K. Pandian. 2018. "What Is Really Happening with Global Inequality?" *Sociology of Development* 4, 261–81.

Alesina, Alberto, Rafael Di Tella, and Robert MacCulloch. 2004. "Inequality and Happiness: Are Europeans and Americans Different?" *Journal of Public Economics* 88, 2009–42.

Alesina, Alberto and Edward L. Glaeser. 2004. *Fighting Poverty in the US and Europe*. Oxford University Press.

Alesina, Alberto, Armando Miano, and Stefanie Stantcheva. 2023. "Immigration and Redistribution." *Review of Economic Studies* 90, 1–39.

Alexiou, Constantinos and Emmanouil Trachanas. 2021. "Health Outcomes, Income and Income Inequality: Revisiting the Empirical Relationship." *Forum for Health Economics and Policy* 24(2), 75–100.

Altonji, Joseph G. and Richard K. Mansfield. 2011. "The Role of Family, School, and Community Characteristics in Inequality in Education and Labor-Market Outcomes." In *Whither Opportunity?*, edited by Greg J. Duncan and Richard J. Murnane, Russell Sage Foundation and Spencer Foundation, 339–58.

Alvaredo, Facundo, Anthony B. Atkinson, Thomas Blanchet, et al. 2021. "Distributional National Accounts Guidelines Methods and Concepts Used in the World Inequality Database." Research Report, World Inequality Lab, hal.science/hal-03307584.

Amate-Fortes, Ignacio, Almudena Guarnido-Rueda, Diego Martínez-Navarro, and Francisco J. Oliver-Márquez. 2023. "Income Inequality and COVID-19 in the USA." *Critical Public Health* 33, 814–27.

Anderson, Christopher J. and Jason D. Hecht. 2015. "Happiness and the Welfare State: Decommodification and the Political Economy of Subjective Well-Being." In *The Politics of Advanced Capitalism*, edited by Pablo Beramendi, Silja Häusermann, Herbert Kitschelt, and Hanspeter Kriesi, Cambridge University Press, 357–80.

Andersen, Torben M., Jesper Roine, Bernt Bratsberg, et al. 2015. *Nordic Economic Policy Review: Whither the Nordic Welfare Model?* Norden.

Andrews, Dan, Christopher Jencks, and Andrew Leigh. 2011. "Do Rising Top Incomes Lift All Boats?" *B.E. Journal of Economic Analysis and Policy* 11(1), article 6.

Andrias, Kate. 2019. "An American Approach to Social Democracy: The Forgotten Promise of the Fair Labor Standards Act." *Yale Law Journal* 128, 616–709.

Angrist, Joshua D. and Jorn-Steffen Pischke. 2009. *Mostly Harmless Econometrics*. Princeton University Press.

Ansolabehere, Stephen, John de Figueiredo, and James M. Snyder Jr. 2003. "Why Is There So Little Money in U.S. Politics?" *Journal of Economic Perspectives* 17(1), 105–30.

Arpaia, Alfonso, Pedro Cardoso, Aron Kiss, Kristine Van Herck, and Annelee Vandeplas. 2017. "Statutory Minimum Wages in the EU: Institutional Settings and Macroeconomic Implications." Policy Paper 124, Institute of Labor Economics (IZA).

Ashok, Vivekinan, Ilyana Kuziemko, and Ebonya Washington. 2016. "Support for Redistribution in an Age of Rising Inequality: New Stylized Facts and Some Tentative Explanations." *Brookings Papers on Economic Activity*, Spring, 367–405.

Ashworth, Jared and Tyler Ransom. 2018. "Has the College Wage Premium Continued to Rise? Evidence from Multiple U.S. Surveys." Discussion Paper 11657, Institute of Labor Economics (IZA).

Atkinson, Anthony B. 2015. *Inequality: What Can Be Done?* Harvard University Press.

Atkinson, Anthony B., Bea Cantillon, Eric Marlier, and Brian Nolan. 2002. *Social Indicators*. Oxford University Press.

Atkinson, Anthony B. and Salvatore Morelli. 2010. "Inequality and Banking Crises: A First Look." Report for the International Labour Organization (ILO).

Atkinson, Anthony B. and Salvatore Morelli. 2014. "Chartbook of Economic Inequality."

Atkinson, Anthony B. and Thomas Piketty, eds. 2007. *Top Incomes over the Twentieth Century*. Oxford University Press.

Aune, Dagfinn, et al. 2016. "BMI and All Cause Mortality: Systematic Review and Non-Linear Dose-Response Meta-Analysis of 230 Cohort Studies with 3.74 Million Deaths Among 30.3 Million Participants." *BMJ*, https://doi.org/10.1136/bmj.i2156.

Auten, Gerald and David Splinter. 2024. "Income Inequality in the United States: Using Tax Data to Measure Long-Term Trends." *Journal of Political Economy*, 132(7), https://doi.org/10.1086/728741.

Auten, Gerald, David Splinter, and Susan Nelson. 2016. "Reactions of High-Income Taxpayers to Major Tax Legislation." *National Tax Journal* 69, 935–64.

Autor, David, Arindrajit Dube, and Annie McGrew. 2024. "The Unexpected Compression: Competition at Work in the Low Wage Labor Market." Working Paper 31010, National Bureau of Economic Research.

Avent, Ryan. 2018. "Economists Understand Little about the Causes of Growth." *The Economist: Free Exchange*, April 14.

Ayres, Ian, Aaron Edlin, and Robert J. Shiller. 2023. "The AI Age Requires Inequality Insurance." *Project Syndicate*, December 27.

Backman, Olaf and Kenneth Nelson. 2018. "The Egalitarian Paradise?" In *Routledge Handbook of Scandinavian Politics*, edited by Peter Nedergaard and Anders Wivel, Routledge, 25–35.

Bailey, Martha and Susan Dynarski. 2011. "Gains and Gaps: A Historical Perspective on Inequality in College Entry and Completion." In *Whither Opportunity?*, edited by Greg J. Duncan and Richard J. Murnane, Russell Sage Foundation and Spencer Foundation, 117–31.

Baker, Dean. 2011. *The End of Loser Liberalism*. Center for Economic and Policy Research.

Baker, Dean. 2021. "Wealth Inequality: Should We Care?" Center for Economic and Policy Research.

Baker, Dean and Jared Bernstein. 2013. *Getting Back to Full Employment*. Center for Economic and Policy Research.
Bakija, Jon, Adam Cole, and Bradley T. Heim. 2012. "Jobs and Income Growth of Top Earners and the Causes of Changing Income Inequality: Evidence from U.S. Tax Return Data." https://users.nber.org/~confer/2010/PEf10/Bakija_Heim_Cole.pdf.
Bakija, Jon, Lane Kenworthy, Peter Lindert, and Jeff Madrick. 2016. *How Big Should Our Government Be?* University of California Press.
Balestra, Carlotta and Richard Tonkin. 2018. "Inequalities in Household Wealth Across OECD Countries: Evidence from the OECD Wealth Distribution Database." Statistics Working Paper 2018/01, OECD.
Barro, Robert J. 2008. "Inequality and Growth Revisited." Working Paper Series on Regional Economic Integration 11, Asian Development Bank.
Bartels, Larry M. 2016. *Unequal Democracy*. 2nd edition. Princeton University Press.
Bartels, Larry M. 2017. "Political Inequality in Affluent Democracies: The Social Welfare Deficit." Working Paper 5-2017, Center for the Study of Democratic Institutions, Vanderbilt University.
Barth, Erling, Henning Finseraas, and Karl Ove Moene. 2015. "Political Reinforcement: How Rising Inequality Curbs Manifested Welfare Generosity." *American Journal of Political Science* 59, 565–77.
Barth, Erling, Kalle Moene, and Axel West Pedersen. 2021. "Rising Inequality in the Egalitarian Nordics." In *Europe's Income, Wealth, Consumption, and Inequality*, edited by Georg Fischer and Robert Strauss, Oxford University Press, 218–45.
Basu, Kaushik. 2023. "To Save Democracy, Fight Inequality." *Project Syndicate*, October 26.
Baumgartner, Frank R., Jeffrey M. Berry, Marie Hojnacki, David C. Kimball, and Beth L. Leech. 2009. *Lobbying and Public Policy*. University of Chicago Press.
Beckert, Jens. 2024. "Varieties of Wealth: Toward a Comparative Sociology of Wealth Inequality." *Socio-Economic Review* 22, 475–99.
Beckfield, Jason. 2004. "Does Income Inequality Harm Health? New Cross-National Evidence." *Journal of Health and Social Behavior* 45, 231–48.
Bentham, Jeremy. 1843. *The Complete Works of Jeremy Bentham*. Vol. 10. Online Library of Liberty.
Beramendi, Pablo and Philipp Rehm. 2016. "Who Gives, Who Gains? Progressivity and Preferences." *Comparative Political Studies* 49, 529–63.
Berg, Andrew, Jonathan D. Ostry, Charalambos G. Tsangarides, and Yorbol Yakhshilikov. 2018. "Redistribution, Inequality, and Growth: New Evidence." *Journal of Economic Growth* 23, 259–305.
Bergh, Andreas and Anders Kärnä. 2022. "Explaining the Rise of Populism in European Democracies 1980-2018: The Role of Labor Market Institutions and Inequality." *Social Science Quarterly* 103, 1719–31.
Bernstein, Jared. 2013. "The Impact of Inequality on Growth." Center for American Progress.
Bernstein, Jared. 2015. *The Reconnection Agenda: Reuniting Growth and Prosperity*.
Bernstein, Jared. 2019. "Recent Wage Trends Are Impressive. Their Levels . . . Not So Much." *Washington Post: Post Everything*, May 8.
Bernstein, Jared and Keith Bentele. 2019. "The Increasing Benefits and Diminished Costs of Running a High-Pressure Labor Market." Center on Budget and Policy Priorities.
Bernstein, Jared, Ben Spielberg, and Keith Bentele. 2017. "The Relationship Between Tight Labor Markets and the Earnings of Low-Income Households." Yankelovich Center for Social Science Research, University of California–San Diego.
Bertrand, Marianne and Adair Morse. 2016. "Trickle-Down Consumption." *Review of Economics and Statistics* 98, 863–79.
Birnbaum, Simon, Tommy Ferrarini, Kenneth Nelson, and Joakim Palme. 2017. *The Generational Welfare Contract*. Edward Elgar.

Bischoff, Kendra and Sean F. Reardon. 2013. "Residential Segregation by Income, 1970–2009." Russell Sage Foundation.

Bishop, Bill with Robert G. Cushing. 2008. *The Big Sort: Why the Clustering of Like-Minded America Is Tearing Us Apart*. Houghton Mifflin.

Bittman, Mark and David L. Katz. 2020. *How to Eat*. Houghton Mifflin Harcourt.

Bjørnskov, Christian. 2008. "Social Trust and Fractionalization: A Possible Reinterpretation." *European Sociological Review* 24, 271–83.

Blanchard, Olivier and Dani Rodrik. 2021. "Introduction: We Have the Tools the Reverse the Rise in Inequality." In *Combating Inequality*, edited by Olivier Blanchard and Dani Rodrik, MIT Press, xi–xx.

Blanchet, Thomas, Lucas Chancel, and Amory Gethin. 2022. "Why Is Europe More Equal Than the United States?" *American Economic Journal: Applied Economics* 14, 480–518.

Blanchflower, David and Andrew J. Oswald. 2013. "Does High Homeownership Impair the Labor Market?" Working Paper 19079, National Bureau of Economic Research.

Blandhol, Christine, Magne Mogstad, Peter Nilsson, and Ola L. Vestad. 2020. "Do Employees Benefit from Worker Representation on Corporate Boards?" Working Paper 28269, National Bureau of Economic Research.

Bloome, Deirdre. 2014. "Income Inequality and Intergenerational Income Mobility in the United States." *Social Forces* 93, 1047–80.

Bloome, Deirdre, Shauna Dyer, and Xiang Zhou. 2018. "Educational Inequality, Educational Expansion, and Intergenerational Income Persistence in the United States." *American Sociological Review* 83, 1215–53.

Bloome, Deirdre and Bruce Western. 2011. "Cohort Change and Racial Differences in Educational and Income Mobility." *Social Forces* 90, 375–95.

Bok, Derek. 2010. *The Politics of Happiness*. Princeton University Press.

Bonica, Adam, Nolan McCarty, Keith T. Poole, and Howard Rosenthal. 2014. "Why Hasn't Democracy Slowed Rising Inequality?" *Journal of Economic Perspectives* 27(3), 103–24.

Booth, Michael. 2014. *The Almost Nearly Perfect People*. Jonathan Cape.

Bordo, Michael D. and Christopher M. Meissner. 2012. "Does Inequality Lead to a Financial Crisis?" Working Paper 17896, National Bureau of Economic Research.

Bosch, Gerhard and Claudia Weinkopf, eds. 2008. *Low-Wage Work in Germany*. Russell Sage Foundation.

Boshara, Ray. 2009. "Combating Poverty by Building Assets." *Pathways*, Spring, 19–23.

Boushey, Heather. 2019. *Unbound: How Inequality Constricts Our Economy and What We Can Do About It*. Harvard University Press.

Boushey, Heather and Adam S. Hersh. 2012. "The American Middle Class, Income Inequality, and the Strength of Our Economy." Center for American Progress.

Boushey, Heather and Carter C. Price. 2014. "How Are Economic Inequality and Growth Connected? A Review of Recent Research." Washington Center for Equitable Growth.

Brady, David and Ryan Finnigan. 2013. "Does Immigration Undermine Public Support for Social Policy?" *American Sociological Review* 79, 17–42.

Branham, J. Alexander, Stuart N. Soroka, and Christopher Wlezien. 2017. "When Do the Rich Win?" *Political Science Quarterly* 132, 43–62.

Brännlund, Anton and Jan Szulkin. 2023. "How Does a Growing Wealth Gap Affect Voting? Evidence from Sweden." *Electoral Studies* 85, 1–11.

Breznau, Nate and Carola Hommerich. 2019. "No Generalizable Effect of Income Inequality on Public Support for Governmental Redistribution Among Rich Democracies 1987–2010." *Social Science Research* 81, 170–91.

Breznau, Nate, Eike Mark Rinke, Alexander Wuttke, and Tomasz Zoltak. 2022. "Observing Many Researchers Using the Same Data and Hypothesis Reveals a Hidden Universe of Uncertainty." *Proceedings of the National Academy of Sciences (PNAS)*, https://doi.org/10.1073/pnas.2203150119.

Buettner, Dan. 2017. *The Blue Zones of Happiness: Lessons from the World's Happiest People*. National Geographic.
Buffett, Warren E. 2011. "Stop Coddling the Super-Rich." *New York Times*, August 14.
Burgoon, Brian and Matthijs Rooduijn. 2021. "'Immigrationization' of Welfare Politics? Anti-Immigration and Welfare Attitudes in Context." *West European Politics* 44, 177–203.
Burgoon, Brian, Sam van Noort, Matthijs Rooduijn, and Geoffrey Underhill. 2023. "Positional Deprivation and Support for Radical Right and Radical Left Parties." *Economic Policy* 34, 49–93.
Burn-Murdoch, John. 2023. "How Disadvantage Became Deadly in America." *Financial Times*, October 12.
Burstein, Paul. 2014. *American Public Opinion, Advocacy, and Policy in Congress: What the Public Wants and What It Gets*. Cambridge University Press.
Burtless, Gary and Christopher Jencks. 2003. "American Inequality and Its Consequences." In *Agenda for the Nation*, edited by Henry Aaron, Pietro S. Nivola, and James M. Lindsay, Brookings Institution Press, 61–108.
Business Roundtable. 2019. "Statement on the Purpose of a Corporation."
Calvert, Emma and Tony Fahey. 2013. "The Impact of Income Inequality on the Family." Geary Working Paper 2013-02, University College Dublin.
Cantillon, Bea, Zachary Parolin, and Diego Collado. 2020. "A Glass Ceiling on Poverty Reduction? An Empirical Investigation into the Structural Constraints on Minimum Income Protections." *Journal of European Social Policy* 30, 129–43.
Cao, Zhiyan, Guy D. Fernando, Arindam Tripathy, and Arun Upadhyay. 2018. "The Economics of Corporate Lobbying." *Journal of Corporate Finance* 49, 54–80.
Caplan, Bryan and Vipul Naik. 2015. "A Radical Case for Open Borders." In *The Economics of Immigration: Market-Based Approaches, Social Science, and Public Policy*, edited by Benjamin Powell, Oxford University Press, 180–209.
Caplan, Bryan and Zach Weinersmith. 2019. *Open Borders*. First Second.
Card, David and Alan B. Krueger. 1995. *Myth and Measurement: The New Economics of the Minimum Wage*. Princeton University Press.
Case, Anne and Angus Deaton. 2015. "Rising Morbidity and Mortality in Midlife Among White Non-Hispanic Americans in the 21st Century." *PNAS* 112, 15078–83.
Case, Anne and Angus Deaton. 2020. *Deaths of Despair and the Future of Capitalism*. Princeton University Press.
Castelló-Climent, Amparo. 2010. "Inequality and Growth in Advanced Economies: An Empirical Investigation." *Journal of Economic Inequality* 8, 293–321.
Causa, Orsetta, Nicolas Woloszko, and David Leite. 2019. "Housing, Wealth Accumulation, and Wealth Distribution: Evidence and Stylized Facts." Economics Department Working Paper 1588, OECD.
Cengiz, Doruk, Arindrajit Dube, Attila Lindner, and Ben Zipperer. 2019. "The Effect of Minimum Wages on Low-Wage Jobs." *Quarterly Journal of Economics* 134, 1405–54.
Cha, Yun and Hyunjoon Park. 2021. "Converging Educational Differences in Parents' Time Use in Developmental Child Care." *Journal of Marriage and Family* 83, 769–85.
Chancel, Lucas. 2021. "Ten Facts About Inequality in Advanced Economies." In *Combating Inequality*, edited by Olivier Blanchard and Dani Rodrik, MIT Press, 3–30.
Chancel, Lucas, Thomas Piketty, Emmanuel Saez, and Gabriel Zucman. 2022. *World Inequality Report 2022*. World Inequality Lab.
Chaudry, Ajay, Taryn Morrissey, Christina Weiland, and Hirokazu Yoshikawa. 2017. *Cradle to Kindergarten*. Russell Sage Foundation.
Cherlin, Andrew J. 2014. *Labor's Love Lost: The Rise and Fall of the Working-Class Family in America*. Russell Sage Foundation.
Cherlin, Andrew J., David C. Ribar, and Suzumi Yasutake. 2016. "Nonmarital First Births, Marriage, and Income Inequality." *American Sociological Review* 81, 749–70.

Chetty, Raj, Will S. Dobbie, Benjamin Goldman, Sonya Porter, and Crystal Yang. 2024. "Changing Opportunity: Sociological Mechanisms Underlying Growing Class Gaps and Shrinking Race Gaps in Economic Mobility." Working Paper 32697, National Bureau of Economic Research.

Chetty, Raj, David Grusky, Maximilian Hell, Nathaniel Hendren, Robert Manduca, and Jimmy Narang. 2017. "The Fading American Dream: Trends in Absolute Income Mobility Since 1940." *Science* 356, 398–406.

Chetty, Raj and Nathaniel Hendren. 2018. "The Impacts of Neighborhoods on Intergenerational Mobility I: Childhood Exposure Effects." *Quarterly Journal of Economics* 133, 1107–62.

Chetty, Raj, Nathaniel Hendren, Maggie R. Jones, and Sonya R. Porter. 2018. "Race and Economic Opportunity in the United States: An Intergenerational Perspective." Working Paper 24441, National Bureau of Economic Research.

Chetty, Raj, Nathaniel Hendren, and Lawrence F. Katz. 2016. "The Effects of Exposure to Better Neighborhoods on Children: New Evidence from the Moving to Opportunity Experiment." *American Economic Review* 106, 855–902.

Chetty, Raj, Nathaniel Hendren, Patrick Kline, Emmanuel Saez, and Nicholas Turner. 2014. "Is the United States Still a Land of Opportunity? Recent Trends in Intergenerational Mobility." *American Economic Review* 104(5), 141–47.

Chetty, Raj, Michael Stepner, Sarah Abraham, Shelby Lin, Benjamin Scuderi, Nicholas Turner, Augustin Bergeron, and David Cutler. 2016. "The Association Between Income and Life Expectancy in the United States, 2001–2014." *JAMA* 315, 1750–66.

Cho, Wendy Tam, James G. Gimpel, and Iris S. Hui. 2013. "Voter Migration and the Geographic Sorting of the American Electorate." *Annals of the Association of American Geographers* 103, 856–70.

Chozick, Amy. 2015. "Hillary Clinton Proposes Tax Credit for Businesses That Share Profits." *New York Times*, July 16.

Cingano, Federico. 2014. "Trends in Income Inequality and Its Impact on Economic Growth." OECD Social, Employment, and Migration Working Papers 163.

Clark, Andrew E., Sarah Fleche, Richard Layard, Nattavudh Powdthavee, and George Ward. 2017. "The Key Determinants of Happiness and Misery." *World Happiness Report 2017*.

Clarkwest, Andrew. 2008. "Neo-Materialist Theory and the Temporal Relationship Between Income Inequality and Longevity Change." *Social Science and Medicine* 66, 1871–81.

Clausing, Kimberly. 2019. *Open: The Progressive Case for Free Trade, Immigration, and Global Capital*. Harvard University Press.

Clemens, Michael A., Claudio E. Montenegro, and Lant Pritchett. 2008. "The Place Premium: Wage Differences for Identical Workers across the US Border." Policy Research Working Paper 4671, World Bank.

Cohen, Joshua. 2009. "Money, Politics, Political Equality." In *Philosophy, Politics, Democracy*, Harvard University Press, 268–302.

Coibion, Olivier, Yuriy Gorodnichenko, Marianna Kudlyak, and John Mondragon. 2014. "Does Greater Inequality Lead to More Household Borrowing? New Evidence from Household Data." Working Paper 19850, National Bureau of Economic Research.

Conchon, Aline, Norbert Kluge, and Michael Stollt. 2015. "Worker Board-Level Participation in the 31 European Economic Area Countries." European Trade Union Institute.

Coontz, Stephanie. 1992. *The Way We Never Were*. Basic Books.

Cooper, Kerris and Kitty Stewart. 2021. "Does Household Income Affect Children's Outcomes? A Systematic Review of the Evidence." *Child Indicators Research* 14, 981–1005.

Corak, Miles. 2016. "How the Great Gatsby Curve Got Its Name." *Economics for Public Policy*, December 4.

Corak, Miles. 2017. "'Inequality Is the Root of Social Evil,' or Maybe Not? Two Stories about Inequality and Public Policy." Discussion Paper 11005, Institute of Labor Economics (IZA).

Cowie, Jefferson. 2016. *The Great Exception: The New Deal and the Limits of American Politics.* Princeton University Press.

Cramer, Reid and David Newville. 2009. "Children's Savings Accounts." New America Foundation.

Curran, Michaela and Matthew C. Mahutga. 2018. "Income Inequality and Population Health: A Global Gradient?" *Journal of Health and Social Behavior* 59, 536–53.

Currie, Janet. 2024. "Health and Inequality." Dimensions of Inequality: The IFS Deaton Review. *Oxford Open Economics* 3, i549–i556.

Cutler, David M. and Edward L. Glaeser. 2021. "When Innovation Goes Wrong: Technological Regress and the Opioid Epidemic." Working Paper 28873, National Bureau of Economic Research.

Cynamon, Barry Z. and Steven M. Fazzari. 2014. "Inequality, the Great Recession, and Slow Recovery."

Dahl, Robert A. 1989. *Democracy and Its Critics.* Yale University Press.

Dahl, Robert A. 2006. *On Political Equality.* Yale University Press.

Dal Bo, Ernesto, Frederico Finan, Olle Folke, Torsten Persson, and Johanna Rickne. 2019. "Economic Losers and Political Winners: Sweden's Radical Right."

Daly, Martin. 2016. *Killing the Competition: Economic Inequality and Homicide.* Routledge.

Daly, Mary C. and Daniel C. Wilson. 2013. "Inequality and Mortality: New Evidence from U.S. County Panel Data." Working Paper 2013-13, Federal Reserve Bank of San Francisco.

Danielson, Taylor. 2016. "Migration, Nationalism, and the Welfare State." PhD dissertation, University of Arizona, Department of Sociology.

Dao, Maria Carlota, Sophie Thiron, Ellen Messer, et al. 2021. "Cultural Influences on the Regulation of Energy Intake and Obesity: A Qualitative Study Comparing Food Customs and Attitudes to Eating in Adults from France and the United States." *Nutrients,* https://doi.org/10.3390/nu13010063.

Davis, Jonathan and Bhashkar Mazumder. 2017. "The Decline in Intergenerational Mobility After 1980." Working Paper 2017-05, Federal Reserve Bank of Chicago.

Deaton, Angus. 2003. "Health, Inequality, and Economic Development." *Journal of Economic Literature* 41, 113–58.

Deaton, Angus. 2013. *The Great Escape.* Princeton University Press.

Delhey, Jan and Georgi Dragolov. 2013. "Why Inequality Makes Europeans Less Happy: The Role of Distrust, Status Anxiety, and Perceived Conflict." *European Sociological Review* 30, 151–65.

Demsas, Jerusalem. 2022. "The Homeownership Society Was a Mistake." *The Atlantic,* December 20.

Derrible, Sybil. 2025. *The Infrastructure Book.* Prometheus.

Diamantopoulou, Anna, Agnieszka Chłoń-Domińczak, Bernhard Ebbinghaus, et al. 2023. *The Future of Social Protection and of the Welfare State.* European Commission, Social Protection Unit.

Diener, Ed, Richard E. Lucas, Ulrich Schimmack, and John F. Helliwell. 2009. *Well-Being for Public Policy.* Oxford University Press.

DiPrete, Thomas A. 2020. "The Impact of Inequality on Intergenerational Mobility." *Annual Review of Sociology* 46, 379–98.

DiPrete, Thomas A., Gregory M. Eirich, and Matthew Pittinsky. 2010. "Compensation Benchmarking, Leapfrogs, and the Surge in Executive Pay." *American Journal of Sociology* 115, 1671–712.

Dobbs, Richard, Corinne Sawers, Fraser Thompson, James Manyika, Jonathan Woetzel, Peter Child, Sorcha McKenna, and Angela Spatharou. 2014. "Overcoming Obesity: An Initial Economic Analysis." McKinsey Global Institute.

Dollar, David, Tatjana Kleineberg, and Aart Kraay. 2016. "Growth Still Is Good for the Poor." *European Economic Review* 81, 68–85.

Dorn, David and Peter Levell. 2024. "Trade and Inequality in Europe and the US." Dimensions of Inequality: The IFS Deaton Review. *Oxford Open Economics* 3, i1042–i1068.
Dreier, Peter and Michael Kazin. 2023. "How Socialists Changed America." In *We Own the Future: Democratic Socialism—American Style*, edited by Kate Aronoff, Peter Dreier, and Michael Kazin, New Press, 15–45.
Drum, Kevin. 2024. "Stress in America: A Deeper Look." *Jabberwocking*, August 28.
Drutman, Lee. 2015. *The Business of America Is Lobbying*. Oxford University Press.
Dube, Arindrajit. 2019. "Using Wage Boards to Raise Pay." Research Brief, Economists for Inclusive Prosperity.
Dube, Arindrajit, T. William Lester, and Michael Reich. 2010. "Minimum Wage Effects Across State Borders: Estimates Using Contiguous Counties." *Review of Economics and Statistics* 92, 945–64.
Dube, Arindrajit and Ben Zipperer. 2024. "Own-Wage Elasticity: Quantifying the Impact of Minimum Wages on Employment." Working Paper 32925, National Bureau of Economic Research.
Duncan, Greg J., Kathleen M. Ziol-Guest, and Ariel Kalil. 2010. "Early-Childhood Poverty and Adult Attainment, Behavior, and Health." *Child Development* 81, 306–25.
Durlauf, Steven N., Andros Kourtellos, and Chih Ming Tan. 2021. "The Great Gatsby Curve." Working Paper 43, Stone Center on Socio-Economic Inequality.
Dyck, Joshua J. and Shanna Pearson-Merkowitz. 2023. *The Power of Partisanship*. Oxford University Press.
Dynan, Karen E. and Donald L. Kohn. 2007. "The Rise in U.S. Household Indebtedness: Causes and Consequences." In *The Structure and Resilience of the Financial System*, edited by Christopher Kent and Jeremy Lawson, Reserve Bank of Australia, 84–122.
Easterlin, Richard A. 2021. *An Economist's Lessons on Happiness*. Springer.
Easterly, William. 2009. "Can the West Save Africa?" *Journal of Economic Literature* 47, 373–447.
Economic Mobility Project. 2012. "Pursuing the American Dream: Economic Mobility Across Generations." Pew Charitable Trusts.
The Economist. 2013. "Special Report: The Nordic Countries." February 2.
Edin, Kathryn and Maria J. Kefalas. 2005. *Promises I Can Keep: Why Poor Women Put Motherhood Before Marriage*. University of California Press.
Eick, Gianna Maria. 2024. *Welfare Chauvinism in Europe*. Edward Elgar.
Elliott, William and Melinda Lewis. 2018. *Making Education Work for the Poor: The Potential of Children's Savings Accounts*. Oxford University Press.
Elsasser, Lea, Svenja Hense, and Armin Schafer. 2021. "Not Just Money: Unequal Responsiveness in Egalitarian Democracies." *Journal of European Public Policy* 28, 1890–1908.
El-Shagi, Makram and Liang Shao. 2017. "The Impact of Inequality and Redistribution on Growth." *Review of Income and Wealth* 65, 239–63.
Engler, Sarah and David Weisstanner. 2021. "The Threat of Social Decline: Income Inequality and Radical Right Support." *Journal of European Public Policy* 28(2), 153–73.
Esping-Andersen, Gøsta. 2008. *The Incomplete Revolution*. Polity.
Esping-Andersen, Gøsta and John Myles. 2009. "Economic Inequality and the Welfare State." In *The Oxford Handbook of Economic Inequality*, edited by Wiemer Salverda, Brian Nolan, and Timothy M. Smeeding, Oxford University Press, 639–64.
Evers-Hillstrom, Karl. 2020. "Majority of Lawmakers in 116th Congress Are Millionaires." Center for Responsive Politics.
Fairbrother, Malcolm and Isaac W. Martin. 2013. "Does Inequality Erode Social Trust? Results from Multilevel Models of US States and Counties." *Social Science Research* 42, 347–60.
Feldmeyer, Ben, Francis T. Cullen, Diana Sun, Teresa C. Kulig, Cecilia Chouhy, and Michael Zidar. 2022. "The Community Determinants of Death: Comparing the Macro-Level Predictors of Overdose, Homicide, and Suicide Deaths, 2000 to 2015." *Socius* 8, 1–24.

Ferrer-i-carbonell, Ada and Xavier Ramos. 2014. "Inequality and Happiness." *Journal of Economic Surveys* 28, 1016–27.
Finseraas, Henning. 2009. "Income Inequality and Demand for Redistribution: A Multilevel Analysis of European Public Opinion." *Scandinavian Political Studies* 32, 94–119.
Fioroni, Sarah and Dan Foy. 2024. "Americans Sleeping Less, More Stressed." Gallup, April 15.
Firebaugh, Glenn. 2008. *Seven Rules for Social Research*. Princeton University Press.
Firebaugh, Glenn and Laura Tach. 2012. "Income, Age, and Happiness in America." In *Social Trends in American Life*, edited by Peter V. Marsden. Princeton University Press, 267–87.
Fisher, Max and Emma Bubola. 2020. "As Coronavirus Deepens Inequality, Inequality Worsens Its Spread." *New York Times*, March 20.
Flaherty, Eoin. 2015. "Top Incomes Under Finance-Driven Capitalism, 1990–2010: Power Resources and Regulatory Orders." *Socio-Economic Review* 13, 417–47.
Fligstein, Neil and Adam Goldstein. 2015. "The Emergence of a Finance Culture in American Households, 1989–2007: Some Preliminary Evidence." *Socio-Economic Review* 13, 575–601.
Fligstein, Neil, Orestes P. Hastings, and Adam Goldstein. 2017. "Keeping Up with the Joneses: How Households Fared in the Era of High Income Inequality and the Housing Price Bubble, 1999–2007." *Socius* 3, 1–15.
Flood, Sarah, Joel McCurry, Aaron Sojourner, and Matthew Wiswall. 2022. "Inequality in Early Care Experienced by US Children." *Journal of Economic Perspectives* 36(2), 199–222.
Follett, Chelsea and Vincent Geloso. 2023. "Global Inequality in Well-Being Has Decreased Across Many Dimensions: Introducing the Inequality of Human Progress Index." Policy Analysis 949, Cato Institute.
Forcillo, Donato. 2017. "Codetermination: The Presence of Workers on the Board." University of Cagliari and Sassari.
Förster, Michael, Ana Llena-Nozal, and Vahé Nafilyan. 2014. "Trends in Top Incomes and Their Taxation in OECD Countries." OECD Social, Employment, and Migration Working Paper 159.
Fox, Justin. 2018. "Why German Corporate Boards Include Workers." *Bloomberg Opinion*, August 24.
Frank, Robert H. 2005. "Positional Externalities Cause Large and Preventable Welfare Losses." *American Economic Review* 95, 137–41.
Frank, Robert H. 2007. *Falling Behind: How Rising Inequality Harms the Middle Class*. University of California Press.
Frank, Robert H. 2016. *Success and Luck: Good Fortune and the Myth of Meritocracy*. Princeton University Press.
Frank, Robert H. and Philip J. Cook. 1995. *The Winner-Take-All Society*. Penguin.
Frank, Robert H., Adam Seth Levine, and Oege Dijk. 2013. "Expenditure Cascades." *Review of Behavioral Economics* 1, 55–73.
Frankfurt, Harry G. 2015. *On Inequality*. Princeton University Press.
Freeland, Chrystia. 2012. *Plutocrats: The Rise of the New Global Super-Rich and the Fall of Everyone Else*. Penguin.
Freeman, Richard B. 1996. "Why Do So Many Young American Men Commit Crimes and What Might We Do About It?" *Journal of Economic Perspectives* 10(1), 25–42.
Fry, Richard and Paul Taylor. 2012. "The Rise of Residential Segregation by Income." Pew Research Center.
Frydman, Carola and Raven S. Molloy. 2011. "Does Tax Policy Affect Executive Compensation? Evidence from Postwar Tax Reforms." *Journal of Public Economics* 95, 1425–37.
Furman, Jason. 2024. "Globalization with Minimal Apologies." Opening Lecture, World Trade Organization Public Forum.
Ganzeboom, Harry B. G., Ruud Luijkx, and Donald J. Treiman. 1989. "Intergenerational Class Mobility in Comparative Perspective." *Research in Social Stratification and Mobility* 8, 3–84.

Garfinkel, Irwin, Lee Rainwater, and Timothy Smeeding. 2010. *Wealth and Welfare States*. Oxford University Press.

Gautié, Jerome and John Schmitt, eds. 2010. *Low-Wage Work in the Wealthy World*. Russell Sage Foundation.

Gilens, Martin. 2012. *Affluence and Influence*. Princeton University Press.

Gladwell, Malcolm. 2008. *Outliers: The Story of Success*. Little, Brown.

Glaeser, Edward. 2010. "Does Economic Inequality Cause Crises?" *New York Times: Economix*, December 14.

Global Burden of Disease (GBD) 2015 Obesity Collaborators. 2017. "Health Effects of Overweight and Obesity in 195 Countries over 25 Years." *New England Journal of Medicine* 377, 13–27.

Goldin, Claudia and Lawrence Katz. 2008. *The Race Between Education and Technology*. Harvard University Press.

Goldstein, Adam. 2012. "Income, Consumption, and Household Indebtedness in the U.S., 1989–2007." Paper presented at the Annual Meeting of the American Sociological Association, Denver.

Gordon, Robert G. 2016. *The Rise and Fall of American Growth*. Princeton University Press.

Hacker, Jacob S. 2006. *The Great Risk Shift*. Oxford University Press.

Hacker, Jacob S. and Paul Pierson. 2010. *Winner-Take-All Politics*. Simon and Schuster.

Hacker, Jacob S. and Paul Pierson. 2020. *Let Them Eat Tweets: How the Right Rules in an Age of Extreme Inequality*. Liveright.

Hajdu, Gábor. 2021. "Perceived Income Inequality and Subjective Social Status in Europe." Discussion Paper 926, Global Labor Organization.

Hanushek, Eric A., Paul E. Peterson, Laura M. Talpey, and Ludger Woessmann. 2019. "The Achievement Gap Fails to Close." *Education Next* 19(3), 8–17.

Harding, David, Christopher Jencks, Leonard Lopoo, and Susan Mayer. 2009. "The Changing Effect of Family Background on the Incomes of American Adults." In *Unequal Chances: Family Background and Economic Success*, edited by Samuel Bowles, Herbert Gintis, and Melissa Osborne Groves, Russell Sage Foundation and Princeton University Press, 100–144.

Haroon, Hiba and Shaun Harrison. 2024. "U.S. Economic Mobility Trends and Outcomes: A Research Update." Washington Center for Equitable Growth.

Harris, Douglas N., Bradley Birzer, Carol Graham, Mona Hanna, Frederick M. Hess, Gary Hoover, Ariel Kalil, Anna Lembke, Joseph Romm, Patrick Sharkey, Heidi Shierholz, Kiron Skinner, Michael Strain, Scott Winship, Anjana Nair, and Emilia Nordgren. 2025. *The State of the Nation: 2025 Report*. State of the Nation Project, Tulane University.

Hastings, Orestes P. 2018. "Less Equal, Less Trusting? Longitudinal and Cross-Sectional Effects of Income Inequality on Trust in U.S. States, 1973–2012." *Social Science Research* 74, 77–95.

Hauser, Robert M., John Robert Warren, Min-Hsiung Huang, and Wendy Y. Carter. 2000. "Occupational Status, Education, and Social Mobility in the Meritocracy." In *Meritocracy and Economic Inequality*, edited by Kenneth Arrow, Samuel Bowles, and Steven Durlauf, Princeton University Press, 179–229.

Hayes, Christopher. 2012. *Twilight of the Elites: America After Meritocracy*. Crown.

Heckman, James J. 2008. "Schools, Skills, and Synapses." Working Paper 14064, National Bureau of Economic Research.

Helliwell, John F., Haifang Huang, Shun Wang, and Max Norton. 2020. "Social Environments for World Happiness." In *World Happiness Report 2020*.

Helliwell, John F., Richard Layard, Jeffrey Sachs. 2017. "Social Foundations of World Happiness." In *World Happiness Report 2017*.

Hemel, Daniel and Rebecca Kysar. 2019. "The Big Problem with Wealth Taxes." *New York Times*, November 7.

Hemerijck, Anton. 2013. *Changing Welfare States*. Oxford University Press.

Hemerijck, Anton, ed. 2017. *The Uses of Social Investment*. Oxford University Press.

Hertz, Tom. 2007. "Trends in the Intergenerational Elasticity of Family Income in the United States." *Industrial Relations* 46, 22–50.

Herzer, Dierk and Sebastian Vollmer. 2012. "Inequality and Growth: Evidence from Panel Cointegration." *Journal of Economic Inequality* 10, 489–503.

Hicks, Alexander. 1999. *Social Democracy and Welfare Capitalism*. Cornell University Press.

Hills, John, Tom Sefton, and Kitty Stewart, eds. 2009. *Towards a More Equal Society? Poverty, Inequality, and Policy Since 1997*. Policy Press.

Hogstrom, Gabriel, Anna Nordstrom, and Peter Nordstrom. 2015. "Aerobic Fitness in Late Adolescence and the Risk of Early Death: A Prospective Cohort Study of 1.3 Million Swedish Men." *International Journal of Epidemiology* 45, 1159–68.

Holmberg, Susan R. 2017. "Fighting Short-Termism with Worker Power." Roosevelt Institute.

Horowitz, Juliana Menasce, Ruth Igielnik, and Rakesh Kochhar. 2020. "Most Americans Say There Is Too Much Economic Inequality in the U.S., but Fewer Than Half Call It a Top Priority." Pew Research Center, January 9.

Hout, Mike. 2018. "Occupational Change in a Generation in the United States, 1994–2016." Population Center, New York University.

Huber, Evelyne, Jingling Huo, and John D. Stephens. 2015. "Power, Markets, and Top Income Shares." Working Paper 404, Kellogg Institute for International Studies, University of Notre Dame.

Huber, Evelyn and John D. Stephens. 2001. *Development and Crisis of the Welfare State*. University of Chicago Press.

Huber, Evelyn and John D. Stephens. 2024. *Challenging Inequality*. University of Chicago Press.

Inglehart, Ronald F. 2018. *Cultural Modernization*. Cambridge University Press.

IPPR Commission on Economic Justice. 2018. *Prosperity and Justice: A Plan for the New Economy*. Polity Press.

Iyengar, Shanto and Sean J. Westwood. 2015. "Fear and Loathing Across Party Lines: New Evidence on Group Polarization." *American Journal of Political Science* 59, 690–707.

Jacob, Brian and Jens Ludwig. 2008. "Improving Educational Outcomes for Poor Children." Working Paper 14550, National Bureau of Economic Research.

Jacobs, Elisabeth and Liz Hipple. 2018. "Are Today's Inequalities Limiting Tomorrow's Opportunities?" Washington Center for Equitable Growth.

Jacobs, Lawrence, Ben Barber, Larry Bartels, et al. 2004. "American Democracy in an Age of Rising Inequality." Report of the American Political Science Association Task Force on Inequality and American Democracy. *Perspectives on Politics* 2, 651–66.

Jäger, Simon, Benjamin Schoefer, and Jorg Heining. 2020. "Labor in the Board Room." NBER Conference Paper.

Jäntti, Markus and Stephen P. Jenkins. 2015. "Income Mobility." In *Handbook of Income Distribution*, edited by Anthony Atkinson, vol. 2A, Elsevier, 807–935.

Jaumotte, Florence and Carolina Osorio Buitron. 2015. "Inequality and Labor Market Institutions." Staff Discussion Note 15/14, International Monetary Fund.

Jencks, Christopher. 2002. "Does Inequality Matter?" *Daedalus*, Winter, 49–65.

Jencks, Christopher. 2009. "The Graduation Gap." *American Prospect*, October 22.

Jencks, Christopher and Susan Mayer. 1990. "The Social Consequences of Growing Up in a Poor Neighborhood." In *Inner-City Poverty in the United States*, edited by Laurence Lynn and Michael McGeary, National Academy Press, 111–86.

Jensen, Carsten and Kees van Kersbergen. 2017. *The Politics of Inequality*. Palgrave Macmillan.

Jerrim, John and Lindsey Macmillan. 2015. "Income Inequality, Intergenerational Mobility, and the Great Gatsby Curve: Is Education the Key?" *Social Forces* 94, 505–33.

Jetter, Michael, Sabine Laudage, and David Stadelmann. 2019. "The Intimate Link Between Income Levels and Life Expectancy: Global Evidence from 213 Years." *Social Science Quarterly* 100, 1387–403.

Jha, Prabhat, Chinthanie Ramasundarahettige, Victoria Landsman, Brian Rostron, Michael Thun, Robert N. Anderson, Tim McAfee, and Richard Peto. 2013. "21st-Century Hazards of Smoking and Benefits of Cessation in the United States." *New England Journal of Medicine* 368, 341–50.

Judge, Ken, Jo-Ann Mulligan, and Michaela Benzeval. 1998. "Income Inequality and Population Health." *Social Science and Medicine* 46, 567–79.

Kalil, Ariel. 2015. "Inequality Begins at Home: The Role of Parenting in the Diverging Destinies of Rich and Poor Children." In *Families in an Era of Increasing Inequality*, edited by Paul R. Amato, Alan Booth, Susan M. McHale, and Jennifer Van Hook, Springer, 63–82.

Kamande, Anthony. 2024. "Governments Across the Globe Are Giving Up on the Fight Against Inequality: Here's What They Should Do Instead." *From Poverty to Power* (Duncan Green blog). October 23.

Kamande, Anthony, Jo Walker, Matthew Martin, and Max Lawson. 2024. *The Commitment to Reducing Inequality Index 2024*. Development Finance International and Oxfam.

Katsaiti, Marina Selini. 2012. "Obesity and Happiness." *Applied Economics* 44, 4101–14.

Kaushal, Neeraj, Katherine Magnuson, and Jane Waldfogel. 2011. "How Is Family Income Related to Investments in Children's Learning?" In *Whither Opportunity?*, edited by Greg J. Duncan and Richard J. Murnane, Russell Sage Foundation and Spencer Foundation, 187–205.

Kearney, Melissa S. 2023. *The Two-Parent Privilege*. University of Chicago Press.

Kearney, Melissa S. and Phillip B. Levine. 2012. "Explaining Recent Trends in the U.S. Teen Birth Rate." Working Paper 17964, National Bureau of Economic Research.

Kelley, Jonathan and M.D.R. Evans. 2017. "Societal Inequality and Individual Subjective Well-Being: Results from 68 Societies and Over 200,000 Individuals, 1981–2008." *Social Science Research* 62, 1–23.

Kelly, Gavin. 2023. "Against Inequality-Pessimism." *Medium*, December 5.

Kelly, Gavin and Daniel Tomlinson. 2017. "Putting Tech to Work: The Urgent Need for Innovation in How the Low-Wage Workforce Is Supported." Resolution Trust.

Kenworthy, Lane. 2004. *Egalitarian Capitalism*. Russell Sage Foundation.

Kenworthy, Lane. 2008a. *Jobs with Equality*. Oxford University Press.

Kenworthy, Lane. 2008b. "Types of Mobility." *Consider the Evidence*, July 4.

Kenworthy, Lane. 2011a. *Progress for the Poor*. Oxford University Press.

Kenworthy, Lane. 2011b. "Step Away from the Pool." *Newsletter of the American Political Science Association Organized Section for Qualitative and Multi-Method Research*, Fall, 26–28.

Kenworthy, Lane. 2013. "Has Rising Inequality Reduced Middle-Class Income Growth?" In *Income Inequality: Economic Disparities and the Middle Class in Affluent Countries*, edited by Janet C. Gornick and Markus Jäntti, Stanford University Press, 101–14.

Kenworthy, Lane. 2015. "Do Employment-Conditional Earnings Subsidies Work?" ImPRovE Working Paper 15-10, Herman Deleeck Centre for Social Policy, University of Antwerp.

Kenworthy, Lane. 2018. "America's Great Decoupling." In *Inequality and Inclusive Growth in Rich Countries*, edited by Brian Nolan, Oxford University Press, 333–62.

Kenworthy, Lane. 2020. *Social Democratic Capitalism*. Oxford University Press.

Kenworthy, Lane. 2025. *The Good Society*. Online at lanekenworthy.net.

Kenworthy, Lane and Leslie McCall. 2008. "Inequality, Public Opinion, and Redistribution." *Socio-Economic Review* 6, 35–68.

Kenworthy, Lane and Timothy Smeeding. 2013. "Growing Inequalities and Their Impacts in the United States." GINI Project.

Kenworthy, Lane and Timothy Smeeding. 2014. "The United States: High and Rapidly-Rising Inequality." In *Changing Inequalities and Societal Impacts in Rich Countries*, edited by Brian Nolan, Wiemer Salverda, Daniele Checchi, Ive Marx, Abigail McKnight, Istvan Gyorgy Toth, and Herman van de Werfhorst, Oxford University Press, 695–717.

Keys, Benjamin. 2024. "Climate Change Should Make You Rethink Homeownership." *New York Times*, October 29.

Kiernan, Kathleen, Sam Crossman, and Angus Phimister. 2024. "Families and Inequalities." Dimensions of Inequality: The IFS Deaton Review. *Oxford Open Economics* 3, i645–i677.

Kim, D., et al. 2008. "Is Inequality at the Heart of It? Cross-Country Associations of Income Inequality with Cardiovascular Diseases and Risk Factors." *Social Science Medicine* 66, 1719–32.

Klein, Ezra and Joe Posner. 2014. "How Wealth Inequality Is Dangerous for America." *Vox*, Episode 75.

Kondo, Naoki, Grace Sembajwe, Ichiro Kawachi, Rob M. van Dam, S. V. Subramanian, and Zentaro Yamagata. 2009. "Income Inequality, Mortality, and Self-Rated Health: Meta-Analysis of Multilevel Studies." *BMJ*, https://doi.org/10.1136/bmj.b4471.

Kornrich, Sabino. 2016. "Inequalities in Parental Spending on Young Children." *AERA Open* 2(2), https://doi.org/10.1177/2332858416644180.

Kristal, Tali. 2017. "What Can Unions Do? An Impact Estimate for an Increase in the Private-Sector Unionization Rate on Workers' Earnings." Yankelovich Center for Social Science Research, University of California–San Diego.

Krugman, Paul. 1992. "The Rich, the Right, and the Facts: Deconstructing the Income Distribution Debate." *American Prospect*, Fall, 19–31.

Krugman, Paul. 1994. *Peddling Prosperity*. W.W. Norton.

Krugman, Paul. 2007. *The Conscience of a Liberal*. W.W. Norton.

Krugman, Paul. 2011. "Oligarchy, American Style." *New York Times*, November 3.

Krugman, Paul. 2013. "The New Growth Fizzle." *New York Times*, April 18.

Krugman, Paul. 2021. "Globalization: An Ambiguous Good." *Econofact Chats*, February 21.

Kruse, Douglas, Richard Freeman, and Joseph Blasi. 2008. "Do Workers Gain by Sharing? Employee Outcomes Under Employee Ownership, Profit Sharing, and Broad-Based Stock Options." Working Paper 14233, National Bureau of Economic Research.

Kumhof, Michael, Romain Ranciere, and Pablo Winant. 2015. "Inequality, Leverage, and Crises." *American Economic Review* 105, 1217–45.

Kuo, Chun-Tung and Ichiro Kawachi. 2023. "County-Level Income Inequality, Social Mobility, and Deaths of Despair in the US, 2000–2019." *JAMA Network Open* 6, 1–12.

Lăcătus, Cristina-Mihaela, Elena-Daniela Grigorescu, Mariana Floria, Alina Onofriescu, and Bogdan-Mircea Miha. 2019. "The Mediterranean Diet: From an Environment-Driven Food Culture to an Emerging Medical Prescription." *International Journal of Environmental Research and Public Health*, https://doi.org/10.3390/ijerph16060942.

Lancee, Bram and Herman G. Van de Werfhorst. 2012. "Income Inequality and Participation: A Comparison of 24 European Countries." *Social Science Research* 41, 1166–78.

Lareau, Annette. 2003. *Unequal Childhoods*. University of California Press.

Larsen, Christian Albrekt. 2013. *The Rise and Fall of Social Cohesion*. Oxford University Press.

Layard, Richard. 2005. *Happiness*. Penguin.

Layard, Richard, Andrew Clark, and Claudia Senik. 2012. "The Causes of Happiness and Misery." In *World Happiness Report*, edited by John Helliwell, Richard Layard, and Jeffrey Sachs, Earth Institute, Columbia University.

Layard, Richard and Jan-Emmanuel De Neve. 2023. *Wellbeing: Science and Policy*. Cambridge University Press.

Layard, Richard, Guy Mayraz, and Stephen Nickell. 2009. "Does Relative Income Matter? Are the Critics Right?" Discussion Paper 918, Centre for Economic Performance.

Layte, Richard and Christopher T. Whelan. 2014. "Who Feels Inferior? A Test of the Status Anxiety Hypothesis of Social Inequalities in Health." *European Sociological Review* 30, 525–35.

Lazonick, William. 2014. "Profits Without Prosperity." *Harvard Business Review*, September.

Lee, Chul-In and Gary Solon. 2009. "Trends in Intergenerational Income Mobility." *Review of Economics and Statistics* 91, 766–72.

Lee, Ronald, et al. 2015. *The Growing Gap in Life Expectancy by Income*. National Academies Press.
Leicht, Kevin T. and Scott T. Fitzgerald. 2007. *Postindustrial Peasants*. Worth.
Leigh, Andrew and Christopher Jencks. 2007. "Inequality and Mortality: Long-Run Evidence from a Panel of Countries." *Journal of Health Economics*, https://doi.org/10.1016/j.jhealeco.2006.07.003.
Leigh, Andrew, Christopher Jencks, and Timothy M. Smeeding. 2009. "Health and Economic Inequality." In *The Oxford Handbook of Economic Inequality*, edited by Wiemer Salverda, Brian Nolan, and Timothy M. Smeeding, Oxford University Press, 384–405.
Leipziger, Lasse, Svend-Erik Skaaning, and Matilde Thorsen. 2023. "Does Economic Inequality Harm Democratic Quality? No, but Yes." In *No Normal Science! Festschrift for Kees van Kersbergen*, edited by Christoffer Green-Pedersen, Carsten Jensen, and Barbara Vis, Politica, 187–201.
Leonhardt, David. 2023. *Ours Was the Shining Future: The Story of the American Dream*. Random House.
Lewis, Michael. 1989. *Liar's Poker*. W.W. Norton.
Lieberson, Stanley. 1985. *Making It Count*. University of California Press.
Lindbeck, Assar. 1986. "Limits to the Welfare State." *Challenge*, January–February, 31–36.
Lindert, Peter H. and Jeffrey G. Williamson. 2016. *Unequal Gains: American Growth and Inequality Since 1700*. Princeton University Press.
Lindh, Arvid and Leslie McCall. 2023. "Bringing the Market In: An Expanded Framework for Understanding Popular Responses to Economic Inequality." *Socio-Economic Review* 21, 1035–55.
Lohmann, Henning and Ive Marx, eds. 2018. *Handbook on In-Work Poverty*. Edward Elgar.
Lowrey, Annie. 2014. "Income Gap, Meet the Longevity Gap." *New York Times*, May 15.
Lukk, Martin. 2024. "Politics of Boundary Consolidation: Income Inequality, Ethnonationalism, and Radical-Right Voting." *Socius* 10, 1–20.
Lundberg, Olle, Monica Åberg Yngwe, Maria Kölegård Stjärne, Jon Ivar Elstad, Tommy Ferrarini, Olli Kangas, Thor Norström, Joakim Palme, and Johan Fritzell. 2008. "The Role of Welfare State Principles and Generosity in Social Policy Programmes for Public Health: An International Comparative Study." *The Lancet* 372, 1633–40.
Lupu, Noam and Alejandro Tirado Castro. 2023. "Unequal Policy Responsiveness in Spain." *Socio-Economic Review* 21, 1697–720.
Lupu, Noam and Jonas Pontusson. 2024. "The Political Puzzle of Rising Inequality." In *Unequal Democracies: Public Policy, Responsiveness, and Redistribution in an Era of Rising Economic Inequality*, edited by Noam Lupu and Jonas Pontusson, Cambridge University Press, 1–25.
Lynch, John, George Davey Smith, Sam Harper, Marianne Hillemeier, Nancy Ross, George A. Kaplan, and Michael Wolfson. 2004. "Is Income Inequality a Determinant of Population Health? Part 1. A Systematic Review." *Milbank Quarterly* 82, 5–99.
Mackenbach, Johan P. 2016. "Changes in Mortality Inequalities Over Two Decades: Register Based Study of European Countries." *BMJ*, https://doi.org/10.1136/bmj.i1732.
Madland, David. 2018. "Wage Boards for American Workers." Center for American Progress.
Malleson, Tom. 2023. *Against Inequality: The Practical and Ethical Case for Abolishing the Superrich*. Oxford University Press.
Manning, Alan and Barbara Petrongolo. 2024. "Monopsony in Local Labour Markets." Dimensions of Inequality: The IFS Deaton Review. *Oxford Open Economics* 3, i951–i958.
Maralani, Vida and Douglas McKee. 2015. "Obesity Is in the Eye of the Beholder: BMI and Socioeconomic Outcomes Across Cohorts." *Sociological Science*, https://doi.org/10.15195/v4.a13.
Marchal, Sarah and Ive Marx. 2024. *Zero Poverty Society: Ensuring a Decent Income for All*. Oxford University Press.

Markey, Raymond, Nicola Balnave, and Greg Patmore. 2010. "Worker Directors and Worker Ownership/ Cooperatives." In *Oxford Handbook of Participation in Organizations*, edited by Adrian Wilkinson, Paul J. Gollan, Mick Marchington, and David Lewin, Oxford University Press, 237–57.

Marmot, Michael. 2004. *Status Syndrome: How Your Social Standing Directly Affects Your Health*. Bloomsbury.

Marmot, Michael, Tony Atkinson, John Bell, et al. 2010. *Fair Society, Healthy Lives: The Marmot Review*. Strategic Review of Health Inequalities in England Post-2010. https://www.parliament.uk/globalassets/documents/fair-society-healthy-lives-full-report.pdf.

Marr, Chuck, Krista Ruffini, and Chye-Ching Huang. 2013. "Strengthening the EITC for Childless Workers Would Promote Work and Reduce Poverty." Center on Budget and Policy Priorities.

Martinsson, Johan, Ulrika Andersson, and Annika Bergström, eds. 2018. "Swedish Trends, 1986–2017." SOM Institute, University of Gothenburg.

Mason, Lilliana. 2018. *Uncivil Agreement: How Politics Became Our Identity*. University of Chicago Press.

Mathisen, Ruben B. 2022. "Affluence and Influence in a Social Democracy." *American Political Science Review* 117, 751–58.

Mayer, Susan E. 1999. *What Money Can't Buy*. Harvard University Press.

McCall, Leslie. 2013. *The Undeserving Rich*. Cambridge University Press.

McCall, Leslie and Lane Kenworthy. 2009. "Americans' Social Policy Preferences in the Era of Rising Inequality." *Perspectives on Politics* 7, 459–84.

McCarty, Nolan, Keith T. Poole, and Howard Rosenthal. 2008. *Polarized America*. MIT Press.

McLanahan, Sara and Christopher Jencks. 2015. "Was Moynihan Right? What Happens to Children of Unmarried Mothers?" *Education Next*, March 22.

McLanahan, Sara, Laura Tach, and Daniel Schneider. 2013. "The Causal Effects of Father Absence." *Annual Review of Sociology* 39, 399–427.

Meltzer, Allan H. and Scott F. Richard. 1981. "A Rational Theory of the Size of Government." *Journal of Political Economy* 89, 914–27.

Merton, Robert K. 1968. *Social Theory and Social Structure*. Free Press.

Mian, Atif and Amir Sufi. 2014. *House of Debt*. University of Chicago Press.

Mijs, Jonathan J.B. 2021. "The Paradox of Inequality: Income Inequality and Belief in Meritocracy Go Hand in Hand." *Socio-Economic Review* 19, 7–35.

Milanovic, Branko. 2009. "Income Inequality and Speculative Investment by the Rich and Poor Led to the Financial Meltdown." *Yale Global Online*, May 4.

Milanovic, Branko. 2011. *The Haves and the Have-Nots*. Basic Books.

Milanovic, Branko. 2016. *Global Inequality*. Harvard University Press.

Milanovic, Branko. 2022. "The Three Eras of Global Inequality, 1820–2020." Working Paper 59, Stone Center on Socio-Economic Inequality.

Milanovic, Branko. 2023. "The Great Convergence." *Foreign Affairs*, July–August, 78–91.

Miller, Lisa. 2012. "The Money-Empathy Gap." *New York Magazine*, July 1.

Mishel, Lawrence, Josh Bivens, Elise Gould, and Heidi Shierholz. 2012. *The State of Working America*. 12th edition. Economic Policy Institute.

Moffitt, Robert and John Karl Scholz. 2009. "Trends in the Level and Distribution of Income Support." Working Paper 15488, National Bureau of Economic Research.

Morelli, Salvatore and Anthony Atkinson. 2015. "Inequality and Crises Revisited." *Economia Politica* 32, 31–51.

Moyn, Samuel. 2018. "Human Rights in the Neoliberal Maelstrom." Human Rights Lecture, Duke Human Rights Center, Duke University, September 6.

Mullahy, John, Stephanie Robert, and Barbara Wolfe. 2004. "Health, Income, and Inequality." In *Social Inequality*, edited by Kathryn M. Neckerman, Russell Sage Foundation, 523–44.

Murphy, Kevin J. 2013. "Executive Compensation: Where We Are, and How We Got There." In *Handbook of the Economics of Finance*, vol. 2A, Elsevier, 211–356.

Murray, Charles. 2012. *Coming Apart: The State of White America, 1960–2010*. Crown Forum.
National Academies of Sciences, Engineering, and Medicine. 2023. *Reducing Intergenerational Poverty*. National Academies Press.
National Research Council and Institute of Medicine. 2013. *U.S. Health in International Perspective: Shorter Lives, Poorer Health*. National Academies Press.
Newman, Katherine S. and Elisabeth S. Jacobs. 2023. *Moving the Needle: What Tight Labor Markets Do for the Poor*. University of California Press.
Nichols, Austin and Jesse Rothstein. 2016. "The Earned Income Tax Credit." In *Economics of Means-Tested Transfer Programs in the United States*, vol. 1, edited by Robert A. Moffitt, University of Chicago Press, 137–218.
Norris, Pippa and Ronald Inglehart. 2019. *Cultural Backlash*. Cambridge University Press.
Nussbaum, Martha C. 2011. *Creating Capabilities*. Harvard University Press.
O'Connor, Kelsey J. 2017. "Happiness and Welfare State Policy Around the World." *Review of Behavioral Economics* 4, 397–420.
OECD (Organization for Economic Cooperation and Development). 2006. *Starting Strong II: Early Childhood Education and Care*. OECD Publishing.
OECD. 2015. *In It Together: Why Less Inequality Benefits All*. OECD Publishing.
OECD. 2019a. *Negotiating Our Way Up: Collective Bargaining in a Changing World of Work*. OECD Publishing.
OECD. 2018. "The Role and Design of Net Wealth Taxes in the OECD."
OECD. 2019. *The Heavy Burden of Obesity*. OECD Publishing.
OECD. 2021. *Does Inequality Matter? How People Perceive Economic Disparities and Social Mobility*. OECD Publishing.
Ogden, Kate and David Phillips. 2024. "The Distribution of Public Service Spending." Dimensions of Inequality: The IFS Deaton Review. *Oxford Open Economics* 3, i1209–i1261.
Okun, Arthur M. 1975. *Equality and Efficiency: The Big Tradeoff*. Brookings Institution Press.
Olshansky, S. Jay, et al. 2012. "Differences in Life Expectancy Due to Race and Educational Differences Are Widening, and Many May Not Catch Up." *Health Affairs* 8, 1803–13.
Osberg, Lars and Timothy M. Smeeding. 2006. "'Fair' Inequality? Attitudes Toward Pay Differentials: The United States in Comparative Perspective." *American Sociological Review* 71, 450–73.
Ostry, Jonathan D., Andrew Berg, and Charalambos G. Tsangarides. 2014. "Redistribution, Inequality, and Growth." International Monetary Fund.
Our World in Data. 2024. "Excess Mortality: Cumulative Deaths from All Causes Compared to Projection Based on Previous Years, Per Million People." https://ourworldindata.org/grapher/cumulative-excess-deaths-per-million-covid?time=2023-12-31.
Owens, Ann, Sean Reardon, and Christopher Jencks. 2016. "Income Segregation Between Schools and School Districts." *American Educational Research Journal* 53, 1159–97.
Oxfam. 2023. "Survival of the Richest: How We Must Tax the Super-Rich Now to Fight Inequality."
Packer, George. 2011. "The Broken Contract: Inequality and American Decline." *Foreign Affairs*, November–December, 20–31.
Page, Benjamin I., Larry M. Bartels, and Jason Seawright. 2013. "Democracy and the Policy Preferences of Wealthy Americans." *Perspectives on Politics* 11, 51–73.
Page, Benjamin and Martin Gilens. 2017. *Democracy in America? What Has Gone Wrong and What We Can Do About It*. University of Chicago Press.
Page, Benjamin I., Jason Seawright, and Matthew J. Lacombe. 2019. *Billionaires and Stealth Politics*. University of Chicago Press.
Palier, Bruno, ed. 2010. *A Long Goodbye to Bismarck? The Politics of Welfare Reform in Continental Europe*. University of Chicago Press.
Palley, Thomas I. 2015. "Inequality, the Financial Crisis, and Stagnation: Competing Stories and Why They Matter." Working Paper 151, Macroeconomic Policy Institute.
Partanen, Anu. 2016. *The Nordic Theory of Everything*. Harper.

Paskov, Marii, Klarita Gërxhani, Herman G. van de Werfhorst. 2013. "Income Inequality and Status Anxiety." Discussion Paper 90, GINI Project.
Pastor, Manuel. 2018. *State of Resistance: What California's Dizzying Descent and Remarkable Resurgence Mean for America's Future*. New Press.
Paulus, Alari, Holly Sutherland, and Panos Tsakloglou. 2010. "The Distributional Impact of In-Kind Public Benefits in European Countries." *Journal of Policy Analysis and Management* 29, 243–66.
Payne, Keith. 2017. *The Broken Ladder: How Inequality Affects the Way We Think, Live, and Die*. Penguin.
Pazzona, Matteo. 2024. "Revisiting the Income Inequality-Crime Puzzle." *World Development*, https://doi.org/10.1016/j.worlddev.2023.106520.
Perret, Sarah. 2020. "Why Did Other Wealth Taxes Fail and Is This Time Different?" Evidence Paper 6, Wealth Tax Commission.
Perry, Ian. "The Effects of California's Public Policy on Jobs and the Economy Since 2011." Working Paper 108-17, Institute for Research on Labor and Employment.
Persson, Mikael. 2023. "Who Got What They Wanted? Investigating the Role of Institutional Agenda Setting, Costly Policies, and Status Quo Bias as Explanations to Income Based Unequal Responsiveness." *Journal of European Public Policy* 31, 1879-901.
Persson, Mikael and Anders Sundell. 2023. "The Rich Have a Slight Edge: Evidence from Comparative Data on Income-Based Inequality in Policy Congruence." *British Journal of Political Science* 54, 514–25.
Peters, Kim, Miguel A. Fonseca, Niklas K. Steffens, and Oliver P. Hauser. 2024. "Do Followers Mind the Pay Gap? An Experimental Test of the Impact of the Vertical Pay Gap on Leader Effectiveness." *Leadership Quarterly*, https://doi.org/10.1016/j.leaqua.2024.101811.
Pew Research Center. 2011. "The Elusive 90% Solution." March 11.
Pfeffer, Fabian T. and Nora Waitkus. 2021. "The Wealth Inequality of Nations." *American Sociological Review* 86, 567–602.
Philippon, Thomas and Ariell Reshef. 2013. "An International Look at the Growth of Modern Finance." *Journal of Economic Perspectives* 27(2), 73–96.
Phillips, Meredith. 2011. "Parenting, Time Use, and Disparities in Academic Outcomes." In *Whither Opportunity?*, edited by Greg J. Duncan and Richard J. Murnane, Russell Sage Foundation and Spencer Foundation, 207–28.
Pickett, Kate E. and Richard G. Wilkinson. 2015. "Income Inequality and Health: A Causal Review." *Social Science and Medicine* 128, 316–26.
Piketty, Thomas. 2014. *Capital in the Twenty-First Century*. Translated by Arthur Goldhammer. Harvard University Press.
Piketty, Thomas. 2020. *Capital and Ideology*. Translated by Arthur Goldhammer. Harvard University Press.
Piketty, Thomas. 2022. *A Brief History of Equality*. Translated by Steven Rendall. Harvard University Press.
Piketty, Thomas, Emmanuel Saez, and Stefanie Stantcheva. 2014. "Optimal Taxation of Top Labor Incomes: A Tale of Three Elasticities." *American Economic Journal: Economic Policy* 6(1), 230–71.
Piketty, Thomas, Emmanuel Saez, and Gabriel Zucman. 2018. "Distributional National Accounts: Methods and Estimates for the United States." *Quarterly Journal of Economics* 133, 553–609.
Pinker, Steven. 2018. *Enlightenment Now*. Viking.
Pollin, Robert. 2011. "Back to Full Employment." *Boston Review* 36(1), 13-19.
Popper, Nathaniel. 2016. "How Much Do We Really Know About Global Trade's Impacts?" *New York Times*, September 6.
Prickett, Kate C. and Jennifer March Augustine. 2021. "Trends in Mothers' Parenting Time by Education and Work from 2003 to 2017." *Demography* 58, 1065–91.
Pritchett, Lant. 2020. "Poverty Reduction and Economic Growth." *EconoFact*, February 2.

Putnam, Robert D. 2015. *Our Kids: The American Dream in Crisis.* Simon and Schuster.

Putnam, Robert D. with Shaylynn Romney Garrett. 2020. *The Upswing: How America Came Together a Century Ago and How We Can Do It Again.* Simon and Schuster.

Qi, Yaqiang. 2012. "The Impact of Income Inequality on Self-Rated General Health: Evidence from a Cross-National Study." *Research in Social Stratification and Mobility* 30, 451–71.

Radcliff, Benjamin. 2013. *The Political Economy of Human Happiness.* Cambridge University Press.

Rajan, Raghuram G. 2010. *Fault Lines.* Princeton University Press.

Rawls, John. 1971. *A Theory of Justice.* Harvard University Press.

Rawls, John. 2001. *Justice as Fairness: A Restatement.* Harvard University Press.

Reardon, Sean F. and Kendra Bischoff. 2011. "Income Inequality and Income Segregation." *American Journal of Sociology* 116, 1092–153.

Reardon, Sean F., Kendra Bischoff, Ann Owens, and Joseph B. Townsend. 2018. "Has Income Segregation Really Increased? Bias and Bias Correction in Sample-Based Segregation Estimates." *Demography* 55, 2129–60.

Reardon, Sean F. and Ximena A. Portilla. 2016. "Recent Trends in Income, Racial, and Ethnic School Readiness Gaps at Kindergarten Entry." *AERA Open,* https://doi.org/10.1177/2332858416657343.

Reeves, Richard V. 2017. *Dream Hoarders: How the American Upper Middle Class Is Leaving Everyone Else in the Dust, Why That Is a Problem, and What to Do About It.* Brookings Institution Press.

Reich, Robert B. 2010. *Aftershock.* Knopf.

Reich, Robert B. 2013. "Inequality for All." Commonwealth Club.

Reich, Robert B. 2015. *Saving Capitalism.* Knopf.

Reich, Robert B. 2020. *The System: Who Rigged It, How We Fix It.* Knopf.

Reid, T.R. 2017. *A Fine Mess: A Global Quest for a Simpler, Fairer, and More Efficient Tax System.* Penguin.

Robeyns, Ingrid. 2024. *Limitarianism: The Case Against Extreme Wealth.* Astra House.

Rodden, Jonathan. 2019. *Why Cities Lose: The Deep Roots of the Urban-Rural Political Divide.* Basic Books.

Rodems, Richard and Fabian T. Pfeffer. 2021. "Avoiding Material Hardship: The Buffer Function of Wealth." *Journal of European Social Policy* 31, 517–32.

Rogers, Joel. 1990. "Divide and Conquer: Further 'Reflections on the Distinctive Character of American Labor Laws.'" *Wisconsin Law Review* 1990, 1–147.

Rogoff, Kenneth. 2024. "Is Capitalism Really the Cause of Global Inequality?" *Project Syndicate,* October 10.

Roine, Jesper and Daniel Waldenström. 2014. "Long-Run Trends in the Distribution of Income and Wealth." Uppsala Center for Fiscal Studies, Uppsala University.

Rosset, Jan. 2016. *Economic Inequality and Political Representation in Switzerland.* Springer.

Rosset, Jan, Jeremie Poltier, and Jonas Pontusson. 2024. "Uneven Responsiveness: Public Opinion and Redistributive Policy Shifts in Western Europe Since 2008."

Rothstein, Bo and Eric Uslaner. 2005. "All for All: Equality, Corruption, and Social Trust." *World Politics* 58, 41–72.

Ruhm, Christopher J. 2018. "Deaths of Despair or Drug Problems?" Working Paper 24188, National Bureau of Economic Research.

Ryan, Rebecca M., Ariel Kalil, Caitlin Hines, and Kathleen Ziol-Guest. 2020. "Trends in Parental Values in a Period of U.S. Labor Market Change." *Journal of Marriage and Family* 82, 1495–514.

Saez, Emmanuel and Gabriel Zucman. 2019. *The Triumph of Justice: How the Rich Dodge Taxes and How to Make Them Pay.* W.W. Norton.

Sampson, Robert. 2012. *Great American City.* University of Chicago Press.

Sanchez Cumming, Carmen. 2022. "A Primer on Monopsony Power: Its Causes, Consequences, and Implications for U.S. Workers and Economic Growth." Washington Center for Equitable Growth.

Sanders, Bernie with John Nichols. 2023. *It's OK to Be Angry About Capitalism.* Crown.

Santos, Mateus Renno, Alexander Testa, and Douglas B. Weiss. 2018. "Where Poverty Matters: Examining the Cross-National Relationship Between Economic Deprivation and Homicide." *British Journal of Criminology* 58, 372–93.

Sawhill, Isabel V. 2014. *Generation Unbound: Drifting into Sex and Parenthood Without Marriage.* Brookings Institution Press.

Schakel, Wouter. 2021. "Unequal Policy Responsiveness in the Netherlands." *Socio-Economic Review* 19, 37–57.

Schanzenbach, Diane Whitmore and Michael R. Strain. 2020. "Employment Effects of the Earned Income Tax Credit: Taking the Long View." Working Paper 28041, National Bureau of Economic Research.

Schechtl, Manuel and Daria Tisch. 2024. "Tax Principles, Policy Feedback, and Self-Interest: Cross-National Experimental Evidence on Wealth Tax Preferences." *Socio-Economic Review* 22, 279–300.

Schmitt, John. 2013. "Why Does the Minimum Wage Have No Discernible Effect on Employment?" Center for Economic and Policy Research.

Schneider, Daniel, Orestes P. Hastings, and Joe LaBriola. 2018. "Income Inequality and Class Divides in Parental Investments." *American Sociological Review* 83, 475–507.

Schneider, Simone M. 2019. "Why Income Inequality Is Dissatisfying: Perceptions of Social Status and the Inequality-Satisfaction Link in Europe." *European Sociological Review* 35, 409–30.

Scholz, John Karl, Robert Moffitt, and Benjamin Cowan. 2009. "Trends in Income Support." In *Changing Poverty, Changing Policies*, edited by Sheldon Danziger and Maria Cancian, Russell Sage Foundation and Harvard University Press, 203–41.

Schroeder, Joris Melchior and Michaela Neumayr. 2023. "How Socio-Economic Inequality Affects Individuals' Civic Engagement: A Systematic Literature Review of Empirical Findings and Theoretical Explanations." *Socio-Economic Review* 21, 665–94.

Schwellnus, Cyrille, Andreas Kappeler, and Pierre-Alain Pionnier. 2017. "The Decoupling of Median Wages from Productivity in OECD Countries." International Productivity Monitor.

Secura, Gina M., et al. 2014. "Provision of No-Cost, Long-Acting Contraception and Teenage Pregnancy." *New England Journal of Medicine* 371, 1316–23.

Sen, Amartya. 1999. *Development as Freedom.* Oxford University Press.

Sepulveda, Edgardo R. and Ann-Sylvia Brooker. 2021. "Income Inequality and COVID-19 Mortality: Age-Stratified Analysis of 22 OECD Countries." *SSM—Population Health*, https://doi.org/10.1016/j.ssmph.2021.100904.

Sharkey, Patrick. 2013. *Stuck in Place: Urban Neighborhoods and the End of Progress Toward Racial Equality.* University of Chicago Press.

Sharkey, Patrick. 2018. *Uneasy Peace: The Great Crime Decline, the Renewal of City Life, and the Next War on Violence.* W.W. Norton.

Sherraden, Michael. 2007. "Assets for All: Toward Universal, Progressive, Lifelong Accounts." In *Ending Poverty in America*, edited by John Edwards, Marion Crain, and Arne L. Kalleberg, New Press, 151–64.

Shiller, Robert J. 2014. "Better Insurance Against Inequality." *New York Times*, April 12.

Shorrocks, Anthony, James Davies, and Rodrigo Lluberas. 2022. *Global Wealth Databook 2022.* Credit Suisse Research Institute.

Sides, John, Michael Tesler, and Lynn Vavreck. 2018. *Identity Crisis: The 2016 Presidential Campaign and the Battle for the Meaning of America.* Princeton University Press.

Smith, Noah. 2012. "Big Government, Small Bellies: What Japan Can Teach Us About Fighting Fat." *The Atlantic*, September 6.

Snowdon, Christopher. 2011. *The Spirit Level Delusion: Fact-Checking the Left's New Theory of Everything*. Monday Books.
Sofocleous, Panayiotis. 2025. "The Change in Sweden's Immigration and Integration Policy after 2015." PhD dissertation, University of California–San Diego, Department of Sociology.
Sommeiller, Estelle and Mark Price. 2018. "The New Gilded Age: Income Inequality in the U.S. by State, Metropolitan Area, and County." Economic Policy Institute.
Stiglitz, Joseph E. 2006. *Making Globalization Work*. W.W. Norton.
Stiglitz, Joseph E. 2009. "Drunk Driving on the US's Road to Recovery." *Real Clear Politics*, January 9.
Stiglitz, Joseph E. 2012. *The Price of Inequality*. W.W. Norton.
Stiglitz, Joseph E. 2013. "In No One We Trust." *New York Times*, December 21.
Stiglitz, Joseph E. 2015. *Rewriting the Rules of the American Economy*. W.W. Norton.
Stiglitz, Joseph E. 2023. "Inequality and Democracy." *Project Syndicate*, August 31.
Stiglitz, Joseph E., Amartya Sen, and Jean-Paul Fitoussi. 2009. *Report by the Commission on the Measurement of Economic Performance and Social Progress*.
Stoetzer, Lukas F., Johannes Giesecke, and Heike Klüver. 2023. "How Does Income Inequality Affect the Support for Populist Parties?" *Journal of European Public Policy* 30(1), 1–20.
Su, Dejun, Khalid Alshehri, and Jose Pagán. 2022. "Income Inequality and the Disease Burden of COVID-19: Survival Analysis of Data from 74 Countries." *Preventive Medicine Reports*, https://doi.org/10.1016/j.pmedr.2022.101828.
Summers, Lawrence H. 2021. "Would a Wealth Tax Help Combat Inequality?" In *Combating Inequality*, edited by Olivier Blanchard and Dani Rodrik, MIT Press, 141–51.
Tan, Anabel X., Jessica A. Hinman, Hoda S. Abdel Magid, Lorene M. Nelson, and Michelle C. Odden. 2021. "Association Between Income Inequality and County-Level COVID-19 Cases and Deaths in the US." *JAMA Network Open*, https://doi.org/10.1001/jamanetworkopen.2021.8799.
Taub, Amanda. 2017. "Why Americans Vote 'Against Their Interest.'" *New York Times*, April 12.
Tavernise, Sabrina. 2015. "Colorado Finds Startling Success in Effort to Curb Teenage Births." *New York Times*, July 5.
Taylor, Timothy. 2021. "Why Have Other High-Income Countries Dropped Wealth Taxes?" *Conversable Economist*, February 1.
Tedeschi, Ernie. 2019. "Americans Are Seeing the Highest Minimum Wage in History (Without Federal Help)." *New York Times*, April 24.
Tett, Gillian. 2009. *Fool's Gold*. Free Press.
Thaker, Anant C. and Elizabeth C. Williamson. 2012. "Unequal and Unstable: The Relationship Between Inequality and Financial Crises." New America Foundation.
Thewissen, Stefan, Lane Kenworthy, Brian Nolan, Max Roser, and Timothy Smeeding. 2018. "Rising Inequality and Living Standards in OECD Countries: How Does the Middle Fare?" *Journal of Income Distribution* 26(2), 1–23.
Thombs, Ryan, Dennis Thombs, Andrew Jorgenson, and Taylor Harris Braswell. 2020. "What Is Driving the Drug Overdose Epidemic in the United States?" *Journal of Health and Social Behavior* 61, 275–89.
Thompson, Jeffrey P. and Elias Leight. 2012. "Do Rising Top Income Shares Affect the Incomes or Earnings of Low and Middle-Income Families?" Working Paper 2012-76, Finance and Economics Discussion Series, Federal Reserve Board.
Tomaskovic-Devey, Donald and Ken-Hou Lin. 2013. "Financialization: Causes, Inequality Consequences, and Policy Implications." *North Carolina Banking Institute Journal* 18, 167–94.
Tooze, Adam. 2018. *Crashed: How a Decade of Financial Crises Changed the World*. Penguin.
Truesdale, Beth C. and Christopher Jencks. 2016. "The Health Effects of Income Inequality: Averages and Disparities." *Annual Review of Sociology* 37, 413–30.

Twenge, Jean M. 2000. "The Age of Anxiety: Birth Cohort Change in Anxiety and Neuroticism, 1952–1993." *Journal of Personality and Social Psychology* 79, 1007–21.
University of Wisconsin Population Health Institute. 2015. "County Health Rankings: Key Findings Report."
United Nations Office of Drugs and Crime. N.d. "Intentional Homicide." dataunodc.un.org/dp-intentional-homicide-victims.
US Centers for Disease Control. 2012. "Overweight and Obesity: Causes and Consequences."
US Congressional Budget Office. 2008. "Growing Disparities in Life Expectancy." Economic and Budget Issue Brief.
US Congressional Budget Office. 2022. "The Distribution of Household Income, 2019."
Uslaner, Eric. 2002. *The Moral Foundations of Trust*. Cambridge University Press.
Van de Werfhorst, Herman G. and Wiemer Salverda. 2012. "Consequences of Economic Inequality." *Research in Social Stratification and Mobility* 30, 377–87.
Van Parijs, Philippe. "What Kinds of Inequality Should Economists Address?" In *Combating Inequality*, edited by Olivier Blanchard and Dani Rodrik, MIT Press, 49–58.
Vandell, Deborah Lowe and Barbara Wolfe. 2000. "Child Care Quality: Does It Matter and Does It Need to Be Improved?" Special Report 78, Institute for Research on Poverty, University of Wisconsin–Madison.
Varbanova, Vladimira, Niel Hens, and Philippe Beutels. 2023. "Determinants of Life Expectancy and Disability-Adjusted Life Years (DALYs) in European and Organisation for Economic Co-operation and Development (OECD) Countries: A Longitudinal Analysis (1990–2019)." *SSM Population Health*, https://doi.org/10.1016/j.ssmph.2023.101484.
Veenhoven, Ruut and Silke Kegel. 2023. "Is Life Really Getting Worse? Change of Average Happiness in Nations 1946–2021." Working Paper 2, International Society for Quality-of-Life Studies.
Verbist, Gerlinde, Michael Förster, and Maria Vaalavuo. 2012. "The Impact of Publicly Provided Services on the Distribution of Resources: Review of New Results and Methods." OECD Social, Employment, and Migration Working Papers 130.
Vitols, Sigurt. 2010. "Board Level Employee Representation, Executive Remuneration, and Firm Performance in Large European Companies." Hans Böckler Foundation.
Vohs, Kathleen D. 2006. "The Psychological Consequences of Money." *Science* 314, 1154–56.
Voitchovsky, Sarah. 2009. "Inequality and Economic Growth." In *The Oxford Handbook of Economic Inequality*, edited by Wiemer Salverda, Brian Nolan, and Timothy M. Smeeding, Oxford University Press, 549–74.
Volscho, Thomas W. and Nathan J. Kelley. 2012. "The Rise of the Super-Rich: Power Resources, Taxes, Financial Markets, and the Dynamics of the Top 1 Percent, 1949 to 2008." *American Sociological Review* 77, 679–99.
Voss, Kim, Michael Hout, and Kristin George. 2024. "Persistent Inequalities in College Completion, 1980–2010." *Social Problems* 71, 480–508.
Wade, Robert. 2001. "Winners and Losers." *The Economist*, April 28.
Waldenström, Daniel. 2024. *Richer and More Equal: A New History of Wealth in the West*. Polity Press.
Waldfogel, Jane. 2006. *What Children Need*. Harvard University Press.
Waldfogel, Jane. 2010. *Britain's War on Poverty*. Russell Sage Foundation.
Wamhoff, Steve and Matthew Gardner. 2019. "Who Pays Taxes in America in 2019?" Institute on Taxation and Economic Policy.
Warner, Jennifer. 2012. "5 Dietary Patterns Most Americans Fit Into." *WebMD*.
Warren, Elizabeth. 2018. "Companies Shouldn't Be Accountable Only to Shareholders." *Wall Street Journal*, August 14.
Waters, Hugh and Marlon Graf. 2018. "America's Obesity Crisis: The Health and Economic Costs of Excess Weight." Milken Institute.

Watson, Tara. 2009. "Inequality and the Measurement of Residential Segregation by Income." *Review of Income and Wealth* 55, 820–44.

Weitzman, Martin L. 1984. *The Share Economy*. Harvard University Press.

Welzel, Christian. 2013. *Freedom Rising: Human Empowerment and the Quest for Emancipation*. Cambridge University Press.

Western, Bruce, Meredith Kleykamp, and Jake Rosenfeld. 2004. "Crime, Punishment, and American Inequality." In *Social Inequality*, edited by Kathryn M. Neckerman, Russell Sage Foundation, 771–96.

Wilkinson, Richard. 1992. "Income Distribution and Life Expectancy." *British Medical Journal* 304, 165–68.

Wilkinson, Richard and Kate Pickett. 2009. *The Spirit Level: Why Greater Equality Makes Societies Stronger*. Bloomsbury Press.

Wilkinson, Richard and Kate Pickett. 2019. *The Inner Level: How More Equal Societies Reduce Stress, Restore Sanity, and Improve Everyone's Well-Being*. Penguin.

Wilson, William Julius. 1987. *The Truly Disadvantaged*. University of Chicago Press.

Wilson, William Julius. 1996. *When Work Disappears*. Vintage.

Winship, Scott. 2013. "The Dream Abides: Economic Mobility in America from the Golden Age to the Great Recession." Policy Brief, Brookings Institution.

Winship, Scott. 2018. "Economic Mobility in America." Part 2: "The United States in Comparative Perspective." Archbridge Institute.

Winship, Scott and Donald Schneider. 2013. "The Great Gatsby Curve Revisited: Does More Inequality Correspond with Less Economic Mobility Across Local Labor Markets?" Manhattan Institute.

Wlezien, Christopher and Stuart N. Soroka. 2011. "Inequality in Policy Responsiveness?" In *Who Gets Represented?*, edited by Peter K. Enns and Christopher Wlezien, Russell Sage Foundation, 285–310.

Yakter, Alon. 2018. "The Heterogeneous Effect of Diversity: Ascriptive Identities, Class, and Redistribution in Developed Democracies." *European Journal of Political Research* 58, 820–44.

Yglesias, Matthew. 2018. "Elizabeth Warren Has a Plan to Save Capitalism." *Vox*, August 15.

Young, Cristobal. 2017. *The Myth of Millionaire Tax Flight*. Stanford University Press.

Young, Kevin A., Tarun Banerjee, and Michael Schwartz. 2020. *Levers of Power: How the 1% Rules and What the 99% Can Do About It*. Verso.